Land and Economy in
Baroque Italy

For S.E.M.

Land and Economy in Baroque Italy

Valpolicella, 1630–1797

Peter Musgrave

Leicester University Press

Leicester, London

Distributed in the United States and Canada by St. Martin's Press, New York

First published in Great Britain in 1992 by Leicester University Press
(a division of Pinter Publishers Limited)

Editorial offices
Fielding Johnson Building, University of Leicester,
Leicester, LE1 7RH, England

Trade and other enquiries
25 Floral Street, London, WC2E 9DS, England
and Room 400, 175 5th Avenue, New York, NY 10010, USA

British Library Cataloguing in Publication Data
A CIP catalogue record for this book is available from the
British Library

ISBN 0 7185 1449 1

Library of Congress Cataloging-in-Publication Data
Musgrave, Peter.
  Land and economy in Baroque Italy: Valpolicella, 1630–1797/
Peter Musgrave.
     p. cm.
  Includes bibliographical references (p.   ) and index.
  ISBN 0-7185-1368-1
  1. Valpolicella (Italy) - Economic conditions. 2. Land tenure -
Italy - Valpolicella - History. 3. Agriculture - Economic aspects -
Italy - Valpolicella - History.   I. Title.
HC307.V26M87   1992
333.3'0945'34–dc20   92–14244
                                                                          CIP

Typeset by Mayhew Typesetting, Rhayader, Powys
Printed and bound in Great Britain by Biddles Ltd., Guildford and King's Lynn

Contents

List of tables

Preface

This book began life some fifteen years ago as the result of a forced, but not regretted change in my plans for research; it was the late Ralph Davis who encouraged me to work on pre-modern Italy and not only for his often stated reason that 'it seemed more sensible to work on somewhere warm and attractive rather than on Wigan'. I have every reason to be grateful to him for both his advice and for his support in the early stages of this work.

Any historian must, first of all, be indebted to the archivists and librarians who make his work possible. I have been lucky in the invariable helpfulness and courtesy of the staff of the Archives in Italy I have worked in. In particular it is a pleasure to record the debt I owe to the Director of the *Archivio di Stato* in Verona, dottoressa Laura Castellazzi, and to her staff, in particular dottoressa Angela Miciluzzo, dottoressa Gloria Maroso, and signori/e Giordano, Lazzarini, Murari, Martini, Finetto, Ligozzi, Gucciardo, Firenza, Perriello, di Lorenzi, Lombardo, Pacciucci, Quaranta, Vesentini, Refatto Oselladore and Giuliano. The Director of the Archivio Storico della Curia Vescovile, don Franco Segala and his predecessor mons. Antonio Fasani made using their archive a pleasure and their knowledge both of the Archive and of the history of the Veronese church made easy many things which could have been difficult. To don Mario Trivulzi, assistant in the Archivio Storico, mons. Alberto Piazzi, Canon-Librarian of the *Biblioteca Capitolare* and his deputy, don Giuseppe Zivelonghi, himself from an ancient Valpolicella family, thanks are also due.

My heads of Department at Leicester, Ralph Davis, the late H.J. Dyos, Derek Aldcroft and Peter Fearon have had faith in me and have supported me, even when others had begun to doubt that the long gestation of this study would ever produce anything. Many colleagues at Leicester and elsewhere have helped, often in ways that they may not be aware of. To all of them, and in particular to Philip Cottrell, Peter Clark, Charles Phythian-Adams, Nick Davidson, Brian Pullen and Gian-Maria Varanini go my thanks. Any errors, misinterpretations or infelicities which remain in the text are mine alone and despite their advice.

Margaret Christie and above all Gillian Austen have performed the miracle of converting first my handwriting and then my word-processing into a form which is comprehensible to normal mortals.

I gratefully acknowledge the financial support I have received in the research upon which this book is founded from the Social Sciences Research Council (now the ESRC), the British Academy, the Twenty-Seven Foundation and the Research Board of the University of Leicester.

If this book has finally reached completion, it is entirely the responsibility of my wife who has supported, encouraged and, as was from time to time necessary, bullied me. To her, this book is dedicated, with all my love.

Peter Musgrave
November 1991

A note on measurements

The most common measure of surface area used in this book is the Veronese *campo* of 24 *vareze*; the *vareza* was divided into 12 *tavolette*. The *campo* was roughly 3000 square metres or about three-quarters of an acre.

Grain was measured normally in *minali*; the *minale* was a measure of volume, equivalent to 38.65 litres. Three *minali* made a *sacco*, while the *minale* was divided into 4 *quarte*, each of 4 *quartaroli*.

Wine and grapes were measured in *brente* of 68.7 litres (about 15 English gallons); the *brenta* was divided into 4 *secchie*. Twelve *brente* made one *botta* and three *botte* made a *carro*. Oil was also measured in *brente*, but the oil *brenta* was divided in to sixteen *bacede*.

The currency normally used was the Veronese *lira* of 20 *soldi*, each of 12 *dinari*, although the Venetian *trono* of 20 *marchetti* was the most usual coinage in circulation. Conventionally the Veronese *lira* was valued at 15 *marchetti*. The *ducato* was the usual money of account although ducat coins did not circulate. The ducat was valued conventionally at 6 *troni* 4 *marchetti*.

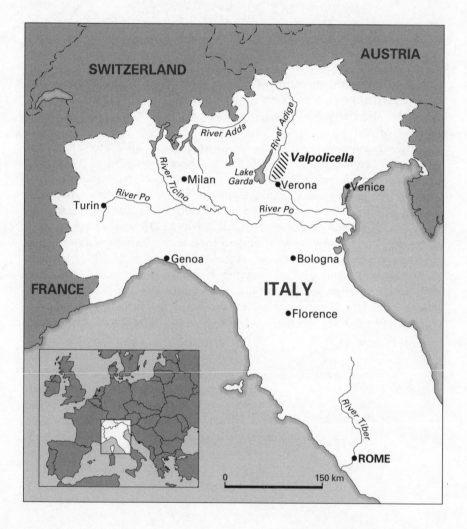

1
Introduction

I

Economic History has traditionally concerned itself with growth and development. Perhaps inevitably, given its origins in studies of the Industrial Revolution, it has tended to concentrate on particular lines of development; in many ways it has become a new 'Whig Interpretation of History', seeing history in terms of the growth of, and preparation for, eighteenth and nineteenth century industrialization. Like Spencerian sociology it has seen good in that which has survived to contribute to the final triumph of industrialization and has consigned to a historical and evolutionary scrap-heap all competing systems which did not do so.

Just like the Whig view of political history, this neo-Whiggery distorts reality, and in particular it distorts the mentalities of the past, consigning most human societies to the status of a set of bunglers searching for, and failing to find, the philosopher's stone of industrialization. Above all, it totally ignores that, for most of human history, what has been valued and sought after has not been growth or change but security and stability. Change, rather than being good, rather than being productive or progressive, was bad and destructive. The importance of stability and survival was as great for individuals as it was for monarchs and states, and formed the central item in any economic or social strategy. Pre-modern people did not in some way fail to achieve an Industrial Revolution; in many ways they sought to avoid it. Far from seeing the Industrial Revolution as a triumph for a progressive society, it may be more instructive to see it as a desperate expedient resulting from a fundamental failure of the societies and economies involved.

The collapse in the 1970s and the 1980s of the myth of continuous, self-sustaining exponential economic growth, coupled with a growing appreciation of the darker side of industrialization, in particular the increasing consciousness of the ecological damage which growth seems to have involved has produced a shift in historical sentiment, towards a reconsideration of the 'historical dead-ends', towards at least the possibility that the pre-industrial past was not stupid but just may have some answers, some pointers forward.

Perhaps inevitably the pendulum has now tended to swing too far in the opposite direction: the extreme rationalism of the old history has been replaced by the extreme romanticism of the new. The pre-modern world has been portrayed in some quarters as being almost mystically in tune with its environment, as possessing some ecological secret denied to Industrial or post-Industrial society. The pre-modern past becomes a repository of ecological wisdom, an Age of Gold to be looked back on almost with longing. This picture of the pre-modern past is as distorting as is the Whig view. Pre-modern economies may have been ecologically neutral – although a Castillian or an Anatolian farmer might disagree[1] – but that ecological neutrality came above all from lack of means rather than from any conscious rejection, or even realization of the possibility of ecological deterioration. Seventeenth and eighteenth century agricultural practices, in the Valpolicella as elsewhere, produced soil exhaustion, deforestation and erosion; elsewhere in the Veronese, the development of rice plantations led to serious and irreversible consequences for the hydrological regime of the plains. If the pre-modern past does not provide us with an example of the stupidity of our ancestors, neither does it provide us with an inexhaustible source of folk-wisdom and ecological rectitude.

The dead-ends of history do not contain any miracle solutions to the problems of the modern world, any more than did the industrial and economic growth of the eighteenth and nineteenth centuries; they are merely indications of differing lines of development, of differing responses to circumstances or constraints. It is crucially important in the interpretation of past economies that it is recognized that an economy or society may well, following a perfectly clear and perfectly defensible economic or social rationale, remain prosperous and growing without changing; indeed that a pre-modern economy operating efficiently and properly could contain within its structure the mechanisms necessary to ensure stability and security, and to prevent revolutionary economic and social change. In crude terms, a prosperous early modern economy which did not, in the late eighteenth century, have, or at least begin to have, an Industrial Revolution, should not be seen as necessarily backward, inefficient or as a failure, but as a success, in that it had succeeded in weathering the crises of the later eighteenth century without being fundamentally changed. It was rather the 'revolutionary' economies, above all England, that were failures – forced by circumstances to change, to accept new and unstable sources of wealth, and all the social consequences, for individuals as well as for society as a whole, that that entailed.

In the context of such an argument the role of northern and central Italy is classic. In the sixteenth century, the region showed all the signs of prosperity and industrial growth. Indeed, it could be argued that many of Rostow's pre-conditions for industrial revolution were already present – perhaps even to a greater extent than in eighteenth century England.[2] Northern Italy was still the mistress of international and intercontinental commerce: the discovery of the Cape Route had no more than temporarily affected her trade.[3] Not merely was northern Italy at the centre of Europe's long-distance trade with the most developed part of the non-European world, but the Italian trading cities also played a dominating role in European trade and in the internal trade of the wealthiest area of Europe – Northern Italy itself. This commercial importance was not limited to the dominating cities – Milan, Venice, Genoa, Florence – but spread also to the lesser cities of the mainland. Northern and central Italy were, too, perhaps the most concentrated industrialized region of sixteenth century Europe, playing a major role in textile production and the supply of metal goods. So important had commerce and industry become that regional specialization had reached the point where the region was, almost certainly, a clear net importer of foodstuffs, dependent upon its manufacturing and service industries to pay for imported food. Furthermore, the financial and credit system of northern Italy was without equal in Europe. Nor had the effects of economic development failed to spread to society. In many ways northern and central Italy had, it could be claimed, an 'industrial society'. The rise of the commercial nobilities of the cities and their replacement of both traditional rulers and traditional systems of government can, with some justification, be seen as a first 'bourgeois revolution'; the economic success of the towns had produced a flow of population to them, producing a society with a very high index of urbanization. Equally, the early disappearance of feudalism in the Italian countryside had produced an agricultural labour force which was further on the way to proletarianization than was any other labour force in Europe: urban labour, too, seems to have been well on the way to modern industrial organization. In every sense, then, here was an economy and society apparently trembling on the brink of an early Industrial Revolution.

Northern Italy did not go over that brink until the late nineteenth or even the early twentieth century. From the end of the sixteenth century northern Italy seemed to stagnate and to go backwards. Her commercial supremacy disappeared, never to revive; her industries began to yield primacy to others, her financiers saw the financial centre of Europe move to Amsterdam. Even her nobilities 'retrogressed', turning from commerce and finance to landholding and to the 'Noble Life'. The seventeenth and eighteenth centuries, the Age of the Baroque, were years of apparent stagnation and decline and, therefore, of poverty. Northern Italy failed; just at the time that the new economies of the North began to surge forward, she stagnated and slipped back. The explanations of that faltering and decline are many, and heavily supercharged with moral and political argument. For some

historians the cause of the 'Decline of Italy' lay in the commercial
decline consequent upon the shift of commercial power from the
Mediterranean to the Atlantic; above all the Dutch capture of the
crucial European grain trade in and after the 1590s, and the subsequent ruthless exploitation by the Dutch of their organizational advantages on the Cape Route turned Italy from a node to a backwater, and
a conservative backwater at that. Starved of the commercial wealth
upon which she had depended for so long, Italy was compelled to sink
to the level of a minor power. For others the fault lay only in part in
the commercial decline but rather more in the moral and economic
failure of the nobilities who, entranced by the chimera of noble
lifestyle and noble power elsewhere in Europe retreated from the
forefront of commerce into 'refeudalization' and land-holding; prefer-
ring the easy noble life to the challenging life of commerce and
entrepreneurship, the nobility, above all the Venetian nobility,
betrayed their nation and their ancestors. Much the most popular
explanation of the decline, particularly in Italy itself, has been the
devastating effect of war and foreign rule. During the Golden Age of
Italian prosperity most of the states were independent and Italian-
ruled; the Age of the Baroque was above all the age of Habsburg
domination. Italy was bled to finance the wars and courts of
foreigners; Italian interests were ruthlessly subordinated to imperial
need and requirements. The ruling groups of cities acquiesced in this
as collaborators with the foreign rulers.[4]

All these explanations have something to be said in their favour, as
well as a great deal against them; all are as polemical as they are
historical. Equally they have much of the flavour of explanations snat-
ched out of the air as much to fit predetermined ideas as to explain
the decline. Above all, the great objection to all these explanations
must be that they seek to explain a phenomenon – the Decline of Italy
– the existence of which is not fully established. The problem is easily
stated; the 'centuries of decline' coincided in most of northern and
central Italy with a continuation of signs of apparent, even growing
prosperity. The clearest physical manifestation of this is the large
amount of building and rebuilding which seems to have been undertaken in these centuries. The building and rebuilding is not merely that
of public or state buildings; all across northern Italy churches were
rebuilt or new ones built in new locations and old churches refur-
bished and beautified in the new Baroque and Rococo tastes. Equally,
private lay building continued apace; not merely the modernising of
the town *palazzi* and rural villas of the nobility but also, perhaps even
more significantly, the reconstruction of town and rural housing. It
would hardly be going too far to say the 'centuries of decline' saw a
large-scale 'rebuilding of Rural (and Urban) Italy'.

To some extent, it is true, this rebuilding can be explained as the
consequence of an increasingly exploitative state and élite, sucking

more and more of the wealth of the economy to them and investing it in conspicuous status. Although this explanation may hold reasonably true for, for instance, Tuscany or the Papal States, in Lombardy and even more in the Veneto it breaks down more or less completely. Certainly the state, the nobility and the wealthier ecclesiastical corporations were building and rebuilding, but both public and private affluence extended further down society. All across the Veneto, as in Lombardy, small rural communes engaged in building works; urban and rural parish churches and chapels were rebuilt and embellished by private donations. Individuals, too, rebuilt houses: the urban bourgeois and their rural counterparts built new, more commodious houses, while even peasant housing – in many cases housing owned by peasants – was being improved.

Of course, the evidence of building activity is not, of itself, decisive, but the rebuilding is on such a scale and so general that it can be taken as at least strongly hinting at relative prosperity. If then, during the period of decline, rather than poverty there is clear, if not incontrovertible evidence of prosperity and, at least for part of the period, of growing prosperity, it is surely justifiable to ask whether the Age of the Baroque was so clearly an age of decline and failure.

II

In any discussion of the 'Age of Decline' Venice and the Veneto play, inevitably, a central role. Venice, after all, had been one of the economic leaders, perhaps *the* economic leader of Italy in the sixteenth century: not merely had Venice outshone her commercial rivals but the industries of Venice and her Terra Firma empire had been leaders all across Europe. Venetian society, both in the city itself and on Terra Firma, had been profoundly affected by her commercial and economic success and, furthermore, was not affected by the imposition of foreign rule; Venice retained her political independence until 1797. As a consequence, too, the Venetian constitutional system, and the relationship between Venice and her subject cities on the mainland were not fundamentally changed from the fifteenth century onwards.

Perhaps because Venice had been so much the leader in the sixteenth century, her seventeenth and eighteenth century decline was possibly the most spectacular of all the crashes of early modern Italy. Her commercial power in the eastern Mediterranean declined rapidly after 1600; her industries became less and less competitive, and more and more restricted to luxuries and fripperies. Her nobility withdrew to the lands and villas they had begun to acquire in the Terra Firma in the sixteenth century, and soon Venice became synonymous with decadence and decline. It must be said that, particularly in the eighteenth century, that reputation for decadence and post-Imperial decline was carefully nurtured. The excesses of Carnival in Venice, the reputation of Casanova, and Venice as 'Sin City', were all carefully used to attract tourists from the north – Venice, after all, became a tourist trap long before the advent of Thomas Cook.[5]

This picture, however, attractive though it may be to the moralist, distorts both the nature of Venice's pre-seventeenth century economy and its later development. Blinded by the splendour of Venice's maritime and commercial wealth, it is all too easy to forget that, from the early fifteenth century onwards, the Venetian state and the Venetian economy had been, in a very real sense, dual. Venice continued to look towards the Levant, but she was also a major Italian land power, with an empire stretching virtually to the gates of Milan. The glories of the overseas empire and of the Levantine trade have, perhaps inevitably, overwhelmed the role of the land empire and the land economy in Venice's overall position. For most historical studies the land empire only begins to play a role with the end of the prosperity of the eastern trade. However, the land empire had, with one short break, been administered by Venice since the early fifteenth century and the relationship, both administrative and economic, established then continued to the fall of the Republic. The land empire had its own industries and its own commerce, to some considerable extent separate from the economy of Venice itself. In many ways the so-called decline of Venice in the seventeenth and eighteenth centuries is, rather, a long process of the redirection of the economy away from maritime trade and towards the land empire. Venice became a regional centre of its land empire rather than an international entrepôt, directed towards local rather than international trade, and dependent upon the prosperity of its land empire rather than on the success of the Levantine fleets. The loss of the Levantine trade and of the maritime empire did not mean that Venice became commercially dead; it certainly did not mean that the commerce or industry of the Terra Firma disappeared. Arguably the history of the seventeenth and eighteenth century Venetian land empire was a tension between, on the one hand, the growing importance economically and to some extent politically of the subject cities such as Verona or Brescia and, on the other hand, the growing efficiency of Venice's control over the Terra Firma cities and economies.

Venice's relationship with the cities of the Terra Firma was always, in European terms, a peculiar one. The fourteenth and fifteenth century expansion of the empire, at first largely for defensive reasons, had brought into Venetian control a series of political units, assimilated as units. The cities, furthermore, were assimilated as *functioning* political units, the constitutional and political structures taken over by a conqueror not sufficiently strong or, to begin with, sufficiently concerned, to replace them with a new colonial structure. This was a colonial empire nearer in form to the Feudatory states of British India or to Lugardian indirect rule rather than to direct rule. Rather than dismantling the independent political structures of the newly subjected cities, Venice incorporated them directly into her system. Indeed, even where the old communal and conciliar structures had been largely dismantled or had atrophied under signorial rule, as, to some extent, had been the case in Verona under the della Scala, the new Venetian rulers restored effective power to the noble councils. Like the British in India, the Venetian state was content to allow the traditional leaders of Terra Firma society to administer their cities and territories, subject to the imposition of 'residents' on the city. The two Venetian *Rettori* in each city, the *Podesta* and the *Capitano del Popolo*, in fact filled traditional, pre-existing positions in the conciliar government of the cities; the only formal difference was that, rather than being elected by the cities' councils, they were appointed by the Venetian Senate, to which they were responsible for the oversight of administration and of justice, and for the payment of taxes. Local administration remained clearly and firmly in local hands, operating through the complex sets of checks and balances evolved by the communes to prevent the concentration of too much power in too few hands. Venice, in the Terra Firma as in her own constitution, was exercised to prevent the threat of new signorial or monarchic concentration of power appearing and, perhaps paradoxically, it may have been the Venetian imperial presence which prevented in the Veneto the sort of revolution which brought the Medici to hereditary archducal power in Tuscany.

Compared with the states around it – Spanish Lombardy, the Prince-Bishopric of Trento, the Papal States – Venice's land empire was a loose confederation of semi-independent cities. Venice imposed governors in the subject cities, but never gave them the time or the absolute power to weld the parts of the Empire into any consistent whole. The Venetian Rectors in a city like Verona, far from being, even in the Age of Absolutism, absolute rulers or the representatives of an absolute state, were firmly trapped between two weighty bureaucratic bodies. One, senatorial government in Venice, at one and the same time demanded results, especially financial contributions from the Rectors and their cities, and jealously worked to ensure that no individual Podesta or Captain gained sufficient local power to allow him to work effectively; the other, conciliar government in the subject city, hedged the Rectors around with traditional, constitutional constraints, jealous above all of the privileges of their cities and was always willing to rush to Venice to gain senatorial support against the pretensions of the Rectors. Beyond everything else, the Rectors were Venetian politicians, in the subject cities for no more than a few months at a time, constantly looking back to Venice lest their political careers in the city might be damaged.

The Venetian land empire was not, of course, exempt from the growing bureaucratic complexity of all European states in the seventeenth and eighteenth centuries. The late seventeenth and eighteenth centuries did see a very definite extension of central control, a much greater involvement of the Venetian government in the affairs of the subject cities and a much greater bureaucratization of the whole process of government. This process, however, took the form of the extension from the centre of the power and influence of Venetian agencies such as the Inquisitors-General in Terra Firma, the *Magistrati ai Beni Inculti*, the *Magistrati ai Beni Comunali*, and many others, centrally controlled, rather than any increase in the power of the Rectors in individual cities. Indeed in some cities, the eighteenth century saw a growing alliance between Rectors and city councils to resist the growth of central power. Local autonomy may have been reduced, but it was still strong at the end of the Republic.

The tie which held the Empire together was above all fiscal; the Terra Firma cities, in addition to providing Venice with a *cordon sanitaire* against invasion, provided her with an income. Even the fiscal relationship, however, was one which emphasized local autonomy. Although the Venetian government determined the level of contribution required from each city, and although Venice too determined the customs duties on some items, the details of tax-assessment and tax-gathering were left to individual cities and their councils. The cities were largely self-taxing; the distribution of taxation, the forms of its levying and collection were left entirely in the hands of the cities, which meant not the Rectors but the city councils. Even so central a question as the land tax, the *estimo*, was left entirely in the hands of the city and its bureaucracy. Equally it was up to the cities to conduct their own economic and trade policies: Verona, for instance, established a trade fair in the 1630s in competition with the Bolzano fairs, despite Venice's close identification with them.

This relatively free economic structure seems to contradict the image of a jealous economic master, wantonly destroying the industries of the Terra Firma cities to protect her own; of an imperial master willingly distorting the economic activities of its subjects for its own ends. It is certainly true that the island government did make a number of attempts to prevent the development of competing production in the Terra Firma, for instance of glass, or to prevent the export of raw materials to competing industries outside its borders, as was the case with the long-run bans on the export of unwoven silk to the Trentino, a ban which was of major concern to the Veronese. The number of areas in which this sort of manipulation in favour of Venice took place were relatively few; above all they were, perhaps inevitably given the structure of the Empire, largely ineffective. In the Veronese, for instance, the export of silk to the silk mills of Rovereto continued through every form of ban. After all, it was the governmental mechanism of Verona which had to enforce such a ban: smuggling of silk across a border largely guarded by a part-time customs force made up of Veronese silk producers was hardly a difficult task: even the nobility, if the reports of the Rectors are to be believed, were using their carriages as conveyances for contraband.

There is another dimension to this peculiar confederate structure which must be discussed. The survival of the communal governments and their incorporation into a political system almost paranoically fearful of the concentration of political or military power in hands other than those of the state, served to keep the nobility of the Veneto in a very peculiar situation. This can best be summed up by saying that, in an age of noble power and noble privilege, the nobilities of the Venetian Terra Firma remained essentially under-privileged. As in Venice itself the nobility retained a monopoly of the most important offices, but, again as in Venice, that was a double-edged privilege; political office and the gaining of it could be extremely expensive, not perhaps as cripplingly expensive as some Venetian offices undoubtedly were, but certainly enough to make them a problem. Furthermore, periods of office-holding were very short – the members of the Council of XII, the chief council of the Commune of Verona, were elected for two months at a time. The costs of election also could be very high. Political office was hardly an unmixed blessing. And against this the Veneto nobleman was excluded from many of the privileges and functions which his noble counterparts enjoyed elsewhere in Europe. The Veneto nobleman was not exempted from any taxation, nor did he possess any legal privileges, being suable and having to sue, in the same courts and under the same laws as commoners. In theory the most distinctive noble form of employment, the military service of the state, was barred to him by Venetian legislation, more honoured in the breach than the observance it is true, forbidding the nobility (and other inhabitants, of the Terra Firma cities) serving as officers in the Republic's armies. The Veneto nobility was, in effect, forced to send its sons abroad to gain military experience and the status which went with it. Military service was, paradoxically, the only form of employment which was forbidden by law or custom to the Veneto aristocracy. The conventions which, elsewhere in Europe, excluded the nobility from involvement in commerce, finance or industry had no place in Veneto society; if some noble or noble families avoided commercial involvement it was through choice or circumstance and not as a result of prohibition. If, in that sense, the Veneto nobilities could hardly be called truly noble, they did have one feature which made them more truly noble than others. The incorporation of the Terra Firma cities and their constitutional structures into the Venetian empire, and Venice's fear of local power, effectively closed the Terra Firma nobilities in the way that the Venetian nobility itself had been closed since 1298; there was no Venetian Louis XIV or Louis XV to swamp the old nobility with the new. The only hope a non-nobleman had of promotion to a form of nobility, although not to the institutional status of nobility, as indeed the only hope a Veneto nobleman had of promotion within the nobility, was through the action of a neighbouring (or other) ruler. The closed nobility meant, of course, that upward social mobility, certainly in terms of the accepted 'official' social structure, was limited; there was no title to nobility to buy, no exclusive noble life-style to emulate.[6]

The peculiar confederation which was the Venetian Terra Firma empire provides an important test bed for the theory of the decline and its possible causes. The empire remained essentially free of foreign control, and indeed remarkably free of central control, until the very end of the eighteenth century. Although it had a large and prosperous nobility, that nobility was not privileged nor cut off from general social and economic activity. Nor, despite the reputation of the Venetian state, was it dominated by an exploitative imperial centre, distorting the economies and societies of its subject cities for its own ends. In some ways, indeed, Venice preserved in the Terra Firma cities as in its own society, a social structure which was a living and changing relic of the age before the Age of Absolutism.

2

Verona, the Veronese and the Valpolicella

I

Verona, the Faithful City, and its surrounding state, the Territorio Veronese, was, in many ways, central to the Terra Firma empire. In purely geographical terms it lies at the very edge of the Veneto, bordering Lombardy, Emilia-Romagna and the Trentino. This gave it two advantages. First, its position placed it at the centre of a series of lines of communications; the parallel routes of the Garda trough and the Adige are the prime link between much of northern and central Italy on the one hand and the Tirol, Germany and the North on the other. Unlike much of the rest of the Veneto, much, probably most, of Verona's trade was not directed to or from Venice, but moved independently. Verona's trade fairs gave it an independent commercial base, and a base which was not too seriously affected by the decline of Venice's foreign trade. Verona also had a crucial position in east–west communications, not merely in the Terra Firma empire, but in the whole communication network of northern Italy; most trade and virtually all travellers through the northern side of the north Italian plain passed through the Territorio. The city's nodal position did, however, have its disadvantages: above all, Verona and the Veronese were crucially on the great military roads between the Habsburg territories in Germany and their colonies or dependants in Italy. Venice's effective neutrality in all Italian land wars after the 1520s reduced the potentially disastrous consequences of the city's position, but the weakness of Venice effectively meant that foreign troops had, from time to time, to be allowed passage through the Territorio, usually along the Adige, crossing at Perarola or Bussolengo and proceeding via the Mincio towards Mantua. Even the peaceful Republic, however, could not totally avoid military intervention, and on a number of occasions troops fought in the Veronese, in some cases, such as in 1704, entering the Valpolicella by the pass of the Rocca Pia.[1] This military centrality was to prove disastrous in the last years of the Republic, as Napoleon's army fought, camped and foraged over a large part of the Territorio.[2]

The geographical centrality of Verona also led to a political centrality. In many ways Verona and its Territorio was the lynchpin of the land empire, providing as it did the link between the 'near terra Firma' – Padua and Vicenza – and the Venetian territories in Lombardy. In the same way, it was also a crucial political link in German–Italian communications, a city whose politics and internal stability were of far wider concern than a mere Venetian city.

In many ways Verona had a realistic claim to be the second city of the Venetian empire; certainly she was virtually the only one of the subject cities who could, even after the decline of Venice's international commerce, begin to challenge her dominance. In part this was a result of Verona's historical importance: the memory of the Scaliger domination was still strong, in Verona at least; again, the capture of the city by Maximillian in 1509 had been the prelude to perhaps the most dangerous crisis in Venice's history. This lasting political and military importance made Verona peculiarly significant in Venice's policies to control and maintain her empire. At the same time, unlike the other Veneto cities, seventeenth and eighteenth century Verona had a sufficiently strong industrial and commercial base to allow her to remain relatively independent of the crises and problems of Venice.

Verona was not, however, just a city. Like all the Terra Firma cities, Verona also controlled the countryside around her, the Territorio Veronese. The boundaries of the Territorio had been fixed by a series of political accidents before the arrival of the Venetians; there had been some minor variations subsequently. The Territorio, those communes which fell under the control of the Commune of Verona did not exactly correspond, for instance with the Diocese of Verona: the diocese included parishes on the Lombard shore of Lake Garda, which politically were part of the Territorio of Brescia, while the Four Vicarates in the Adige valley lay, politically in the Principality of Trento, but ecclesiastically in the Diocese of Verona. Ostiglia, in the Marquisate of Mantua, was Veronese ecclesiastically speaking, while a number of parishes in the east of the Territorio fell into the jurisdiction of the Bishop of Vicenza.[3]

The Territorio was very varied. The great mass of the population and a high proportion of the geographical area lay in the plains. In fact the plain region of the Veronese itself was varied: the heavy and wet soils of the Grandi Valli in the far south-east contrasting with the much lighter soils of the west. The plains were above all the land of great estates and of cereal production – wheat, rye, maize and rice – albeit a cereal cultivation mingled, as elsewhere, with vine and olive production, and the production of mulberry leaves and silk. Some areas of the plain also specialized in fruit production. To the north of the plains lay the alpine foothills and valleys – the Valpolicella, the

Valpantena, the Val d'Illasi. This was very much a mixed area of agriculture, mixing arable plain land with hoe-cultivated terraces, grain with grapes, olive, fruit and mulberry and agriculture with industry: although it was an area with large estates, it also had large numbers of smaller landholders, including quite large areas of 'peasant' landholding. On the high tops of the Lessini and Monte Baldo, an unusual mixture of agriculture was to be found; in addition to the pastoral farming which is to be expected at heights of over 4500 feet, complete with complex patterns of transhumance, there existed an important, though declining, cereal sector.[4] Around Lake Garda, the Veronese had a taste of a more truly Mediterranean agriculture in which cereals, grapes and olives were coupled with lake fishing.

The variety of the Veronese was not found merely in its variety of agricultural types. The 'Proprietorial Body' of the Veronese was extremely varied. Although some areas, such as parts of the plains, were heavily dominated by noble landholders, in general no single group – Venetian or Veronese nobles or ecclesiastical landholders, for instance – can be said to be dominant. In particular a considerable quantity of land was in the ownership of what, for the sake of neatness, can be called the urban and rural bourgeoisie, almost a Veronese gentry; equally, not all the land of the Veronese had by any means passed into non-peasant hands and in some communes the majority of the land was in the legal ownership of its cultivators.[5] Again the variety of the Veronese is to be seen in the diversity of its economic activity: although it was a predominantly agricultural economy, it was an agricultural economy with an important industrial sector, not merely the textile industries which were so widespread in seventeenth and eighteenth century Europe but also industries such as boat-building and marble extraction. Furthermore, the Veronese's central communications position meant that commerce and transportation were major sources of wealth and employment.

II

In many ways the Territorio Veronese was a microcosm of the whole Terra Firma empire; to some extent, too, the Valpolicella can be seen as a microcosm of the Veronese. Within the boundaries of the Vicarate were to be found a very high proportion of the types of agriculture and economy to be found in the Territorio. Equally the Valpolicella was, as was the whole of the Territorio, typified by a widely varied range of types of society and of patterns of landowning. It would be tempting but wrong to see the Valpolicella as being for these reasons representative of the Veronese as a whole. It must be made clear that the Valpolicella was *not* 'typical'. Above all its proximity to the city, which made it possible for all but the inhabitants of the most distant communes to go to and to return from Verona in a single day, meant that its economy was disproportionately related to that of the city. Although daily or periodic markets existed in a number of centres, the city and suburban markets were at least as important as the more local ones both, as buying and selling places for the Valpolicella population. The proximity of the city also made employment in the city at all levels an extremely attractive alternative to life and work in the Valpolicella. All the evidence suggests that there was a high and consistent level of migration from the Valpolicella into the city; furthermore Valpolicella families profited from the flow of income from the city. Equally the physical nearness of the Valpolicella coupled with its reputation for a pleasant and salubrious summer climate made it a popular centre of *villegiatura* for the nobility. While the Valpolicella was never quite as fashionable as the Val d'Illasi, a large number of the nobility built villas on their Valpolicella estates and, indeed, built up Valpolicella estates for that purpose. The presence of the noble households during the summer certainly had some effect on the Valpolicella economy as a whole, while the demand for Valpolicella land helped to keep land prices high and reduced the scale and speed of land transfers amongst the nobility. It is also the case that a number of non-noble Valpolicella families, whose members made money in Verona and elsewhere, established themselves in 'gentry houses' in the Valpolicella, again providing another focus for consumption.[6]

Although the Valpolicella included many of the agricultural types of the Territorio its coverage was not complete: obviously the Valpolicella had no share in the lake-side agriculture of Garda, but, above all, it had little or no real plains land. As a consequence it developed few of the great *podere* or *latifundia* of the plains, great noble-owned estates worked by a relatively impoverished peasantry, dominating land-ownership, the renting of land and the availability of employment over a wide area. The lack of this kind of estate coupled with the physical geography of the region meant that the Valpolicella was little affected by the development in the seventeenth and eighteenth centuries of large-scale rice farming which, in the plains proper, changed the economy very considerably.

The other feature which made the Valpolicella atypical was the existence of a clear consciousness of a regional identity over and above communal loyalty. Both by its inhabitants and by outsiders, the Valpolicella was perceived as a separate and clearly identified region within the Veronese. More than this, it was widely perceived as a rich and prosperous area throughout the period of this study and hence is one of the areas most likely to have been deeply affected by the 'decline' and its attendant disasters.

The origins of this local identity go back at least to the fourteenth century, traditionally to the grant to Federico della Scala of, effectively, palatine rights in a 'County of the Valpolicella'. Federico's short-lived Palatinate, however, although its founding diploma defined the boundaries of the Valpolicella for the future, seems to have been no more than a recognition and formalization of an existing situation: the strong feelings of community of the population of the *Pievi* of S. Giorgio, S. Floriano and Negrar.[7]

In formal terms the Valpolicella was no more than one of the Vicarates into which the Veronese was divided for judicial and some administrative purposes. The vicarate was an institution lying between the rural commune and the Territorio. Its functions were largely judicial: the Vicar was, in essence, a small claims judge of the first instance. The Vicar had in addition a number of more strictly administrative functions: it was the Vicar, for instance, who licensed, and often presided over, the meetings of the *vicinie* of the communes. The vicarial, and hence judicial, geography of the Veronese was extremely complex, the result of a complex series of historical accidents. The vicarates were by no means equal in size, either physically or in population; nor indeed were they necessarily geographically continuous. The vicarates were also, in a sense, private, in that the right to appoint vicars did not inevitably lie with the state – in the case of the Veronese with the communal councils of Verona. A wide range of nobility, the Bishop of Verona, some communal councils and others had the right and duty of appointment of vicars. Furthermore vicarial rights were alienable. It must also be pointed out that the existence of the vicarates in no way affected the access of individuals or communes to the organs of central government in Verona, either the civil authorities or the communal and rectorial law courts.[8]

Within this framework the Valpolicella vicarate was unusual. In terms of numbers of communes and population, although not of surface area, it was the largest of the non-urban vicarates of the Veronese. Furthermore, unlike most of the other vicarates, it had administrative and above all fiscal functions beyond the purely judicial. Above all, the Valpolicella was an intermediate fiscal unit; the vicarate as a whole was responsible for the payment of certain taxes, for their distribution and for the auditing of the tax gatherers' accounts. This taxation function was exercised through a number of vicariate institutions, above all the Council of Eighteen and the Great Council. These institutions were in themselves exceptional: although other vicarates, such as the Vicarate of the Mountains,[9] had vicarial councils, their functions were concerned solely with the use and distribution of the common lands of the vicarate. The Valpolicella councils, in addition to dealing with the common lands of the vicarate, above all the Campagna della Valpolicella in the commune of Pescantina, were concerned with such matters as roads and, in particular with the defence of the rights and privileges of the Valpolicella against the claims and pressures both of the communes which made up the Valpolicella and of the city and Venetian governments. These privileges, in particular exemption from financial and other levies to provide food for and security from foreign troops passing through the Veronese, were valuable and jealously guarded.[10]

The vicarate institutions were of two sorts. The vicar himself, the presiding official and judge of the vicarate, with wide powers over, amongst others, weights and measures, licensing of drinking houses, control of mills and boats, and supervision of road maintenance,[11] was selected by the Great Council of the Valpolicella from a list drawn from the Veronese nobility. The appointment had to be approved by the councils of the city and by the Venetian rectors, but after the early sixteenth century that became no more than a formality. The vicarate almost certainly brought its occupant little by way of profit; although court fees brought in some income, and although each of the communes made a small, fixed payment to the vicar annually,[12] the cost of hospitality and the display the office made incumbent on the vicar was almost certainly greater. Equally the problems for an active city politician of holding a weekly or bi-weekly court in the vicarial headquarters in S. Pietro in Cariano were considerable: most, although not all, found it necessary to employ a deputy, usually a law graduate, to carry out the day-to-day functions of the Vicar. Nonetheless the Vicarate of the Valpolicella was regarded as an honour and one which was hard sought by the Veronese nobility, particularly those families, such as the Verita Poeta, the Maffei, the dal Bene or the della Torre who held considerable Valpolicella lands; Benedetto dal Bene records in the 1780s both his own pleasure at his appointment and the considerable feasting and jollification involved in his installation.[13] The coats of arms of the vicars which adorn the Casa della Valpolicella, now the *Municipio* in S. Pietro in Cariano, include many of the most illustrious of the Veronese.[14] Much of the day-to-day administration of the Valpolicella vicarate, and above all of the law courts, was in the hands of the vicar's deputy and as in all Veronese and Venetian justice, the Notary of the courts. It was the notary who dispatched most of the business, in many cases reconciling possible litigants, issuing summonses to appear and issuing the orders for the implementation of court judgments. Unfortunately, the role of the court notary in the administration of justice in pre-modern Italy is a largely ignored and unstudied one; his key role, in the Valpolicella as elsewhere, is undoubted. The final element in the judicial structure were the *viatori*, a mixture of bailiff, process-server and messenger, who represented the power, such as it was, of the vicarate in the communes. The viatori were few in number, usually two or three for the whole vicarate, and heavily dependent upon the support of the communal officials and the broader local community for any success they might have in enforcing their instructions.

Other than its size, the Valpolicella differed little in these institutions from all the other rural vicarates of the Veronese. What did set it apart, however, were its 'representative' institutions. It must be said that these institutions are clearer in theory than they ever seem to have been in practice. Few of the records of the Vicarate councils seem to have survived, and it is possible to look at the Valpolicella records for considerable periods without discovering any clear reference to the councils or their deliberations. Nonetheless they seem to have played a crucial role in the local perception of the identity of the vicarate. There were in essence two councils: the Council of XVIII and the Great Council. The Council of XVIII, was made up of six representatives of the three *piovadeghi* – corresponding to the ecclesiastical *pievi* – into which the Valpolicella was divided. The Great Council was made up of the Eighteen, representatives of the individual communes and the officials of the Valpolicella, above all the *sindico*, effectively the chairman, chief executive and representative of the Valpolicella outside its boundaries, and the *consiglieri*, in effect his deputies and advisers.

It must be emphasized that the vicarial institutions existed in parallel and to some extent in competition with the institutions of the individual communes. The organization of the communes of the Valpolicella was, in general, standard and followed the same pattern as all communes, rural or urban, outside Verona itself. There was no institutional or constitutional distinction in the Veronese between incorporated town and unincorporated countryside. The basic unit of the commune was the *vicinia*: in principle, this was a meeting of all the heads of households within the commune, meeting with the license of and usually in the presence of the vicar or his deputy. The vicinia appointed, annually, the officials of the commune, amended the *statuti* (in essence the rural or urban bye-laws), approved the distribution of taxation and the tax gatherer's accounts and acted as the legal embodiment of the commune, being the only body permitted to carry out a wide range of legal and administrative functions. The decisions of the vicinia were taken by secret ballot and were, where necessary, recorded in notarial documents. Although in theory the membership of the vicinia was clear, the high mobility of families and individuals led to very major difficulties. Much of the seventeenth and eighteenth century history of the Valpolicella communes is taken up by a long-run and bitter controversy between the *originari*, in theory the heads of the original households of the commune, and the *forestieri*, the incomers – many of which families had arrived a century or more before – who were required to pay taxes in the commune, but were *de jure* and in most cases *de facto* excluded from a share in communal government (or at least from the vicinia) and also from the benefits of, for instance, rights to grazing or wood-gathering on the communal lands. A number of judicial decisions taken at the highest levels resolved the issue in theory, but until the very end of the Venetian

Republic, *forestieri* are to be found being excluded from membership of the vicinia and from shares in the communal lands.[15]

Between meetings of the vicinia the day-to-day administration of the commune was in the hands of its elected officials. The chief official was the *massar*, the equivalent of the modern sindaco; paid a salary from the communal exchequer, he was the officer who not merely administered the commune but acted as its official external representative. The massar was responsible for reporting untoward events – sudden deaths, crimes, beggars and so forth – to the government in Verona, and was the official to whom the central government directed its orders in the first instance. The massar was, in theory, both aided and supervised by two or more (depending on the size of the commune) *consiglieri*, who also received an honorarium from the commune. The vicinia also elected an *essator*, who was the communal tax gatherer, responsible above all for the collection of the *estimo*, and two or more *stimadori*, whose basic function was the assessment of the *estimo* but because of this became also the official and unofficial valuers of land in the commune for both public and private purposes. Some of the larger communes had other, more specialized officials in addition to these, but the other official common to all communes was the *scrivan(o)*, in effect the communal secretary and scribe. This was almost certainly an office of some power and greater influence, and in many communes the scrivan, rather than the consiglieri acted as the effective deputy of the massar; in many communes the *scrivania* was the highest office which forestieri could effectively gain. What is very clear from this structure is the very high level of self-government which the organization of Veronese local government gave to the rural community and, of course, the very high level of amateur government. The position of the communes was, perhaps, weakened during the seventeenth and eighteenth centuries by the growing involvement of central government in the management of the communal lands, and indeed by the development of increasing numbers of 'central government agencies'. That decline was, however, only relative and in the Valpolicella as elsewhere, the commune remained the fundamental unit of effective local government until the fall of the Republic.

III

The wide variety of crops cultivated in the Valpolicella has been remarked upon previously; the large number of different crops which could be grown and which would provide a worthwhile return was one of the major advantages which the Valpolicella had over many other regions, and which made its economy more prosperous and more stable than that of much of the rest of the region.

Food grains were, of course, the central crop of this non-specialized

economy. Food grains were grown primarily to provide the basic food
of the population and fodder for the animals. As will be seen, the line
which divided human food from animal food was not a clear one: the
exigencies of the season and the particular situation of a household
might convert animal fodder into human food. As in most of the rest
of Europe at this period the basic food grain was wheat. Although the
bread of the towns was being increasingly blackened in the seventeenth century by growing imports of Baltic rye, and although there
was an increase in rye production in the Valpolicella itself in the
seventeenth century,[16] nonetheless it was wheat which dominated
cultivation and wheaten flour which formed the basis, certainly of
rural bread, throughout the seventeenth and eighteenth centuries.
Kind rents were very frequently specified in terms of volumes of
wheat, and doles to the poor are frequently specified in terms of
volumes of wheat *ridotto in pan*.[17] If wheat was the chief and
central food grain it was in some ways also the most precarious: wheat
was at the edge of its range of secure yield in western Europe – less
so perhaps in the Valpolicella than in England or France – and
relatively minor fluctuations in the climate could produce very sharp
variations in production ranging from glut to total failure. This
precariousness of wheat was one of the features which produced great
instability in France and Spain in the seventeenth and eighteenth
centuries, and which led to a very marked shift in these areas away
from wheat towards rye and other less risky grains. The climate of the
Valpolicella was rather better suited to wheat production than that of
France and the wide variety of land types ensured that, except in the
most disastrous years, some wheat was produced; but even in the Valpolicella wheat seems to have been a very variable, very unpredictable
sort of crop. Had the Valpolicella been entirely dependent upon
wheat, even given the advantages the region possessed over other
regions, it is unlikely that its economy would have been as stable or
as prosperous as it was.

During the seventeenth century the second most important food
grain seems to have been rye (*segala*). In many senses the seventeenth
century was, throughout Europe, the age of rye. Although rye
produces in optimum conditions a lower yield than does wheat,[18] the
real disadvantage of rye had always been the distaste which much of
the population felt at having to eat rye bread. Particularly in the
Mediterranean region, where, until the late sixteenth century wheat
supplies had been sufficient for all levels of society, rye bread was
regarded as being inferior in taste and also in status to wheaten bread:
black bread was a sign of poverty and in some Mediterranean cities the
poor refused to eat it.[19] The great advantage of rye was, however, its
much greater tolerance of extreme weather conditions: in particular
rye continued to yield reasonably well in damp and cool conditions
in which wheat yielded poorly or not at all. There is some evidence

of an increase in rye production in the Valpolicella during the seventeenth century. This expansion seems to have been of two sorts. First some parts of the Valpolicella, such as the very high villages and the damper parts of the lower plains, which were relatively unsuited to the production of wheat even in normal climatic conditions and where the climatic changes of the seventeenth century may have made things worse, seem to have shifted over at least some of the area they cultivated to rye. Even in these areas, however, the principle of insurance, coupled with the dislike of rye bread, meant that quite considerable acreages remained under wheat: the seventeenth century certainly did not see the development of areas specializing in the production of rye. The second area of expansion was an increase in the acreage of rye cultivated in the more favoured parts of the Valpolicella as, presumably, agriculturalists there sought to shift at least in part to a more secure producer than wheat. Here again wheat did not disappear; increased rye production may well have been at the expense of other 'minor' grains. What was happening was a shift of the balance within a mixed economy rather than a total structural shift.

In good times rye was basically an insurance grain – to be used if the wheat supply failed or as an animal food. If the supply of wheat was insufficient, the rye became a larger part of the human diet at an earlier stage than otherwise would have been the case. Rye seems to have been used mostly as an additive to eke out wheat supplies – except at times of the greatest crisis – rather than a grain on its own.

The third great group of grains was the millets, including, from the late seventeenth century onwards, maize. The mix of food grains had always included some millet (*miglio*), but the millets had always occupied a position in the hierarchy of food grains below rye: if the wheat crop was poor, rye was substituted for wheat, but only if both wheat and rye failed did the millets play a role in human food. They were, before the mid-eighteenth century, in essence animal fodder. The position of the millets was, to some extent, revolutionized by the late eighteenth century expansion of maize; by the early nineteenth century maize flour and *polenta*, the porridge made from it, had become one of the staples of the poor. The major advantage of maize was its productivity: a similar area put down to wheat or rye would produce a much lower return. That higher return was dependent upon a much more intensive input of labour: the maize, too, needed much greater supplies of water. In some ways then maize was peculiarly suited to the holders of relatively small landholdings who, as a result of turning over part of their land to maize production could, in the short term considerably increase their production.

Wheat, rye, millets and maize do not by any means exhaust the list of the grains grown in the Valpolicella. There are frequent references to oats and less frequent ones to barley and buckwheat. Also of importance were the mixtures of grains: wheat and rye, millet and rye, wheat and barley, rye and barley. It is often very difficult in the confusion of dialect names for these mixtures to be sure exactly what was being grown or what constituted the mixtures and in what proportions. Undoubtedly grain mixtures did play a considerable part in the agricultural economy. The growing of mixtures may of course be seen as a sign of a primitive and relatively poor agricultural system, but it is as well to point out here that mixtures did also play a part in insurance and risk-spreading. A mixture of grains on the same field in some ways performs the same function as dividing the field up and growing the two crops separately in the parts: if one fails, the other may well succeed. The resulting harvests, although not as desirable as, say, a good harvest of pure wheat, would be an advantage compared with a totally failed crop.

This was a grain based economy but it was not an economy entirely monopolized by grain. In addition to commercial and semi-commercial crops such as vines, olives and fruit, there were also a large number of other crops cultivated chiefly for food or fodder. Leguminous crops, in particular peas, beans and vetches, seem to have played a large part in the agricultural economy. The importance of leguminous crops in any system of rotation, in particular in an economy where livestock and manure was in increasingly short supply, hardly needs emphasizing. The leguminous crops also played an important role in the insurance economy: their prime role seems to have been as animal fodder or as a vegetable crop, but in times of very severe crisis, beans and peas could be ground into coarse flour which could temporarily solve the hunger problem. There also seems to have been a quite wide range of other vegetable crops which were added to the basic food grains: melons and pumpkins, for instance, played quite a major role in the economy of some of the plains areas. It is quite clear that the Valpolicella was capable of producing a widely varied range of food crops, and a sufficiently wide range to make it possible to avoid the devastating effects of the failure of a single, monocultural crop.

The range of agricultural production did not stop with the food grains and other basic foodstuffs. In particular the Valpolicella produced a range of commercial crops and fruit which made its economy even less dependent upon a single type of production. The most famous product of the Valpolicella, in the seventeenth and eighteenth centuries as now, was wine. In addition to producing wine for its own consumption, the Valpolicella produced wine which was consumed in Verona and increasingly shipped beyond the Veronese.[20] Although large numbers of vines were cultivated, it was unusual, although not totally unknown, for an area to be entirely devoted to vines. Where vineyards as such existed they were usually adjuncts of large estates, usually indeed part of the home farm of the villa.[21] In general, vines, in conjunction often with mulberry trees, were grown in field boundaries and on small plots of land otherwise uncultivatable. Following the patterns of the classical *coltura mista* system of agriculture, the vines shared their land with grain and often with other tree crops. The one major exception to this pattern may be found in the steeply terraced lands of the foothills; here the size and shape of terraces often prevented mixed cultivation and, where the strip was too narrow to permit the cultivation of grain, it might well be given over completely to vines.

The history of the olive in the Valpolicella has certain peculiarities. In particular, lying as it does at the very limit of olive cultivation, the production of the olive trees was extremely unpredictable. Since olive production was so unsure, they were, again, grown where they could share the land with other, more securely productive crops. Olives were frequently grown along field boundaries, often with vines growing up them; they were often grown on pasture land. This pattern also applied to the major 'industrial crop' of the Valpolicella, the mulberry. The mulberry was the vital raw material of the silk industry and without a high level of production of mulberry leaves the high levels of silk production could not have been maintained. Like vines, mulberries thrive best on poor soils and on marginal land, and the great majority of mulberries seem to have been grown in the margins of fields and along roadsides.

The picture of the agriculture of the Valpolicella is then a very mixed one. Rather than the great prairie fields or open fields of the wheat lands of northern France, basically producing a single crop, this was a highly complex mixed farming system with a large number of relatively small fields growing a wide variety of crops. The fields, or even strips within them, were divided by lines of vines, mulberries, olives or fruit trees, which in addition to providing a crop themselves also provided shade, shelter and some moisture retention for the crops growing around them. This was an agriculture in which little land was wasted; in which each plot was expected to produce a number of different crops. It is important to point out that this careful use of land was not, in itself, necessary evidence of land shortage or poverty. Rather it was a system in which prudence and the prudent use of the land to ensure some kind of return whatever the season, was the primary concern.

Not all food crops were produced by agriculturalists. Like all rural populations throughout Europe, the people of the Valpolicella and in particular the poorest amongst them made wide use of wild food crops. Perhaps the most important of these and certainly the most vital for the poor in times of severe shortage were nuts. There is little evidence of the gathering of chestnuts and the grinding of the dried nuts into flour, except possibly in the very worst years, but certainly trespassing in search of nuts or damage to nut trees was a common cause of litigation.[22] Nuts were not the only wild food available. Much of the green vegetables which were eaten seem to have been collected from the wild, although some houses and cottages do seem to have had kitchen gardens. The other great source of wild food was fungi. The woods of the valley sides must have been major producers of numbers of different types of fungi, and for the people of the valley side communes they must have been a source not merely of food but also of income, since there was an active market in fungi in Verona and the other urban centres of the Territorio. It was not merely the more common edible fungi which were to be found: truffles were found in some of the woods and their illicit collection and sale formed part of the basis of a complex series of law suits in the late eighteenth century.[23]

The economy of the Valpolicella was basically arable, but a mixed arable economy, even leaving on one side the pastoral areas of the high hills, requires a considerable amount of livestock – for milk, cheese and other dairy produce, for meat, but above all for manure – without which an intensive and productive agriculture was not possible. The history of the livestock of the Valpolicella is surprisingly difficult to write: despite, or perhaps because of, the taxation of most agricultural animals and despite the official interest of the *Ufficio di Sanita*, there is very little evidence to go on in such a discussion.[24]

Leaving aside for the moment the partially pastoral economies of the high hills, the major livestock population was undoubtedly the draught animals which played an obviously vital role in the rural economy. Horses seem to have been quite rare and to have been used chiefly as a means of transport for the relatively wealthy or as draught animals for boats on the Adige; certainly there is little evidence of horses being used as agricultural draught animals or as pack animals. The chief draught animals were donkeys, asses, mules (which were used also to convey people and goods particularly in the hills) and oxen, bullocks and cows, which seem to have been the principal form of traction, whether of carts or of ploughs. Provision of pasture and winter-feed for plough-teams was an often vital and central part of the contracts for sharecropping tenancies, and his plough animals were often the sharecropper's chief and most valuable asset. The number of plough teams registered in the taxation returns for most communities was much less than the total number of holdings and, even allowing for the hand-cultivation of some of the smaller holdings, it is clear that plough-teams must have been shared or rented out.

Cattle do not, in general, seem to have been kept for meat or for milk; it seems such dairy products as were consumed came largely from sheep or goats. Even in the plains communities it is clear that many households possessed a few sheep and goats which provided some wool and meat, but basically provided milk, cheese and manure. The law suits are full of cases arising from the damage caused by sheep and goats, usually herded together in the classical fashion, being allowed to eat vines and other plants growing along the edges of fields.[25] It might be expected that, as the population grew denser and as more and more of the communal waste land was transferred into private hands, so the population of sheep and goats in the lowlands would decline, leading ultimately to a shortage of dairy produce and manure. Certainly there is clear evidence of these problems in the nineteenth century and it may well be that this process was of some significance in the late eighteenth century crisis in the Valpolicella.

If the larger livestock is extremely difficult to chronicle, this is even more the case with smaller livestock, in particular pigs and poultry. There can be no doubt that many, perhaps most, households in the Valpolicella, rich and poor, kept pigs: the dal Bene agent at Volargne, for instance, records sums of money paid for feed for the pigs,[26] while the law suits again provide a picture of pigs damaging crops and, on at least one occasion, buildings.[27] There may well have been a distinction between the way in which a wealthy household – or rather its home farm – raised pigs in sties, and the much more 'free-range' approach of the poorer households, allowing the pigs to roam the fields and woods, usually with one of the children of the household in charge. It seems likely that, in so far as meat featured in the diet of the poorer sections of the population, that meat was in the seventeenth and eighteenth centuries as in the nineteenth, chiefly pig meat preserved by salting.[28]

The other great source of meat seems to have been poultry. It is quite clear from the very frequent appearances of hens in the records that the poultry population of the Valpolicella was large. Many of the surviving feudal *regalia* were paid in hens or eggs, while the account books of noble families speak of very large quantities of eggs arriving from the estates to feed the household. The poultry seem to have been herded rather like the sheep and goats, by youths and children, and, like the sheep and goats, they seem to have strayed from time to time into places where they were not wanted. Virtually all households seem to have had at least a few chickens, but more exotic fowl are to be found, including turkeys. It seems likely that the more exotic birds were kept chiefly for sale to the Verona market, or as part of the stock of the noble home farm, rather than primarily for local consumption.

The livestock of the Valpolicella was, then, as varied as were its arable crops; this was not in any sense a monoculture, nor indeed an agriculture based on a single type of cultivation. It was a broadly mixed system with at least a partial balance between arable and livestock farming. The Valpolicella system was dependent upon a series of complexly interrelated balances, between land, population, livestock and outside pressures, and it was the livestock which constituted one of the most delicate points in that balance.

IV

The geography of the Valpolicella was complex and varied. Perhaps the most helpful way of distinguishing the regions of the Valpolicella is in terms of relief and climate. The relief of the two *piovadeghi* of S. Giorgio and S. Floriano can perhaps be seen as a kind of bowl, with Verona and the river at its base, with the land rising as it moves away from the centre; the highest land of the Valpolicella is also the land furthest away from Verona and the main centres of population in the plain. The *piovadego* of Negrar does not fit exactly this bowl analogy, but is rather a single valley, running north–south with Negrar at its centre and land on the hills rising on either side; in many ways Negrar repeats the geographical structure of the other two *piovadeghi* in miniature.

The lowest level of the bowl, the 'lower plains' or 'valley' land, is the region along the north bank of the Adige running from Ponton and Settimo, ultimately to Parona and Verona itself. To the south it is bounded by the river while along the northern edge stretches a relatively steep slope dividing the lower plain from the upper. The lower plain contains some of the main centres of population, in particular Pescantina, the largest urban centre of the Valpolicella. It is an area of basically alluvial soils, distinguished also by a relatively scattered settlement pattern outside the few major centres. The mixed cultivation of this region seems to have been dominated by grains and by fruit and market gardening; the peaches, from which popular etymology derives the name of Pescantina, were produced for the Verona market throughout the seventeenth and eighteenth centuries. The physical problems of the plain differ from those of the rest of the Valpolicella in that drainage is more of a problem than is water supply. Not merely the high water table, but also the problems generated by flash floods from the mountains and from the Adige itself made water control a matter of major concern and of some capital investment. Geographically at least, the lower plains belong more to the great plains of the Basso Veronese rather than to the hills which lie behind them. The lower plain had considerable waste lands, in particular close to the river and its tributaries, which provided grazing for cattle.

In Pescantina the lower plain had the largest urban concentration of the Valpolicella; its population, which varied from 1500 to 3000 during this period, made it an important market centre and an important centre of consumption. Its importance both locally and regionally was, however, based on its importance as a transportation centre. The *Burchieri* of Pescantina had, from an early period, established a monopoly on river navigation, and above all on the transportation of goods between Verona and the Veronese border with the Trentino, a monopoly which they successfully defended until 1797. The *Parons* of Pescantina, the owners and 'captains' of the boats constituted the élite of Pescantina and were one of the wealthiest groups in the Valpolicella.

The second level of the bowl, the upper plain, lies between the lower plain and the foothills proper; it includes the lower, more cultivated hills such as the Castelrotto-Negarine spur and the low hills of the Negrar valley, as well as the upper plain proper. The upper plain is approximately ten to twelve metres above the lower plain, and there is a relatively sharp and clear dividing line between the two levels. The major streams, the *Progni* of Fumane, Maran and Negrar, cut through the higher plains in deeply-incised valleys; flooding, both as a result of heavy rains and of the flash-flooding of the progni, was a serious problem, as was the water supply during the dry months of summer. The progni also created major problems for communications, particularly when in spate.

The agriculture of the upper plain was, as everywhere, a mixed one; the production of vines and olives as well as fruit was combined with a wide range of grain production. In many ways the agriculture of the upper plains was intermediate between that of the lower plains and that of the terraced land of the foothills proper. In most cases, the units of cultivation were large enough to allow the use of ploughs and the development of relatively extensive farming. Furthermore, the exploitation of the land did not involve the time-consuming and expensive construction of terraces. The lack of broad river beds and, in general, of wooded slopes meant a very limited area of waste land for the grazing of cattle, and it is in this region that the importance of the provision of pasture *per la soventione del lavorente* is greatest.

The tenurial geography of the upper plain was extremely compli-cated; the region possessed a complex mixture of large estates, large bourgeois holdings and 'peasant' farms. A community like S. Ambrogio displays this variety very clearly: much of its land was held, in relatively small units, by resident landowners, but a not inconsiderable proportion was in the hands of absentee landlords like the Serego Allighieri, or bourgeois like the Bernardi family whose wealth sprang originally from their notarial business in Verona.[29] Fumane displays an even more complex pattern: its land holding was dominated, as the village still is, by the great estate of the della Torre family. The della Torre were not the only outside holders of land: the great abbey of S. Zeno in Verona continued to hold feudal rights in the village and to collect dues, mostly in kind, from many of the landholders; resident landholders also held a considerable proportion of the land of the commune.[30]

The physical division between the lower and upper plains is a relatively clear one: the division between the upper plains and the foothills and valley sides, even though in some senses a more signifi-cant one is, physically, a less distinct one. The relatively gentle slope of the lower hills of Castelrotto, S. Pietro and Gargagnago, and the level plain gives way relatively rapidly to the much steeper slopes of S. Giorgio, Mazzurega and Maran. The dividing line does not coincide even roughly with communal boundaries. Equally, the upper boundary of the foothills is indistinct, merging with little change into the high hills.

The agriculture of the foothills and valley sides is, in some ways, more typically 'Mediterranean' than is that of the two levels of the plain. It is distinguished, first, by the steepness of the land which creates not merely problems of communication and drainage, but also requires the establishment and maintenance of terraces, producing fields which, although they vary considerably in size are, at their largest, smaller than the average on the plains. As a result of the steepness of the land considerable amounts of land are uncultivatable: this is an economy with relatively large amounts of waste land and also of woodland, a valuable asset in an economy like that of the Veronese which suffered from permanent and serious shortages of firewood. Secondly, this was an economy of poor soils, leached by the winter rains and suffering severely from summer and autumn drought. The foothills were very much an area of small producers and small owners; the larger units of the plain stopped, in effect, at the point at which the slope grew steeper and terraces replaced fields. To some extent this pattern reflects the unattractiveness of hill and slope land to the larger landholders; hill land was too unproductive and too unpredictable to constitute a valuable addition to an estate. The foothills, relatively poor though they were, were largely free from the pressures of the great landlords.

If the transition from plain to foothills marks a major change in agricultural organization, it represents also a major change in settlement patterns. The upper plain is an area of basically nucleated settlement; the foothills are typically an area of much more scattered settlement. Typically, the foothills commune consists of a concentration of population around the parish church and a series of hamlets: in some cases, such as Purano and S. Rocco in the commune of Maran, with their own chapels or churches; in others no more than a group of small farms such as the hamlet of la Ca in Mazzurega.

The outermost rim of the Valpolicella is the high hills, lying above 450 metres and rising in places to over 1100 metres. These high lands combine an extensive pastoral agriculture, including the summering of cattle from the lower levels, and indeed from the more distant plains, with considerable extensive arable production, in particular of wheat. The high hills, again, are largely an area of relatively small scale local ownership, although there is some evidence of the growing importance of large estates in the high hills in the eighteenth century. It is also an area of dispersed settlement, perhaps inevitably given the scattered location of the cultivated land.

In addition to its major importance as an area of agricultural production, the Valpolicella was also a major industrial area. Silk was produced virtually everywhere in the Valpolicella, but it was the stone of the Valpolicella which constituted the largest single industrial activity. The pink marbles of the Valpolicella were very much in demand in Verona, in Venice, to which they were shipped down the Adige on rafts, and further afield.[31] The main quarries were in the high hills at Prun, Fane and Torbe and in the upper plain at S. Ambrogio which, throughout the period, was the Valpolicella centre par excellence of the stone-cutting industry.

The complexity of the geography of the Valpolicella has been underlined. There is one final practical point which must be made. Although the Valpolicella was divided into the regions discussed above, the division of the region into communes does not follow that pattern; communes lap over the divisions between the upper and lower plains, and between upper plain and foothills. As a consequence, since virtually all of the records used in this study deal with communes rather than geographical types, a rather different and somewhat less sophisticated grouping of the Valpolicella into three regions – the Valley, the Foothills and the High Hills – has had to be adopted, particularly in Chapter 3.

V

It is quite clear that this was by no means a static or stagnant economy. Even if its major concern was stability or security, this did not mean – could not mean – that the economy could turn its back on change. What is significant is that the change which took place was not necessarily 'change in the right direction', meaning change leading towards industrialization. Equally it is significant that this change 'in the wrong direction' was not the result of a failure to understand, nor yet the reaction of an economy which was driven by crisis and desperation to backward-looking changes, but rather the result of a clear and logical rationale: a rationale which led, for much of the seventeenth and eighteenth centuries to prosperity and not to poverty. Pre-modern man sought survival and prosperity through stability and risk-reduction rather than through modern man's change with risk; this was an aim which is perfectly comprehensible. It is wrong to identify survival with stagnation or with inefficiency; a surviving economy can be highly efficient, as Mark Elvin's investigations of the High Level Equilibrium Trap in China has shown.[32] In the same sense, a survival economy was not necessarily unchanging; indeed survival may well require as much change as does growth. The difference between pre-modern and modern economies lies not in the presence or absence of growth, but rather in the nature and consequences of that growth.

The idea of a 'total history' of any pre-modern economy or society, although theoretically tempting is, practically, an impossibility. A total history of the Valpolicella economy is even more so than most. In part this is a consequence of the lack of that background material upon which even the most dedicated 'total historian' must rely. Understandably, Veronese historians have tended to concentrate on the history of the city in the pre-fifteenth century period; although the period from 1405 onwards is now beginning to attract more attention, a great deal of fundamental information, particularly about the rural sector is lacking. Both the administrative and legal systems, for instance, are virtually unstudied and both are so vital in the operation of the society and economy that without such detailed study, any conclusions must be preliminary; although some attempt has been made in this study to explain their general outlines, it must be emphasized that a great deal of original research still remains to be done before the details of their operation and their effects upon society and economy are clear.

This lack of previous research is in one sense entirely comprehensible. The sources for the rural history of the Veronese during the seventeenth and eighteenth centuries are in some ways voluminous; it would be fair to say that, compared with the records available for the economic and social history of most other regions of Europe during the early modern period, they are spectacularly rich. However, they are scattered, both between archival collections and within them. Public records, lay and ecclesiastical are, rightly, still divided into the groupings which they were given for day-to-day administrative purposes; an efficient bureaucracy, like that of seventeenth and eighteenth century Verona, disposed its activities and its records over a wide range of specialist departments, and hence the search for information inevitably covers a wide range of departments and their records. Furthermore, the records have suffered in their lifetimes a series of disasters and disruptions. 'Weeding', the disposal of 'unnecessary' records by governments chronically short of storage space, has affected virtually every governmental collection of archives in Europe, and in the Veronese and elsewhere it has been pursued with a ruthless lack of logic which has left single years or single decades of records intact while all around them have been destroyed. To this conscious and voluntary destruction must be added the accidental destruction caused by natural (and other) catastrophes. The Veronese records have not been immune from those: a disastrous fire in 1724, for instance, virtually completely destroyed the city's notarial archive, while the flood of September 1882 rendered a large part of the curial archive unusable. In addition, the official records have been removed from time to time, often in circumstances which made the maintenance of order in them virtually impossible: such of the curial records as were saved in 1882 were literally pulled from the shelves as the flood waters rose and tipped into sacks in total disorder; it is only in very recent years that the patient work of the (grossly overworked) curial archivists and their assistants has begun to bring any kind of order to them. The records of the *Archivio di Stato* were similarly, if not so seriously, disorganized by their removal under the threat of Allied bombardment in 1945.[33]

If the official 'central' archives have survived only patchily and in some disorder, the records of the communes have been even less lucky. It is clear from contemporary records that even the smallest communes had, in the eighteenth century, communal archives usually kept in a chest either in the parish church or in the *Casa Comunale* where one existed. The political and economic vicissitudes of the nineteenth and twentieth centuries have wiped most of these out. Some were destroyed by French or Austrian armies during the Napoleonic period, or by military or partisan activity in the First and Second World Wars. Many, particularly of the communes suppressed in the Napoleonic reorganization of government, have disappeared and almost certainly were burnt during the nineteenth century. Large amounts of 'unnecessary' records were destroyed on government instruction in the 1930s to provide raw materials for the Abyssinian campaign. The pattern of survival is very patchy, but very poor.[34]

Similar problems affect private records. Again it is clear that, in the late eighteenth century as before, many families, from the peasant level upwards, had collections of papers – deeds, documents concerning land transfers, wills and so forth. Few of these collections seem to have survived; again the vicissitudes of poverty and war seem to have ensured their destruction. Many of these private documents exist now solely in the form of certified copies kept by notaries; of course the very high proportion of transactions which were carried out by *scrittura privata* have not even left this evidence behind. The survival of notarial copies is, of course, a bonus, but it does create its own problems; the destruction of the notarial archive means that it is only where a notary, or a notarial family, was in business both before and after 1724 that their records before 1724 survive. Unfortunately there seems to be little concept in the Veronese of the 'family solicitor', handling all a family's notarial business; families and individuals seem to have shifted from notary to notary with considerable freedom. The closeness of the Valpolicella to Verona means that not merely were local notaries involved, but in addition any city notary could be drawing up Valpolicella documents. The scale of the notarial records and the lack of usable indexes for many of the notaries makes the discovery of Valpolicella material very difficult and the identification of individual documents effectively impossible.

Estate records too seem to have suffered many similar problems. Some estate records – the dal Bene, the Sagramoso, the Rizzardi,[35] for instance – have survived, albeit in somewhat fragmentary form, and in many cases in such locations and conditions as to make their consultation, even with the generous assistance of the present owners, extremely difficult. In addition, the complex patterns of inheritance, of joint ownership and of transfer of land within and between families have meant that estate records have tended to become fragmented and ultimately lost, or to have remained fixed on the estates rather than being transferred from family to family. Therefore, in the nineteenth and twentieth centuries, they tend to have suffered the same fate as other rural records.

The period of this study is fortunately one which in many ways selects itself. The Plague of 1630, probably the worst epidemic to hit the region since the fourteenth century, marks a very real turning point in the history of the Veronese. The sixteenth century had been a period of general prosperity, based both on agriculture and industry, but it was also a period of growing population and growing economic difficulty; by the 1620s very real problems were beginning to appear, with growing food shortages and increased industrial problems. The Malthusian shock of 1630 and the two decades which followed not merely reduced population levels and thereby ushered in a new pattern of agrarian and industrial development, but it also coincided with the end of Venice's Golden Age and with the realignment of relations between Venice and her Terra Firma empire.

The fall of the Venetian Republic in 1797 is not an economic or social event in the way that 1630 is. The prosperity of the eighteenth century was clearly coming to an end before 1797; from the mid-1760s, economic and social problems were beginning to multiply. Although the problems were to get worse after 1797 – disastrously so by 1815 –1797 was no more than a stage on the way. The fall of the Republic did, however, mark a very clear change in the nature of both central and local government; the effective local self-government and decentralization of the Venetian state gave way to the much greater centralization of two more truly foreign governments, the Austrian and the French. After 1797, neither the Valpolicella nor the Veronese would be able to deal with local problems in the same way again; in a very real sense, in 1797, the history of the Valpolicella as a unit within a Veneto-Veronese confederation came to an end.

This study, then, makes no claim to be a total history of the Valpolicella economy during the last 170 years of Venetian domination but is rather intended to outline some of the basic framework of that history. The starting point for any such study must be, despite all the inherent difficulties, some consideration of the performance of the economy. Chapter 3 offers, through a consideration of levels of population, production and prices, a partial indication of the performance of the economy. All these indicators are, in some way, incomplete; taken together, although they cannot offer a total picture, they do give a reasonable indication of the performance of the base economy. However, it cannot be emphasized enough that what they perforce leave out of the performance of this diversified, commercialized and mobile economy is almost as significant as what is included. Chapter 4 examines the agricultural basis of this structure and considers methods of cultivation, crops and agricultural change. Chapter 5 examines the units of management and exploitation of the land and the organization of the productive units. Chapter 6 examines the tenurial and social bases upon which this agrarian structure rested and the ways in which it changed. Chapter 7 examines the non-agricultural sector of the economy: trade, commerce, industry and migration.

The overriding concern of this study, then, is not to provide a complete or comprehensive coverage of all aspects of the early modern Valpolicella economy or society. Rather, its aim is to examine a pre-modern economy which, despite its seventeenth and early eighteenth century prosperity and its proven ability to change and grow, 'failed' to industrialize. That 'failure' – although it was no failure – has been seen by some historians as a consequence of the imposition of foreign rule and foreign exploitation, that is to say, an early form of the 'Development of Under-Development'. By others it has been seen as a failure of the Mediterranean south, be it for racial, cultural, climatic or other reasons, to take up the manifest advantages of industrialization. By yet others it has been seen as the result of the inflexibility, the stagnation, of a particular pattern of society. The evidence seems to point neither to a failure to achieve a perceived goal, nor yet a stagnant 'anti-enterprise' culture and society, but to a society which was with some considerable success pursuing different, but entirely comprehensible ends.

3
The performance of the economy

I

The performance of any economy is notoriously difficult to evaluate: the large range of variables and the problems of bases of comparison make the clear calculation of any real measure extremely difficult for any modern economy. Now that the myth of the relatively unsophisticated nature of pre-modern economies has been finally destroyed, it is clear that the calculation of performance indicators for pre-Industrial Revolution economies is, if anything, even more difficult. Setting aside the problems of sources, a number of other difficulties arise.

First, it is clear that diversity, rather than simplicity, was the keynote of most pre-modern economies. It is no longer possible to argue that agriculture and agriculture alone constituted the key to the economic success or failure of pre-modern societies: certainly this is the case in the Valpolicella. Agriculture was the major single element in the economy, but it was by no means the only element, and the success or failure of other elements in the economic mix could and did have great importance both for individual families and for the prosperity of the total economy.

Secondly, it is clear that these pre-modern economies were neither static nor stable: change was a permanent feature of their structure. In particular, the complex mix of their economies was constantly shifting: new goods, new crops and new employments constantly appearing, old ones declining and disappearing. To follow a single crop or a single theme through a period as long as that covered by this study is to run the risk of being seriously misled, and of seriously misrepresenting the nature and operation of the economy.

Thirdly, the idea of the pre-modern local economy as being in some way isolated or insulated from change and developments elsewhere, while it does have some truth, particularly in times of general crisis such as the 1630s and 1640s, needs very considerable modification in everyday reality. This is particularly true for a local economy like the Valpolicella lying close to a major source of supply, demand and employment such as Verona. Movements of goods and migration of population played a major part in such economies and make the calculation of performance indicators extremely hazardous.

Finally, it must be stressed that the calculation of performance indicators also begs a very major issue. In a sense indicators are based upon assumptions about what performance should be: they have built into them a set of preconceptions about what is 'good' or 'bad' about the way an economy performs – for example, 'growth' is 'good', 'stagnation' is 'bad'. The unhappy story of Third World development should be a warning of the dangers of such an approach. The same holds true for pre-modern economies, whether they are to be classified as 'developing' or not. One of the worst aspects of the Whiggism of economic historians has been to convert pre-modern economic man into a chronologically earlier version of Industrial Revolution man. This is a historical error as dangerous as Macaulay's conversion of the framers of the Glorious Revolution into early nineteenth century politicians. If the Industrial Revolution has any significance in European (or world) history, part of that significance must lie in a change in the overall economic context and, above all, in economic expectations. At least prima-facie economic rationalities should have changed to confront changing economic and social conditions. Pre-modern economic man may have had the same economic rationality as nineteenth or twentieth century man, but it cannot be taken as axiomatic that he did. Performance indicators must be treated as no more than an indicator of a number of things considered important by the modern world. It may well be that the 'true' performance indicators by which seventeenth and eighteenth century Italians judged their economy were not strictly even quantifiable: stability, security or otherwise from devastating crisis, for instance, may have been much more important than growth, and, therefore, to identify their economy as one in decline because of falling indicators of production is, in one ahistorical sense true, but in reality grossly distorts the actual state of the economy and certainly the response of contemporaries to a 'crisis' which they did not perceive as such.

On these very general levels performance indicators for pre-modern economies, helpful though they are, must be distrusted. They quite literally indicate; they do not answer. At a second level, too, they must be distrusted. A crucial difference between the modern state and its pre-modern ancestor is the modern state's concern with information, with 'statistical evidence' and with the idea that that evidence should be in some way accurate. The Venetian state, like most other seventeenth and eighteenth century states, was beginning the long process of the collection of information. By the mid-eighteenth century the Venetian historian begins to get a flow of apparently useful statistical evidence; this evidence has to be treated with great care. First, the Venetian state was not a disinterested collector of information: no pre-modern state had the resources or the inclination to be that. The information gathered was gathered for specific political, military or economic ends, perceived to be important by eighteenth century rulers. It is a salutary experience, and frequently a frustrating one, to assess the priorities of these eighteenth century men through this lens: if the economic historian ever had any doubts that preceding ages saw the world very differently, this should be an object lesson. These eighteenth century concerns can, and do, still impinge on the study of pre-modern economic history: the temptation to assume that, because the Venetian state was concerned with the extension of rice farms (*risarie*) in the plains of the Veronese in the late seventeenth and eighteenth centuries, rice cultivation was of crucial importance in the Veronese economy, is an easy one to succumb to, but it would have surprised many Venetian governors, whose concern was with river navigation and not with agriculture.

This collection of information for very specific practical ends also has another important consequence. When the practical occasion for the collection of information passed, the collection of information ceased or – since this was eighteenth century Venice – gradually faded away. Again frustratingly, the pattern of information is one of sudden, intense, if frequently misleading illumination, preceded and followed by almost total darkness. The idea of a 'run' of information covering more than a few decades at the most is not one which has much place in the study of eighteenth century Venetian statistics.

The reasons why official information was collected also place another fundamental limitation on their use. The Venetian state had no disinterested statistical service to collect its information for it. Such information as it could gather had to be gathered through the agency of the existing governmental structure and, in essence, that meant through lay agency, the elected officials of the communes. These officials and those who elected them were also the tax-payers, and the collection of information was seen in the Veronese, as elsewhere in Europe, as the first stage in the imposition of taxation. The flow of information to the state must then be seen as flawed for this reason. It is the same reason which must throw doubt on, for instance, the circumstantial evidence provided in literary form by the *Relazioni* of the Venetian rectors.[1] Presented to the Senate in Venice at the end of their period of office, they are both a justification for their own actions and also, given the tendency of the Rectors to 'go native', pleas from the Terra Firma cities for special consideration based upon the poverty of the 'poor subject city'. The Relazioni of the Rectors of Verona are in no way different to those of the Rectors of other subject cities, and as political manifestos and special pleadings they need all be considered suspect.

Officially gathered information, which is of such great importance in the study of modern economies, is flawed and has to be treated as such. It is to private information, to estate and other accounts, that attention has to shift. Private sources provide at least as many problems as do the official ones. First is the problem of survival.

It is very clear that from long before 1630 the Veronese was a literate society in which virtually all major and most minor trans-actions were faithfully recorded on paper. Only a minuscule fraction of this material has survived: there is nothing so uninteresting or disposable as last year's petty cash book or even last year's accounts. This disposability is emphasized by the relatively rapid transfer of ownership of land and the confusing interchanges of interests through marriage, death, remarriage, gift and sale which characterize the Veronese, and in particular its landed groups, in the seventeenth and eighteenth centuries. Few estate accounts seem to have survived and certainly very few indeed covering more than a few years.

The one institution which partially escaped from the disposal trap was the Church, or rather the large number of ecclesiastical corpora-tions, secular and regular, which made up the organizational church. In part the natural hoarding instinct of the Church but also the grow-ing centralization of the post-Tridentine Church has led to the accumulation of a large body of information of very considerable use to the economic and social historian which, in the case of Verona, is only now beginning to be explored. This material, split between the Archive of the Curia and the State Archive, provides one of the key-stones of any study of the early modern Veronese economy.

The ecclesiastical records are not without their problems, however. Above all, the ecclesiastical corporations were themselves very peculiar institutions and were part of an even more peculiar institu-tion. In part this peculiarity sprang from the aims and functions of the corporations: monasteries, the *Pievi*, the whole Church itself can very easily be presented as, indeed in many ways presented themselves as, business corporations, concerned with profit and loss, managerial effi-ciency and career structures; but they still retained and, it is fair to say, still attempted to live up to, other aims and ideals. Equally, the corporate immortality of the Church gave its parts rather different priorities to those of secular society. The ecclesiastical corporations, too, were required to manage their estates and collect many of their revenues indirectly through agents. As so often in the Venetian state, these agents were frequently also the payers, and hence the yield of tithes and other revenues were filtered through a system which tended to minimize them. The corporations were not, however, isolated from the overall operation of the economic and social system – indeed the growing dominance of the lower and middle levels of the Church in the Valpolicella by important local families pulled the Church into closer contact with lay society and the general economy in the

seventeenth and eighteenth centuries – and the same economic pressures and problems which produced changes in the economic practices
of the lay landlord also produced changes in the operation of the
ecclesiastical estate. The ecclesiastical corporations were no more
unchanging in their economic organization than were lay estates, and
their accounting systems changed to reflect this.

The Church may have been immortal, but its agents and accountants
were not. One of the major problems with using ecclesiastical
accounts as a source for long run indicators is the inconsistency of the
accounts themselves. Attempts were made by the episcopal *curia* in
the late seventeenth century and the eighteenth century to impose
some kind of standardization on the accounts of the *Pievi* and
monastic houses: the efforts had sufficient success for it to be possible
to isolate three or four basic systems. Each monastic or capitular
accountant, however, made, consciously or unconsciously, changes
and modifications within these basic systems; the change between
accountants frequently also means quite major changes in technique.
Even the apparent continuity of the ecclesiastical record is subject,
then, to quite alarming and sudden lacunae or shifts. The Church,
outwardly the most stable and conservative of organizations, betrays
on closer inspection a bewildering propensity to change and to
modify.

Any performance indicators drawn from this mixture of half-
information, misinformation and silence can only, then, be an indication (and an indirect one at that) of the real performance, the real
prosperity of an economy. The present chapter seeks to draw some
themes out of this tangled mass, but it must be emphasized that they
can be no more than indicators. Any appearance that they may give
of providing a clear, certain and detailed history of economic performance must, from the outset, be rejected. Particularly in the eighteenth century, and to a considerable extent in earlier periods, there
are strong reasons to believe that, while the overall picture is essentially correct, the detail may well be extremely misleading. To avoid
any spurious claim to any more than overall accuracy, the figures have
been subjected to no more than the most basic manipulation; to do so
would have given the results drawn from them a definitiveness which
the sources themselves do not allow.

Three indicators – population, arable production (in particular of
wheat) and prices – have been chosen. In part any such choice is
inevitably determined by the availability of sources, but it is clear that
these three indicators do have a very real claim to be crucial to the
general performance of the economy. They allow some measure, albeit
impressionistic, of the relationship between key variables in the
economic situation and hence some indication of how well or how
badly the economy was able to deal with the problems it confronted.
It must again be emphasized that the picture they give is only partial

and hence potentially misleading. The Valpolicella economy in the seventeenth and eighteenth centuries was not a simple monocultural, or mono-activity one, and to insist on the permanency of one activity, or to base indicators on a single activity, although it may be necessary in practical terms and although it may give some indication of performance, is to risk not merely misinterpreting but also misunderstanding the total economy.

II

Levels of population, and the movement of population, lie at the very centre of the performance of any agriculturally related economy. It is to go too far to claim for population levels an absolute primacy in the overall history of any economy and in particular of an economy like that of the Valpolicella. Equally, levels are not in any sense an inescapable and fixed element in the economic structure: not merely do 'natural' factors, Malthusian or otherwise, produce self-corrections but in addition migration, temporary or permanent, plays a major role in the population history of every pre-modern economy yet studied.

In a sense the population historian of the seventeenth and eighteenth centuries is privileged over the historian of previous centuries. For the first time, in the early modern period, states began to perceive population as a problem or an opportunity – as something of which the state could and should profitably take heed. For some states, such as England, population was seen as a problem, as a source of pressure and social disorder, as one of the causes of poverty in late Tudor and Stuart England; as a problem to be, if not solved, at least mitigated by the more or less forcible emigration of surplus population to North America or to the Caribbean. Increasingly, however, the mercantilist states of the later seventeenth and early eighteenth centuries saw population as a source of strength. Whether as a threat or as a strength, population levels came to be of much greater concern to every European state in the eighteenth century. In addition, the prevalence in many parts of Europe of poll taxes, gave the state a second concern with the counting and registration of at least one section of the population; it also gave a sector of the population a very good reason for seeking to elude the state's attempts to register it.

A second major concern of the state also produced a growing interest, if not in absolute population levels, at least in some of the basic raw materials of demography. The growing efficiency of the state's machinery led, in the Venetian territories as elsewhere from the late sixteenth century onwards, to attempts to control more effectively the spread of epidemic disease, usually plague, but later all forms of epidemic. As part of this process, the *Ufficio di Sanita*, established in Verona in 1575, began to collect information on the level of births and above all deaths, beginning in the city in 1630 and extending to the whole of the rural Veronese in 1732.[2]

The state then was beginning to take an interest in population levels, but it must be emphasized that the state's interest was not a modern demographer's interest. The figures which are available allow estimates and guesses to be made: very rarely do they allow any real estimation of total levels of population and in most cases only indirectly allow any more than an estimate of the scale of population fluctuation.

The first indication of population levels which comes from state sources is a series of censuses undertaken as part of the reassessment of the land tax, the *Estimo*, in 1628. These censuses were undertaken by the elected taxation officials of each commune; despite worries expressed by the Rectors in their *relazioni* in the years after 1600 that the Territorio was becoming depopulated due to the flight of cultivators to the Trentino and Mantua, driven by high taxation and food shortages,[3] the real purpose behind the census was taxation. In some communes of the Veronese – Caldiero in the foothills to the east of Verona, for instance – the assessors took their instructions to mean that they should enumerate the total population, male and female, of whatever age.[4] Unfortunately none of the Valpolicella communes adopted this wider interpretation, or if they did their efforts have not survived: indeed the survival of the censuses is extremely patchy. That for S. Ambrogio, which is typical of the few which have survived, merely gives a total for each category (Men 18–70, Boys, Women and Girls) and it also includes a mysterious group of *cittadini* – citizens of Verona – who do not appear in the fuller list of 'Persone dali 18 ali 70', that is to say those paying the *testadego* or poll tax. It seems likely that these *cittadini* are merely those citizens holding land in S. Ambrogio and not, except possibly for the months of the summer *villegiatura*, resident in the commune.[5]

The first and, in a sense, the only total enumeration of the population which is available for this period comes from the *Ufficio di Sanita*, in the aftermath of the disastrous outbreak of plague in 1630. In the Valpolicella, as indeed in most of the north-west of the Veronese, the plague of 1630 was the most destructive of life for at least 200 years: it has been suggested that in places the proportional loss of life was actually greater than in 1347–9. The effects on the rural economy and on the economy of the city were, in the short term, devastating: the trade of the city declined, houses were ruined, whole hamlets depopulated. The census of 1630–1 was a desperate attempt by the *Sanita* to assess the extent of the disaster which had struck the Territorio and also to ensure that the contagion had been contained. The information was gathered from the communes by travelling commissioners from the *Sanita* charged with enquiring not merely into the level of losses in each commune but also into the zeal

Table 1   Population 1630 and 1631

	1630 No. (%)	1631 No. (%)
Plains	5500 (52.0)	2272 (53.6)
Hills	2990 (28.3)	1070 (25.3)
Valley	2145 (20.3)	895 (21.1)

Sources: ASVR: Sanita Busta 191

Notes
Plains: Arbizzan (= Arbizzano), S. Ambrosio (= S. Ambrogio), Burri (= Bure),
Castelrotto, S. Florian (= S. Floriano), Fumane, Gargagnago, Marano, Negrarine
(= Negarine), S. Pietro in Cariano, Settimo (di Castelrotto), S. Sofia, Vargatara
(= Valgatara), S. Vido (= S. Vito di Negrar).
Hills: Breonio, Cavalo con Volane, Fane, S. Giorgio, Mazzarega (= Mazzurega), Monte,
Prun, Torbe.
Valley: Pescantina, Porton (= Ponton), Volargne.

and completeness with which the *Sanita*'s instructions had been carried out.[6] The census data were based upon returns drawn up by the Parish clergy from their burial records: obviously the survival or otherwise of a priest could have quite significant effects on the accuracy of the final information. The form in which the information was finally recorded by the *Sanita* was not prescribed and varies sharply from commune to commune, to the extent that direct comparisons of, for instance, family size are impossible. What the returns do have in common is a total for all those alive at the end of the Plague in late 1630, and a total for those who had died between Easter and Autumn 1630; by adding the two together it is possible to reach a total for the population before the Plague which, if not absolutely accurate is likely to be nearly so. These figures are summarized in Table 1.

It is possible that this census overestimates the population before 1630 by including in the deaths a number of immigrants: there is considerable evidence in 1630 (as at other times of plague) of considerable movement of population, in particular of migrants fleeing the infected cities to the apparently safer countryside. Unfortunately the form of the 1630–1 census does not allow any very clear correction on this basis. Where the figures for 1630 can be checked against roughly contemporary figures, as they can for Caldiero, they give a very close correspondence. It is reasonable then to accept the 1630 and 1631 figures as being roughly accurate, both in the absolute level of population they indicate and also the proportional fall in the population (about 60 per cent) in that year. This level of population decline, although extremely high, seems typical on the basis of the census of the whole of the north-western Veronese. Verona lay on the edge of the major band of infection: although the plague was serious in Venice itself and the other cities of the eastern Veneto, there is a very sharp tailing-off of rural deaths across the Veronese, the 60 per cent mortality in the north west falling to about 30 per cent in Nogara and Villa Bartolomea in the south east of the Territorio.

A number of features are clear from Table 1. The first, supported by evidence from other sources such as the *Estimo*, is the very high level of population immediately before the Plague. It is not clear, and comparison of the earlier figures where they exist does not make it any clearer, whether the population of the Valpolicella and indeed of the Veronese as a whole, reached its peak in 1630 or whether, as Antonio Bragadino reported in his *Relazione* in 1627, the population was already in decline in the mid-1620s.[7] Certainly a considerable amount of evidence suggests that the population of the *Territorio* never, before 1797, reached again the levels of the 1620s. The second is the scale of the demographic disaster. Population fell to some 40 per cent of its pre-1630 level and rates of mortality were not equal: in Cavalo population fell by 71 per cent, in Ponton by 71 per cent and in Monte by 74 per cent. This inequality of mortality also produced a significant shift in the population balance of the Valpolicella. The communes of the high hills, especially, which had almost certainly seen the most rapid population growth in the late sixteenth and early seventeenth centuries as new marginal land was opened for grain production, were disproportionately affected, their share of the overall population falling from 28.3 per cent in 1630 to 25.3 per cent in 1631. This process of slow decline in the high hills seems to be continued throughout the demographic history of the seventeenth century and much of the eighteenth century.

The census of 1630–1 is unique in the demographic history of the Veronese in the seventeenth and eighteenth centuries: it had no successor. There is also a very real problem; the demographic disaster of 1630 was the most spectacular event of the century, but much evidence suggests that the disasters were not limited to 1630. In particular, outbreaks of plague in 1635 and 1639 almost certainly reduced the population still further. In 1639, Valier, in his *Relazione*, claimed that the population of the *Territorio*, which had fallen to 85 000 in 1631 had further fallen to 80 000 by 1639.[8] The crisis of 1647–52 may well have resulted in further population contraction. Certainly it would be dangerous to assume that the seventeenth century population trough occurred immediately after 1630; it may well be that the true low should be placed in the early 1650s.

Until the collection of figures for births and deaths by the *Sanita* began in 1732 the only evidence for population change is, inevitably, indirect and dubious. There are two major sources: taxation records and episcopal visitations. Both are relatively infrequent, particularly in the eighteenth century, and both are open to the very real criticism that they do not register total population but only taxpayers or communicants and therefore are only usable by the application of a multiplier. The episcopal records, although in theory they offer a useful indicator for this 'dark' period, are so limited as to make their use impossible in practice. Again, they cannot be used as any more than an approximate indicator of absolute population levels, but they do provide, in a period when other indicators are lacking, an indication of the direction of movement of the total population.

The *testadego* – the poll tax – was levied throughout this period on all males aged between 18 and 70, with certain exceptions for, for instance, the members of the *Cernide* – the locally-raised army and customs force. It was not, then, a tax on households, but on individuals, which makes the application of a multiplier to the crude figures even more complex than it would be with, say, a hearth tax. It is quite clear from evidence from other communes of the Veronese (no strictly comparable evidence exists for the Valpolicella) that, certainly in the early seventeenth century, rural households varied very widely in size and composition, even within quite small communities. Furthermore, much of the evidence upon which the calculation of a multiplier must be based comes from the 1620s: it seems reasonable to suppose that a catastrophe like that of 1630 would have some effects on household size and upon the age distribution of the population, and probably that a multiplier based on the 1620s would, at least for much of the seventeenth century, tend to overestimate the population. The *testadego* figures also offer further problems: first, as taxation figures collected by those who were to be taxed, they are subject to all the doubts which must attach to such figures. Secondly, they are by no means complete: not every commune by any means included the *testadego* in its *estimo*: in others the *testadego* is included in such a way that it is impossible to produce a number of taxpayers.

The indication, then, is even more partial than from the 1630 census. As an example, the *testadego* from S. Ambrogio illustrates some of the problems and also ultimately perhaps gives some indication of population movement during the century after 1630. Table 2 is based on the *testadego* returns for the commune from 1634 to 1752 (no figure for 1766, the last Venetian reassessment of the *estimo*, has survived). Two multipliers have been used. The first (column A) is derived from the 1628 S. Ambrogio return: since this does not identify households, and since it almost certainly included a number of exempt taxpayers, it cannot be accepted without some qualification. The second (column B) is based upon information drawn from similar censuses in other communes (Caldiero, Villa Bartolomea, Oppeano) in the late 1620s: this tends to increase population levels slightly. Such a process is not without its dangers. In particular, since the *testadego* was only levied on males over the age of 18 and under 70, the age distribution of a particular community at the point at which the census was taken is obviously crucial.

Table 2 Population of S. Ambrogio based on the *Testadego*

		Heads	A	B
1628	580			
1630	711			
1631	279			
1634		56	206	219
1639		76	279	297
1652		80	294	318
1670		81	297	323
1690		100	367	391
1710		79	290	309
1752		93	341	364

Sources: ASVR AEP 609; 1630, 1631, ASVR Sanita 191

Two important preliminary points need to be made about Table 2. The *estimo* and hence the *testadego* was not assessed at regular or fixed intervals. Although there was a relatively regular 20-year pattern from 1650 to 1710, before 1650 the *estimi* were very much more frequent: after 1710 no new *estimo* was made until 1752 and the records of the last Venetian *estimo*, that of 1766, have not survived for all the Valpolicella communes. Secondly, the tendency of the records to over-emphasize swings after periods of difficulty are clear: almost certainly the sharp drop (of over 25 per cent) between the census figure of 1631 and the calculated figure for 1634 is the result of a general lowering of the age profile; the equally sharp revival from 1634 to 1639 is probably in part the result of many of the young men of 1634 attaining their 'taxation-majority'. It may also be the case that the decline in population between 1690 and 1710 is, in part, the result of such an age shift.

S. Ambrogio has some claims to being considered slightly atypical in the Valpolicella during this period. It was one of the major centres of marble production, and for that reason may well have attracted population in search of employment. In addition it was not dominated by a few large landholders or by noble estates and villas. Both of these factors may well have tended to place S. Ambrogio amongst those areas of the Valpolicella which grew relatively rapidly. Certainly as a 'plains' commune it is likely to have seen more rapid growth than did the hill communes which surround it on the north and west. If S. Ambrogio was not an absolutely typical community, nonetheless it is sufficiently typical to allow some general conclusions to be drawn. The S. Ambrogio figures show very clearly the sharp fall in 1630/1 and, although they may over-estimate it, the continuing falls in the 1630s. From 1639 onwards the growth of population increased slowly until the 1670s and 1680s, although the figures almost certainly conceal greater fluctuations up and down in, for instance, the late 1640s. A sharp rise in the 1670s and 1680s was followed by an equally sharp fall between 1690 and 1710: again this fluctuation is almost certainly exaggerated by shifts in age distribution. The first half of the eighteenth century saw sharp and apparently sustained growth, a growth again underestimated by the *testadego*. It is significant that by the mid-eighteenth century the population had not yet, apparently, reached the levels of 1628. Indeed, on the basis of the return of births and deaths in the *Sanita* after 1732, it is possible to calculate that even in the early 1790s the population of S. Ambrogio had still not reached its 1628 level.

Demographic evidence becomes somewhat fuller from the early 1730s. Since the plague of 1630, the *Sanita* had been collecting information on births and deaths within the city; in 1732 that system was extended also to the *Territorio*. From 1732 until the end of Venetian rule information on births and deaths is centralized in the *Sanita*. The agency for the collection of this information was the parish clergy who were required to submit lists (*fede*) of baptisms and burials in their parishes to the *Sanita*. In Verona the returns were transcribed into large registers which effectively represent a partial transcription of the baptism and burial registers of the individual parishes. Not merely is this convenient but it also fills the very large gaps in survival of the registers in the individual parishes. These compilations, however, are not without their problems. The multiple series of transcriptions has inevitably produced errors, chiefly, although not solely, of omission; as registers of baptisms and burials they are not strictly limited to the resident population of the communes. There is considerable evidence, for instance, that women chose to give birth, particularly to their first child, in their maternal home or the house of a sister or aunt rather than in their own home, which frequently meant that children were born in communes away from that of their parents' usual residence. Equally men and women did not necessarily die, or live at the time of their death, in the commune where they had spent most of their lives. The returns include also the birth of children to travellers, vagrants and temporary migrants, and the deaths of the same categories. Above all, they do not take any account of, nor give any indication of, migration – either in or out. Other evidence suggests the crucial importance of migration in the economy and demography of the Valpolicella, indeed of the whole Veronese, and hence this lack is a major and significant one. The final problem is that the figures deal with annual increments in the population; at no point do they provide a total figure for the population of any commune. It is possible to use the population totals calculated from the *testadego* as a basis and this is done in Table 2.

Table 3 summarizes the movements revealed by the *Sanita* registers: totals are organized into five-year periods (except for 1732–4 and

1795–7) and an annual movement of population has been calculated. One very clear feature is the relative stability of the number of births: leaving aside 1732–4 and 1795–7 when special factors, both real and of recording are present, the difference between the highest and lowest quinquennial totals for births is less than 10 per cent. Very strikingly, too, although the population was clearly increasing naturally by about 120 a year until 1795, the highest levels of births are not solely at the very end of the period, implying a falling birth rate at the end of the eighteenth century. The number of deaths on the other hand shows much greater variation and a tendency to grow suggesting a death rate at least not falling and possibly static or increasing. What is also clear are the dramatic demographic difficulties of the second half of the century, in particular the 1770s and the last years of crisis before the fall of the Republic in 1797. Using the figure for total population for S. Ambrogio (Table 2) it is possible to calculate not merely total population figures for the commune, but also to combine these with the recorded births and deaths to produce an indication of the movement of birth and death rates. It must again be emphasized that these figures are not absolute. The figure for total population in 1752 on which they are based is open to considerable criticism; in addition, the inability of the material available to take account of migration means that the figure for total population is an artificial one based on 'natural' factors only. Table 3 does, however, provide a basis for an indication of the movement of birth and death rates if no more.

Tables 3 and 4 taken together point to much the same pattern: relatively high birth rates in the 1750s (and before), falling pretty consistently until the later 1780s when, for some reason, they leap suddenly upwards. On the other hand, a death rate which falls very much more slowly until the 1780s and then fluctuates widely. The global figures conceal a number of other variations and in particular a number of very bad years for population in periods of general population growth; both 1753 and 1758 saw deficits while nine years before 1770 (1733, 1742, 1751, 1752, 1754, 1760, 1762, 1764 and 1768) saw overall surpluses of births over deaths less than 100 for the whole Valpolicella.

It is important to emphasize that within the general trends, individual years, or individual communes or regions could demonstrate very widely varying fluctuations; mortality in particular was characterized in part by large local variation, epidemic disease or local coincidence leading to very high deficits in years which were generally good. In 1737, for instance, a year in which the whole Valpolicella has a total surplus of 132, Maran suffered a deficit of 5, in 1744 (+207), Arbizzano had a deficit of 6. In 1759 over half (59) of the total surplus was accounted for by the single commune of Pescantina. Examples of this sort could be multiplied, but it is clear

Table 3 Movement of population in five-year periods 1732–97

Period	Births	Deaths	+/–	Annual average
1732–4	1551	1210	+341	+113.6
1735–9	2928	1951	+977	+195.4
1740–4	2971	2094	+877	+175.4
1745–9	3058	2311	+747	+149.4
1750–4	2792	2564	+228	+45.6
1755–9	2910	2285	+625	+125
1760–4	2814	2284	+530	+106
1765–9	2923	2306	+617	+123.4
1770–4	2855	2380	+475	+95
1775–9	3088	2893	+195	+39
1780–4	3065	2460	+605	+121
1785–9	3025	2486	+539	+107.8
1790–4	3050	2430	+620	+124
1795–7	1624	2074	–450	–150

Sources: ASVR: Registri Battezzatti: Provincia 112–173; ASVR: Registri Morti: Provincia 247–308

Table 4 Population of S. Ambrogio

	Average population	Average number of births p.a.	Percentage	Average number of deaths p.a.	Percentage
1750–4	358	41.8	116.7	32.8	91.6
1755–9	381	39.6	103.9	35.4	92.9
1760–4	405	41.0	101.2	36.8	90.8
1765–9	436	42.6	97.7	36.4	83.5
1770–4	449	37.0	82.4	36.6	81.5
1775–9	444	39.8	89.6	39.0	87.8
1780–4	474	37.2	78.4	32.6	68.7
1785–9	474	46.8	98.7	46.0	97.0
1790–4	507	61.2	120.7	48.2	95.1
1795–7	506	47.7	94.2	72	142.3

Sources: As Table 3

that population movements were not simple, clear or universal and that local factors are frequently as important as general influences in dictating patterns of fluctuations.

This compilation of local factors makes any attempt at interpreting the material from 1732 onwards on a communal basis rather more difficult than might otherwise be the case. Table 5A attempts to

Table 5A   Proportion of total births per decade by region 1735–94

	Plains %	Hills %	Valley %
1735–44	55.3	21.6	23.0
1745–54	53.6	22.7	23.7
1755–64	54.5	20.8	24.6
1765–74	53.4	21.5	25.0
1775–84	54.7	21.0	24.3
1785–94	56.8	19.5	23.6

Sources: As Table 3

Table 5B   Proportion of total surplus per decade by region 1735–94

	Plains %	Hills %	Valley %
1735–44	50.5	18.5	31.0
1745–54	50.75	15.9	33.3
1755–64	63.2	10.0	26.8
1765–74	53.8	21.9	24.3
1775–84	62.8	26.3	10.9
1785–94	58.7	17.1	24.1

Sources: As Table 3

analyse shifting proportions of births between the three major geographical zones of the Valpolicella. The picture is, as would be expected, somewhat confused, in particular after 1775 when the effects of frequent and continuing crisis begin to produce new complications. Equally, it has to be said that the relative proportion of births region by region is only a very indirect and partial indicator of the relative position of the regions. Table 5B analyses the proportion of the total surplus for each decade attributable to each region: the information here, for the period after 1770, is even more confused and difficult to interpret. The tables do seem to indicate reasonably clearly that, at least until the late 1760s and possibly thereafter, the population of the hill communes was declining as a proportion of the total population of the Valpolicella. Less clear is the relationship between plains and valley communes but, again until the mid-1770s, there are strong hints that a growing proportion of the population was to be found in the valley communes which were, however, badly hit by the crisis of the 1770s and early 1780s.

It is now possible to attempt a broad sketch of the movement of the

population over the whole period. In the 1620s the population of the
Valpolicella had reached levels which it was not, it seems, to exceed
before the nineteenth century. The evidence suggests that the growth
of population had slowed down, and may even have stopped in the
1620s. The massive crisis of 1630, in which the population fell by
perhaps 60 per cent was, however, the real turning point in the demographic history of the period: not merely did the population fall but
in addition there was a shift in the geographical balance away from the
grain-producing communes of the hills towards the plains and the
valley. The population may have recovered slightly in the early 1630s
and again in the early 1640s, only to be held down again by new crises
in the mid-1630s and the late 1640s. Despite the S. Ambrogio figures
(Table 2), it may well be that the minimum came not in 1631 but in
the late 1640s or early 1650s. For the next century the evidence is
sparse, but it all points to a steady if slow growth, probably reaching
a peak around 1700, but falling again in the succeeding decade. After
about 1715 a period of growth set in which was to continue until at
least the mid-1770s, and which may well have continued until the
mid-1790s. The most rapid period of this growth probably fell in the
two decades before 1750, although that must remain conjecture; even
in these demographically good years there were crises, years of deficit.
From the 1750s onwards, if not earlier, birth rates began to fall, and
to fall much more rapidly than death rates. The third quarter of the
eighteenth century was one of slowing population growth. After 1775
the population was hit by a series of major economic and political
crises, which, with an interlude in the early 1780s, continued until the
fall of the Republic: by the late 1790s falling birth rates and rising
death rates combined to produce, even without the complications of
migration, a net fall in population levels.

III

In an economy in which agriculture played a major role, the level of
agricultural production is the second major determinant of overall
economic performance. It must be emphasized from the outset that
the economy of the Valpolicella was not an entirely agricultural
economy, having also major industrial and commercial activities
which played an important complementary role in the total economy,
nor was it a closed economy in which locally-produced food was
merely locally-consumed. For some centuries before 1630 Verona,
along with the other north Italian cities, had been a major importer of
food; the grain and other foodstuffs imported, either officially or
commercially, into the city found their way also into the general
economy of the Veronese. The people of the Valpolicella had access,
albeit restricted – on occasion by civil ordinance and permanently by

the tax (*dacio*) on the imports and exports of grain from the city – to the markets of the city both as sellers and buyers. The crude relationship between production and population, even if it were calculable in unambiguous terms, is only a part of the total picture.

For something as obviously central to the economic history of the Valpolicella, and to the day-to-day economic perception of contemporaries, it is surprisingly difficult to find information on levels of production in the seventeenth and eighteenth centuries. To some extent this reflects the nature of the agricultural economy. Even in the hill communes, the economy of the Valpolicella was not monocultural. Food grains played a major part, but pulses, fodder crops, fruit, grapes, olives and mulberries were also major elements. Furthermore, within this mixed economy, the balance between particular crops was constantly changing; new crops, most famously maize, rose to importance, then declined and even disappeared. In addition, a common feature of Valpolicella agriculture was the use of mixed crops – for example wheat and barley, wheat and rye, or mixed pulses. This makes the problem of calculation extremely difficult. In addition, a highly complex vocabulary of terms for these mixtures existed: *grana*, *formenton*, *spelta*, *formenton nero* (which is distinguished from *segala* [rye]) and many others. It is never clear what is meant precisely by these terms, nor is it clear whether the terms have any stable meaning since at different times, and in different places at the same time, terms which elsewhere are synonymous are apparently clearly distinguished from each other. A further complication is that, particularly before 1630, there is some evidence to prove that, when in tithe records a particular volume of *formento* (wheat) is referred to, the volume may be the converted value of a quantity of mixed grains, rather than a true measure of wheat produced. Similar sorts of problems arise with grape and wine production: the actual volume of production obviously is only one of a number of factors determining the quality and quantity of the wine finally produced.

The most immediate source of information about agricultural production should come from the producers themselves. It is unlikely that any records from the smaller producers have survived: a combination of highly complex inheritance patterns and the grinding poverty of the nineteenth and early twentieth centuries have certainly guaranteed the destruction of anything as ephemeral as old accounts, other than perhaps a few, covering single years or short runs of years. It is inevitably to the larger owner, lay and ecclesiastical, that attention has to be turned. In fact, consultable lay estate records from the Valpolicella are, at present, largely non-existent. The dal Bene archive contains some estate accounts from Volargne from the mid-seventeenth century and rather more from the late eighteenth, but none of these are in a form which makes any real assessment of production levels possible. More private accounts, such as those of the

Sagramosa family or the Guerrieri-Rizzardi group of families, have recently become available to scholars, but only in such a way and under such conditions as to make the search for and study of production data extremely slow.

It is, then, to the ecclesiastical records that it is necessary to turn. Following the dissolution of the monastic houses under the Napoleonic *Regno d'Italia*, the 'economic and administrative' records of the houses (but not their 'spiritual' records) passed first into the hands of the *Demanio* and ultimately, therefore, into the *Archivio di Stato*. This mass of material, as yet largely untouched by economic and social historians, contains information on the day-to-day life of the houses as well as of their wider economic activities. Unlike lay accounts, the accounts of monastic houses were audited annually, first by a committee of monks appointed by the monastic chapter and then by the Vicar-General of the diocese or his agent. The requirements of this system had two consequences for monastic accounts. First it imposed some form of partial standardization on them, and also a series of complex internal cross-checks which make it much easier for the historian to follow what was actually taking place. Secondly, and perhaps more significantly, the system required the drawing up each year (in a few cases, every three years) of what can best be described as a profit and loss account; the financial officers of the house had to present to the chapter a statement of income and expenditure and an inventory of the goods still in the monastery's hands. This meant that each sub-head of the account had to be totalled and ruled-off each year. The final balance (*summa summarum*) which was the obvious major concern of the other members of the house and of the Vicar-General, interests the economic historian rather less than the detailed statements of income and expenditure, in cash and kind under each head.

Unfortunately the ecclesiastical estate accounts for the Valpolicella present a number of major problems. The first is, simply, their scarcity. Despite the economic importance of the church in the Veronese, in the Valpolicella the church was not a major landowner and certainly not a major agricultural operator. The vast majority of the considerable income which ecclesiastical corporations drew from the Valpolicella came not from directly managed or even rented estates, but from *livelli*. The *livello* was a charge on land, in cash or in kind, paid by the effective owner of property to someone else, usually, though not inevitably, an ecclesiastical corporation. The size of the payment was normally permanently fixed and the property on which the *livello* fell was freely alienable by the *livello*-payer; the transfer of the property involved also the transfer of the duty to pay the *livello*. Much the largest share of most monastic houses was made up of this kind of payment, largely unaffected by fluctuations in production, although obviously the value of payments in kind fluctuated with general price movements. Ecclesiastical estates, and especially large ecclesiastical estates were very few in the Valpolicella, the most important of them being those of S. Zeno Maggiore at Fumane, of S. Leonardo at S. Pietro in Cariano, of S. Fermo Maggiore at S. Pietro in Cariano and Bure, and of S. Eufemia at Negarine.

The second problem concerns the management of the estates. Venetian law effectively forbade the large-scale direct farming of monastic demesne; the social composition of the community of most houses, equally, made direct cultivation by the brothers and sisters rather improbable. Monastic estates were normally worked through agents, the normal forms of these agencies being either a rent (*affitto, affittanza*) or the large-scale form of sharecropping common in the Veronese known as *lavorencia*. *Affitti* were always for fixed cash payments and usually for terms of years, most commonly three or five, and most usually renewed. As a guide to levels of production, these fixed rents are of little direct use. It is basically the *lavorencia* contract which offers the greatest prospect for information; here too there is a problem. There was no standard form of *lavorencia* contract, the distribution of production between *lavorente* and owner being varied between contracts: obviously it is necessary to have the details of contracts, which are only sporadically recorded in the account books of the monasteries, or in their collections of legal documents. To complicate matters even further, the decision as to which form of exploitation to use was constantly open to review: changing economic conditions led to changes from *affitto* to *lavorencia* and back again. To produce a usable run of production figures, it is necessary to have an estate managed on a *lavorencia* basis, on known terms, over a run of years.

The ecclesiastical estate which comes nearest to fulfilling these conditions is the estate of the great Franciscan house of S. Fermo Maggiore in Verona in the adjacent plains communes of S. Pietro in Cariano and Bure. Even here there are major problems. First the estate, of a declared area of 70 Veronese campi (1763), had been bought in June 1671 for 5500 ducats from the property of the suppressed monastery of S. Angelo in Monte.[9] From then until 1684 the estate was rented to Fra Gian-Francesco Maffei, one of the brothers of the house, for an annual rent of 120 ducats.[10] The arrangement broke down in 1683–4, ending finally in litigation which concluded with a decision of the *Magistrati sopra Monasteri* on 13 August 1684 removing Maffei from the estate from November 1684 and leaving him owing the monastery some 1405 lire, some elements of the debt going back to the first acquisition of the estate in 1671. From November 1684, the estate was granted on a *lavorencia* contract to Silvestro Fioratti and his sons. The terms of their *scrittura*, dated March 7 1685, provide for a division of the produce which is typical: the grapes and all the grain, with the exception of millet, were divided equally between *lavorenti* and owner; the owner received 45 per cent of the total production of legumes (other than beans) and millet. Maffei seems to have remained as overseer of the estate.[11] The Fioratti and their successors continued to work the estates until November 1710, when the estate was rented on a cash basis at 500 ducats per annum until March 1714 and then 450 ducats per annum until November 1719, when the arrival of new *affictualli* led to an increase to 500 ducats. There was a brief return to *lavorencia* from November 1726 to November 1729, when the estate was rented to Antonio Zillotto for 450 scudi per annum. Litigation ensued in 1735,[12] and from November 1735 to the fall of the Republic, the estate was worked by a series of *lavorenti*. Their contracts differ in detail, in particular in the details of supplies of seed and implements, but in terms of the dimension of production, they are consistent with each other and with Fioratto's *scrittura* of March 1685.

Consistent and usable figures, therefore, are only available after 1735. This, in itself, adds a further problem: it is clear, by the mid-eighteenth century, that grains other than wheat were becoming increasingly important; to gauge total production, therefore, it is necessary to include the production of other food grains. Table 6 presents five-yearly averages for wheat production and for other food grains, and also the proportion of total production of grains made up by the non-wheat grains: this information is not available for the period before 1735.

Two features appear clearly from these figures. The first is the clear growth in total production until the mid-1760s, growth which was checked in the later half of the 1760s, chiefly in 1765 and 1766 and the early 1770s, to revive and then decline again after the mid-1780s. The second point is that, although the production of other food grains was, until the mid-1760s, increasing, that increase was slow, and was paralleled by an increase in wheat production. After the mid-1760s wheat production fell and only slowly recovered to anything like its previous levels, while the crisis of the 1760s and later did not affect so seriously the production of other food grains, which as a consequence increased their proportion of total production. It is worth pointing out that, even in the mid-1790s, other food grains only accounted for just over one-third of total grain production, and that the other grains produced were not just maize, but included a variety of other grains.

Direct evidence of production, then, only covers a relatively small proportion of the period, and also a tiny proportion of the total area of the Valpolicella. To get a longer term view, and a somewhat more complete one, it is necessary to turn to indirect evidence. This evidence comes again from an ecclesiastical source – the records of tithe payment. The work of Le Roy Ladurie, Goy and others have brought tithe records much closer to the centre of the historian's

Table 6 Possessions of S. Fermo Maggiore in S. Pietro in Cariano and Bure. Five-yearly averages of production of wheat (1685–90, 1700–10, 1735–95) and other grains (1735–95). Landlord's share (*parte dominicale*) in *minali*: Harvest year (July–June)

	Wheat	Other grains	Percentage	Total
1685–90	116.75			
1700–4	116.6			
1705–9	128.23			
1735–9	135	37	21.5	172
1740–4	133	46	25.7	179
1745–9	137	42	23.5	179
1750–4	155	54	25.8	209
1755–9	153	67	30.5	220
1760–4	173	65	27.31	238
1765–9	127	63	33.5	190
1770–4	119	74	38.3	193
1775–9	138	73	34.6	211
1780–4	160	82	33.9	242
1785–9	146	80	35.4	226
1790–4	161	91	38.1	260
(1795–7)	132	74	34.0	206

Sources: ASVR SFM 118, 119, 120, 122, 124, 125, 128, 130, 132, 134, 138, 140, 145, 149, 150, 152, 154, 157, 161, 164, 166, 170, 173, 175, 180, 185, 189, 191, 193, 196, 198, 200, 203, 204, 207, 209, 211, 212, 218, 221, 223, 225, 227, 230, 232, 235, 236, 240, 244, 247, 248, 250, 252, 254, 256, 259, 265, 266, 269, 271, 274, 277, 280, 284, 285, 290, 294, 297, 298, 304, 307, 309, 312, 315, 318, 320, 323, 326, 330, 333, 339, 343, 349, 351, 356, 365, 368, 373, 375, 378, 379, 384, 388, 392, 397, 401, 407, 411, 415, 417, 421, 425, 429, 433, 436, 439, 442, 446, 448.

perception.[13] The Diocese of Verona is fortunate in the survival of a large body of tithe information, contained in the *Curia Vescovile* and stretching back in some cases to the fifteenth century. Like all tithe material, that record is complex and difficult to interpret; like virtually all Veronese material, it has lacunae. The theory of tithe is relatively straightforward, but the reality, in Verona as elsewhere, was far more complicated.

The tithing system in the Veronese, and in much of northern Italy, varied in one important respect from tithing elsewhere; that variation was itself a consequence of the development of ecclesiastical organization in the region. Central to this was the unit called the *pieve*. The *pieve* can best be understood as a group of parishes linked together administratively and by the payment of tithe to a central body, the *Chierichi*. The *Chierichi* were the nominal successors of the original central clergy group who had, in earlier times, served the subordinate parishes, now provided with their own parish priests. With the passage of time, the *Chierichi* had become no more than tithe receivers, in most cases non-residents and in some cases other ecclesiastical corporations. Tithe was paid to the *Chierichi* who were usually represented on the spot by an official, the *sindico*, charged with supervising the local economic administration of the *pieve* and informally with keeping watch over the other local official the *Arciprete*. The *sindico* was responsible for the collection of tithes from each of the parishes, the payment of the accepted financial responsibilities of the *pieve* which included, for instance, the stipends of some of the parish priests, the upkeep of some of the churches, the *sindico*'s own salary, the taxes due to the state and, finally, for the distribution of any surplus remaining at the end of this process to the *Chierichi*. As with all the financial operations of the Church after the Council of Trent, the Bishop and the Curia were charged with supervising the operation of the *pieve* and of the *sindico* and *Arciprete*: the other *Chierichi* also required some kind of check on the operations of their officials. This supervision was operated by the annual preparation and submission of detailed accounts to the Bishop and to each of the *Chierichi*. This account, known as the *tangit*, was approved (or not) by the Vicar General and ultimately found its way into the Archive of the Curia; it is upon these curial copies of the *tangits* that we have to rely for information on tithe yields.

Historically, the Valpolicella was divided into three *Pievi*: S. Giorgio in the west, S. Floriano and Negrar in the east. Arbizzano also had *pieve* status, but its territory lay partly outside the historical Valpolicella. Breonio made claims in the later seventeenth century to *pieve* status, but these were firmly rejected by the *Chierichi* of S. Floriano of which Breonio remained part. Unfortunately the tithe records of the three *pievi* have not survived equally. Indeed one of the major problems facing the historian wishing to use the *pievi* records for the seventeenth and eighteenth centuries, not just for the Valpolicella but for the whole of the Veronese, is their survival and state of preservation. The *tangits* passed into the hands of the Curia Vescovile and were stored, along with most of the rest of the curial archive in ground floor and cellar rooms in the Vescovado in Verona. The disastrous flood of September 1882 devastated the whole of the Ponte Pietra quarter of the city, including the Vescovado. Much of the curial archive was submerged in silt-laden river water for some days: furthermore in a commendable attempt to rescue as much as possible they were literally stuffed into sacks in total disorder and carried to higher rooms in the Vescovado, where many of them remained. The confusion in which much of the Archive remains was compounded by their frantic second movement in April 1945 to protect them from the threat of allied bombardment. As a result of these adventures the Curia's holdings have suffered severely. The floods have rendered much of the records partially or wholly illegible, reducing many bundles of material to compacted papier mache; furthermore the disruptions of 1882 and 1945 have left the tattered remains totally disordered. Although the work of re-ordering the Archive is proceeding, it is inevitably slow and records such as those of the *pievi* occupy a low position in the rank of priorities. Thus, for virtually all of the *pievi*, many bundles of material remain inaccessible; almost certainly they are somewhere within the still unreordered material. Even where the material has been traced and identified, the flood damage may be serious, rendering whole bundles unusable.

Of the three Valpolicella *pievi*, S. Giorgio has, at present, the most complete and accessible records. Although there are considerable gaps, particularly in the mid-seventeenth century, the records run from before 1600 to the late 1790s. S. Floriano has material from 1609 to 1618 and from 1683 to 1749 and again from the 1790s. The Negrar records run only from 1600 to 1659. Hence, for any completeness it is necessary to rely on the S. Giorgio records, supplemented by the others for the periods when they are available. This has both advantages and disadvantages. S. Giorgio kept a greater proportion of the tithes of its *pieve* in its own hands, a lower proportion of the tithe having been alienated to laymen; S. Giorgio includes within its territory all three of the major geographical types of the Valpolicella. On the other hand, as the most distant of the *pieve* from Verona, it was perhaps the most backward of the three, perhaps the least affected by the pull of the city economy; it must be said, however, that there seems to have been little effective difference in the economic position of the three regions.

As Le Roy Ladurie and others have demonstrated, the use of tithe figures as the basis of performance indicators is fraught with problems. What is true for the rest of Europe is certainly true for the Valpolicella. The difficulties, as far as the Valpolicella is concerned, can be summed up under two major headings – the system of collection and the growing opposition to tithe and, more significantly, the growing evasion of payment.

Despite the theoretical universality and ecclesiastical nature of tithes, tithes in the Valpolicella were neither. In common with much of Europe, at times of financial or political difficulty the Veronese church had engaged in a policy of alienating tithes, of selling their rights to collect tithes to non-ecclesiastics; the right to tithes then became a piece of alienable lay property which passed from hand to hand, often for large sums. This means that the figures recorded in the *tangits* are not records of the whole amount paid by communities in tithe, but merely of the share of the tithe collected on behalf of the *Chierichi*. To get some indication of the total production of tithes, it is necessary to know the distribution of the tithe amongst all those with rights to a share. Neither was the tithe universal: the production of many fields was exempt from tithe, or paid tithe at a reduced rate. Some crops were largely exempt, or the community paid a fixed total amount; these *regalie*, which are paralleled by similar payments of, for instance, eggs or poultry, obviously provide no clue to the production of any actual year. If crops and fields were exempt, so too were some estates or individuals. For instance the Avanzi family of Gargagnago in the *pieve* of S. Giorgio established in the early eighteenth century that, as purchasers of land which had belonged to the Abbey of S. Zeno, they were entitled under a Bull of Innocent III to exemption from tithe.[14] A number of new individuals and institutions successfully claimed similar exemptions. Finally, it must be emphasized that the proportion of production taken as tithe was not standard, varying from one-ninth to one-fifteenth.

If the theoretical structure of the tithe creates a number of problems so too does the system of collection. Although the *sindico* might, on a few occasions, take direct responsibility for the collection of tithe, that was normally the result of a failure to find satisfactory agents; obviously the *sindico* could not hope to be in every community at the same time as the harvest came in. The normal means of collection was through agents, *decimali*. Two systems were followed: in the first, the *decimale* was required to collect the whole tithe and hand it over at the *pieve* centre, or elsewhere, to the servants of the *sindico*, at which point the *decimale* was paid a proportion of his collection or in some cases a fixed commission. The other system, *affitto*, was followed less frequently in the Valpolicella: it was in essence a farming system. The *decimale* contracted with the *pieve* to pay, on a named date, a fixed quantity of goods, or a fixed cash sum, in return for the right to collect the tithe of a given crop in a given parish or community. In the Valpolicella these tithe-farming contracts were normally for a single year and were concluded about a month before the harvest, when it was possible for the potential *decimale* to assess the probable outcome of the harvest and hence tender or bid for the tithe farm. These farming contracts create problems for the use of the tithe figures as performance indicators; obviously the farmer's return does not represent the yield of the tithe fully accurately, but on the other hand it is not simply an artificial figure.

The *decimale* was a key figure in the whole system. Upon his trustworthiness and self-interest depended the whole operation of the system. There is enough evidence to identify and categorize the *decimali*, although no detailed or conclusive analysis is possible. Particularly in the earlier part of the seventeenth century and above all in the larger communities, some of the *decimali* were clearly Verona-based investors, looking on *decimale* status as a form of useful income. Most of the *decimali*, and increasingly so as the period progressed, were drawn from well-to-do Valpolicella families, usually from the communities in which they were *decimali* or from neighbouring communities. This takeover (or continued dominance, since little is known of tithe collection before 1600) of the tithe system by the leading local families runs in parallel with their growing dominance of the Valpolicella parish clergy and amongst the *sindici*. As the tithing system became more deeply enmeshed with the patterns of local society, so too the balance of self-interest of the *decimali* shifted from maximizing the *pieve*'s tithe return. Tithe evasion came, in part at least, to be in the interest of the tithe collectors as well as of the tithe payers.

All across Europe the eighteenth century saw growing resistance to and evasion of, tithe, and the Valpolicella was not exempt from this. The records of both *pievi* for which eighteenth century records survive, show clearly a growing use of litigation by *decimali* in their attempts to enforce tithe payments and a growing rate of default. Symptomatic, too, of the growing resistance to tithe was the growing number of suits started by tithe payers against either the *sindico* or the *decimali* claiming exemption; in the late seventeenth and the earlier part of the eighteenth century in the Veronese, including the Valpolicella, this struggle engendered a series of complex and lengthy cases concerning the tithing of new crops, above all maize. Although the litigation finally ended with a declaration of the Church's right to a tithe on the production of maize, the victory was a pyrrhic one: the costs of the case, and its associated bribes, were immense. In addition, for much of the period of the litigation maize had escaped tithing and even after the Church's victory, tithe returns for maize remained suspiciously low.[15]

The tithe figures must, then, be approached with considerable care. They do not provide a direct measure of agricultural production; they are subject to manipulation by the collectors; even from the outset – since the tithe was hardly popular even in the sixteenth century – they were subject to evasion which got worse as the eighteenth century progressed. To these difficulties must be added some of the problems raised by the estate figures; changing crops and practices produced new types of problems and as the problem of the tithe on maize indicates, the tithing system was not particularly good at responding to changes. Equally the problems of nomenclature of crops and of mixtures of crops is, if anything, worse in the *pievi* records, since it seems that each community had its own mixtures of crops and its own names for them. Tables 7A and 7B, then, must be seen purely as indicators; they do not provide a totally accurate nor a complete picture of production, but merely begin to outline trends. On their own they are dubious and they must be taken in combination with the other information which is being assembled in this chapter. Table 7A provides an analysis of the production of the tithe of wheat of the *pievi* collected by the *Chierichi* of the three *pievi*; Table 7B illustrates the wide spread of ownership of the tithe.

The figures are inevitably confusing and they do conceal a great deal, in particular the sharp fluctuations from year to year which are

Table 7A Production of the wheat tithe of the *Pievi* of S. Giorgio, S. Floriano and Negrar belonging to the *Chierichi* 1605–1797. Five-yearly averages in *minali*

Period	S. Giorgio	S. Floriano	Negrar
1605–9			549
1610–4	624		485
1615–9	626		492
1620–4	–		429
1625–9	–		485
1630–4	246		
1635–9	342		
1640–4			276
1645–9	271		265
1650–4			295
—			
1675–9	399		
—			
1685–9		381	
1690–4	460		
1695–9	522	436	
1700–4	529		
1705–9	531		
1710–4	418	326	
1715–9	431	402	
1720–4	363		
1725–9	466		
1730–4	430	363	
1735–9	372	357	
1740–4	334	378	
1745–9	379	373	
1750–4	570	408	
1755–9	372	375	
1760–4	476		
1765–9			
1770–4	326		
1775–9	384		
1780–4			
1785–9	365		
1790–4	413	298	
(1795–7)	316	275	

Source: ASCVVR, Pievi, S. Giorgio, S. Floriano, Negrar

Table 7B Proportion of tithe belonging to *Chierichi* in *Pieve* of S. Giorgio

	Number of shares belonging to *Chierichi*	Total number of shares
S. Ambrogio	38	70
Cavalo	20	74
Gargagnago	46	92
S. Giorgio	12	17
Mazurega	12	24
Monte	15	43
Ponton	32	51
Volargne	45	45

Source: ASVR, Camera Fiscale Reg. 134

such a feature of all pre-modern agricultural statistics. The broad outline can, however, be seen. The very high levels of tithe payments and therefore almost certainly of high production of the 1610s and 1620s are very striking, as is the collapse after 1630: the revival in the later 1630s hides the second disaster of 1635 when in most communes the production of the tithe fell back almost to the crisis levels of 1630–1. The next decades are very clouded, but the figures do seem to indicate further difficulties in production until at least the late 1640s, followed by a recovery reaching its height around the first decade of the eighteenth century, followed by a fall to generally lower levels in the eighteenth century. The eighteenth century decline is almost certainly exaggerated by growing resistance to tithe payment: it is also rather misleading on its own since, as the S. Pietro estate figures indicate, the eighteenth century saw a considerable increase in the importance of other food grains. Table 8 presents the eighteenth century figures for total tithe on grains in the *pieve* of S. Giorgio alone: the S. Floriano figures for other grains are too incomplete to be usable.

From Table 8 it seems clear that, although production of grain did decline in the eighteenth century, the decline was not as great as the fall in the wheat tithe suggests, the additional production being provided by greater production of other food grains. In particular, the crisis of the 1760s and the 1770s saw a more rapid expansion of other food grains coupled with a fall in wheat production. Again, it must be emphasized that evasion of tithe, particularly on the new grains, almost certainly produces an under-estimation of the final total; it must also be emphasized that the increase in production of other food grains is not simply a consequence of increased production of maize but of a much wider increase in production.

Food grains are the major crop which the tithe records are concerned with; the information for other crops is much less complete

Table 8 Production of tithe on wheat and other food grains, *Pieve* of S. Giorgio 1690–1797 (in *minali*)

	Tithe on wheat	Tithe on all other food grains	Total	Percentage of other grains in total
1690–4	460	40	500	8.0
1695–9	522	37	559	6.6
1700–4	529	76	605	12.6
1705–9	531	50	581	8.6
1710–4	418	57	475	12.0
1715–9	431	15	446	3.36
1720–4	363	70	433	16.2
1725–9	466	28	494	5.7
1730–4	430	62	492	12.6
1735–9	372	46	418	11.0
1740–4	334	57	391	14.6
1745–9	379	81	460	17.6
1750–4	370	113	483	23.4
1755–9	372	93	465	20.0
1760–4	476	140	616	22.72
1765–9	—	—	—	—
1770–4	326	191	517	36.9
1775–9	384	183	567	32.3
1780–4				
1785–9	365	145	510	28.4
1790–4	413	151	564	26.8
1795–7	316	110	426	25.82

Source: ASCVVR, Pievi, S. Giorgio

and even more difficult to use. Mulberry leaves, which were the basic raw material of one of the region's major commercial activities – the production of raw silk – the *tangits* provide very little useful information about. Almost certainly, since the leaves were cropped not in a single harvest, but in relatively small quantities over the period of the feeding of the silkworms, the supervision of the collection of tithe was too complex and difficult to justify the returns. For two other non-grain crops of some commercial importance some information is available. The production of grapes and hence of wine has been one of the most typical elements in the Valpolicella's economy since Roman times, and inevitably the *Chierichi* had established their right to a share of production. The tithe was paid in grapes, which were normally shipped in carts or barrels to the *pieve* headquarters and there vinified. The interpretation of the statistics is especially difficult. The quantity of grapes produced is only one factor in the production of wine, both in terms of quantity and quality, and hence an

Table 9A   Tithe on grapes
belonging to *Chierichi*,
Pieve of S. Giorgio
1600–1797. (Decade
averages, in *botte*)

1600–9	26.0
1610–9	32.5
1620–9	24.5
1630–9	26.0
1640–9	24.0
1650–9	31.3
1660–9	—
1670–9	19.5
1680–9	32.8
1690–9	25.0
1700–9	33.5
1710–9	35.0
1720–9	44.0
1730–9	40.0
1740–9	30.0
1750–9	24.0
1760–9	29.5
1770–9	29.5
1780–9	37.0
(1790–7	28.5)

Source: As Table 8

Table 9B   Production of grapes,
possession of S. Fermo
Maggiore in S. Pietro in
Cariano and Bure
1735–97. Landlord's
share (decade averages,
in *botte*)

1735–9	14
1740–9	11.5
1750–9	12.5
1760–9	14
1770–9	13
1780–9	17
1790–7	20

Source: As Table 6

Table 10 Tithe of olive oil, *Pieve*
of S. Giorgio, belonging
to *Chierichi* 1600–1797.
(Decade averages, in
bacede)

1600–9	9
1610–9	18
1620–9	19
1630–9	25
1640–9	20
1670–9	38
1690–9	71
1700–9	53
1710–9	0
1720–9	7
1730–9	13
1740–9	14
1750–9	28
1760–9	25
1770–9	41
1780–9	30
1790–9	7

Source: As Table 8

apparently good year for grape production might in fact produce less wine and less good wine than an apparently less productive year. Grape production fluctuated more from year to year than wheat production and was more susceptible to problems such as storm damage. Table 9A presents the decade averages for the tithe of grapes in the *pieve* of S. Giorgio; Table 9B presents, for comparison, the production figures from the S. Fermo Maggiore estate at S. Pietro.

The increasing production of grapes is clear from both runs of statistics; what is quite clear, and perhaps expected is that the fall in grain production after 1630 is not matched by a fall in grape production, and that the first half of the eighteenth century sees very high relative levels of grape production. Again the eighteenth century figures are almost certainly depressed by growing evasion and opposition to tithe payment.

The other classical element in Mediterranean diet and agriculture is the olive: in fact the Veronese diet seems to have included rather less olive oil and rather more animal fats than the received idea of diet suggests. In the seventeenth and eighteenth centuries olive oil was used rather more for lighting than as an item of diet. Nonetheless, olive oil was a valuable and marketable commodity. Table 10 presents

Table 11   Proportion of total tithe on food grains, *Pieve* of S. Giorgio
              1600–1797. (Decade averages, percentages)

	Plains	Hills	Valleys
1600–9	33.2	51.4	15.4
1610–9	31.9	52.2	13.5
1620–9	33.8	50.5	15.7
1630–9	36.5	51.0	12.5
1640–9	37.0	48.8	14.2
1670–9	40.2	40.2	19.6
1690–9	39.6	43.5	16.9
1700–9	42.1	42.7	15.2
1710–9	39.0	47.3	13.6
1720–9	—	—	—
1730–9	35.5	51.6	12.9
1740–9	34.4	49.7	15.8
1750–9	40.2	47.4	12.5
1760–9	40.3	43.7	16.0
1770–9	43.1	38.9	17.9
1780–9	43.9	39.9	16.2
(1790–7	41.5	40.8	17.7)

Source: As Table 8

the S. Giorgio evidence for olive oil production: the tithe in this case
was paid in oil rather than in raw olives.

One ancient myth can be laid to rest by these figures; although the
winter of 1709–10 did have a devastating effect on the existing olives
of the Valpolicella, it did not mark the permanent end of oil production in the region, nor a permanent shift of the northern limit of the
olive. By the late 1720s olives were again being produced either from
new trees or, perhaps more likely, from the regenerated old trees,
which had been killed to the ground by the cold but which were able
to begin again. By the second half of the century, olive production had
returned, if not quite to the highest pre-1709 levels, at least to levels
which were in excess of those of the first half of the seventeenth
century.

Finally the tithe figures for the *pieve* of S. Giorgio make it possible
to indicate possible changes in the pattern of production between the
regions of the *pieve*, in food grains. To do this it is necessary to
calculate, using the information in Table 7B, the theoretical total yield
of the tithe to all the tithe owners not just to the *Chierichi*. Table 11
presents that evidence.

Here again is clear evidence of the decline of the hill communes
which had been the predominant good grain producers in the late

sixteenth and early seventeenth centuries: their decline is even clearer
if only wheat is considered. It is striking, though, that in the period
from 1690 to almost 1750, the hills stage something of a revival as a
food producer, falling back again from the 1760s onwards.

To summarize the indication of these production figures: the 1630s
and the 1640s saw, in grain production, a very sharp decline from the
very high levels of the first decades of the seventeenth century.
Production of food grains increased for much of the seventeenth
century, possibly reaching a peak around 1700. In the eighteenth
century, although wheat production fell back, greater quantities of
newer food grains were produced, resulting in continued high production until the crises of the period after the mid-1760s. The whole
period is also characterized by the growing importance of other, non-
grain crops such as grapes, olives or, by inference, mulberries. The
period is also typified by a shift of production away from the hill
communes to the valley and the plains, although that shift was to
some extent reversed between 1690 and the mid-eighteenth century.

IV

The most obvious indicator of the relationship between population
and production is price, in particular the price of the basic
commodities of consumption. The separate price history of the
Valpolicella is, however, impossible to describe, and even if it were
possible to do so, a price history of the region which separated it from
the pattern of prices in Verona – which was by far the most significant
market, both for sales and purchases, for the Valpolicella – would be
both entirely artificial and totally misleading. In any case, significantly,
few prices and no consistent runs of prices, exist for the small markets
at Pescantina, Fumane and elsewhere. Purchases and sales in these
markets were always on a very small scale and hence, as were small
sales in the 'free' Verona market, liable to very large, day-to-day fluctuations. To get some clear idea of the price history of the Valpolicella
it is, then, more useful to turn to the markets of Verona, and their
prices.

There are, however, further problems with the Verona price indices.
First it must be remembered that the market in wheat in Verona was
a partially controlled one. As a measure of public order and security,
the rulers of Verona, back to the della Scala, had sought to stabilize
wheat prices in the city, in part by formal price control by proclama-
tion, but chiefly by the direct management of the market using
officially-held stocks to depress prices, chiefly in years of crisis. The
Fonte di Mercato Vecchio in effect acted as a seller of last resort, to
which purchasers, inside and outside the city, could turn.[16] The
Fonte's series of prices for wheat are, for obvious reasons, of immense

significance. Two major problems militate against a total reliance upon them. The first is that, particularly towards the end of the eighteenth century, the *Fonte* seems to have played a much less economically significant role than previously, in part reflecting the economic and fiscal decline of the city. Secondly, and perhaps more significantly, the controlled market of Mercato Vecchio was only one of the grain markets of the city: the markets at Riva S. Lorenzo, Piazza Bra and Isolo di Sotto all seem to have been at least as active as Mercato Vecchio. Increasingly, too, grain was purchased from grain dealers outside the markets: either from grain brokers trading from their own shops or from producers or grain receivers, for instance noble landlords or monastic houses. The rise of the 'non-market' traders is also roughly paralleled by a tendency, particularly amongst larger purchasers, to shift from day-to-day purchases of grain to bulk-purchasing. The eighteenth century saw a further factor which led to a relegation of Mercato Vecchio; as bulk-buying became more common, there was an increasing tendency to turn from Verona's largely local market to the much larger regional and international one at Legnago lower down the Adige, but still in Veronese territory.[17] The development of Legnago and its growing importance as a supplier of Verona and hence of the Valpolicella, drew the region back into the international grain market from which it had escaped as a consequence of the crisis of the 1630s. In particular during the crises of the later eighteenth century, Veronese prices have to be seen as being, in part at least, related to more general European prices in a time of general European shortage.

A further difficulty in using the Verona prices for the Valpolicella arises from the demonstrable differences between city prices and prices outside the walls. This difference can be accounted for by two factors. First, the cost of transporting grain and other goods, particularly away from the Adige, could add considerably to prices: this factor came even more to the fore with the growth in the importance of Legnago. Valpolicella grain shipped to Verona would be more expensive in Verona than in the Valpolicella; conversely, grain from Legnago was considerably more expensive in the Valpolicella than in Verona. The second element was taxation. Although all grain movements in the Veronese were, theoretically, licensed and taxed, the chief taxation on grain was on its importation into and out of the city. This tax, the *dacio*, varied in value through the period, and also in the proportion of final price taken up by the *dacio*. The situation is further complicated since many of the large noble and monastic houses were exempt from some or all of the *dacio* on the produce of their own lands brought into the city. Furthermore, many of these grain receivers had all or part of their grain carted to the city or to the boats to bring it to the city, by their tenants as one of the elements of their rent: the *lavorenti* of S. Fermo Maggiore in S. Pietro were required to convey eighteenth cart loads from S. Pietro to the granary in Verona, at their own expense. Although additional loads were paid for, and the *lavorenti* and the men who accompanied the carts could expect to be fed in Verona by the friars, nonetheless, this free transport was a very valuable asset to the landlord, and one which frequently features in litigation between landlord and tenant.

A final and serious difficulty in the calculation of the price listing of any region or period is the inflation or deflation of money. The monetary history of the Veneto in the seventeenth and eighteenth centuries is a virtually totally unknown field, and it is not the aim of this study to rectify that gap in detail. However, a number of points can be made.

First, the monetary system, at least as far as the level of transaction which forms the subject of this section, was almost entirely metallic. Long distance trade and large-scale transactions were made by written instruments, usually denominated in moneys of account, but most smaller-scale and local payments were made using metallic money, valued at its precious-metal value. This, of course, produced a situation in which coin circulated at values other than its nominal value, to allow for debasement and also for loss of weight due to used and worn money.

Secondly, the circulating medium in Verona and the Territorio, particularly of precious metals, was of extremely varied origins: perhaps because of Verona's nodal communications position and because of its role as an international trading centre, gold and silver from a large number of sources was in common circulation, alongside Venetian and Veronese money.

Thirdly, value in most large transactions and, for accounting purposes all transactions, was expressed in moneys of account, nominally fixed to a given weight of precious metal. In the case of the monastic accounts used here, the money of account was, almost universally, the *trono* of 20 *marchetti*. The *trono* began life as a Venetian silver coin, first issued in the fifteenth century and was rapidly transformed into a purely fictional basis of account. Other moneys of account were used by some accountants particularly in the early seventeenth century, the most important being the Veronese *lira* of twenty *soldi*, again by this stage purely fictitious and nominally fixed to the *trono* at the rate of 15 *soldi* Veronese = 1 *trono*. Where accounts were kept in *lire* Veronese, they have been tacitly converted into *troni* for the calculation of prices. The whole issue of the devaluation of moneys of account is an extremely complex one; in particular relative movements in the prices of precious metals play a significant role in the process. In fact, the relative movement of metal prices in the Veronese is perhaps less significant than it might be: the moneys of account were silver, and the chief circulating medium of the Veronese would appear to have been silver. Although gold coins were used, it was mostly silver coins – the *scudo*, the *doppia*, the *ongaro* – which cropped up in transactions. Although it is, of course, dangerous to ignore the element of monetary fluctuation in such a calculation, it seems not unreasonable to say that until the very end of this period, and indeed really until the issue of paper money after 1797, the precious metal value of the money of account remained roughly stable.

The second set of problems arises from the difficulty of finding long enough runs of prices. Private sources are few and sparse, and public sources largely concerned with the operation of the *Fonte*. The only major runs available are those from the great municipal relief organizations, such as the *Casa di Pieta*, the foundlings' hospital, or the *Casa della Misericordia* or from the monasteries. The great civil organizations were frequently provided with grain at subsidized prices by the Commune of Verona or by the Rectors. It is to the monastic houses, male and female, and to the records which passed to the *demanio* in 1807 that it is necessary to turn for a consistent run. Unfortunately, few of the monasteries have material which is both complete and contains sufficient detail to allow them to be used for the calculation of unit prices. What is particularly unfortunate is that the accounts of two of the greatest of the monastic communities – S. Zeno Maggiore and S. Maria in Organo – both of them major grain sellers, survive in such a fragmentary form that they can only be used for part of the period. The records used in the compilation of price information are detailed as sources in Table 12.

The use of monastic sources for this information gives rise, unavoidably, to a number of problems. Many of the monasteries were large-scale dealers in grain – receiving not merely their share of the grain produced in their own estates, but also a considerable amount from the production of *livelli* in kind. Conversely, some of the monasteries were large-scale grain buyers, particularly when, as in the early eighteenth century, many of their estates were rented out for cash. It must not be thought that the dealings of the monastic houses or their advisers in the grain market were in any way unworldly or naive. It is clear that many of the larger houses – male and female – were, in effect, playing the market: buying and selling to gain the best prices. As will become clear, as the period advanced, and as the Legnago market and all its international connections became more important, this speculative element became more and more significant: by the 1770s the larger houses, and the Chapter of the Cathedral were maintaining permanent agents at Legnago.

This shift to a more 'speculative' approach to the grain market was also reflected in the pattern of grain purchases and sales by the houses. In the seventeenth century and the first years of the eighteenth century, monastic purchases were essentially on a 'retail' basis, grain being bought in small quantities (one or two *minali*) from the miller contracted to the house or from a large number of small traders. A number of small purchases were often made from different sources on the same day, and frequently at different prices. Purchases (and sales) were distributed widely across the year. By the mid-eighteenth century the pattern had shifted to a few bulk purchases and sales, from a limited number of individuals. Purchases tended to be limited to relatively few months a year, usually between July and September, and at a single price. The implications of this change in the organization of the grain market for the economy and society of the city are obvious, but there were equally obvious consequences for the price figures being calculated. It was normally only in crisis years in the late eighteenth century that the monasteries were forced to re-enter the grain market between harvests, and the prices they paid then were obviously much more typical of those paid by the small-scale consumer.

Not all grain was of the same quality and hence not of the same price: new wheat was of greater value than old wheat stored from a previous harvest. In some cases, the accountants recorded that wheat bought and sold was of poor quality, *sporco* (dirty, meaning contaminated with other grains), *vecchio* (old), or *per li poveri* (for the poor), but unfortunately practice was not consistent on this point and it seems likely that, in some years at least, lower quality grain was entered without comment, producing apparently wildly aberrant prices.

Wheat has proved to be the most convenient commodity to produce price statistics: at least at the beginning of the period there is considerable evidence that wheat was the major grain produced in the Valpolicella and in the diet of its population. As has been indicated earlier, other grains were increasingly important in production and consumption, but it has proved difficult to gain clear runs of information on other food grains. In part this is a consequence of the difficulties of identifying crops as a result of the confusing nomenclature mentioned earlier: particularly in the seventeenth century, the crops tended to be grouped together or blurred into each other. Despite the theoretical austerity of their lifestyle, the monastic houses do not, in general, seem to have been major consumers or purchasers of other food grains. The communities of the Veronese houses tended to be dominated by members of noble families or of well-to-do non-noble families, both from Verona and further afield. The nunneries, in particular, acted as centres of education for the children of the same noble and well-to-do families, and the diet of nuns and *donzelle* was essentially the same – based on the diet of the nobility and hence wheat dominated. Even the lay-sisters (*converse* or *sore della Vella Bianca*) who were of lower social origins than the nuns themselves, and the servants of the monastery, were fed on a largely wheat diet: until the 1770s, when other grains were bought, it was as animal feed and appears not in the kitchen accounts but in the accounts of the pig-keeper or *gallinara*. In addition, in most *lavorencia* contracts, sixty per cent or more of the other grains (*minuti*) were allowed to the *lavorente* as his share of the production. Other food grains are, then, under-represented in the monastic records, particularly before the 1760s: in some years a single transaction is recorded from all the monasteries concerned. These gaps are particularly glaring in the years from 1710 to 1730, at the high point of the cash-renting of monastic estates.

The two great non-grain commodities of the Valpolicella present other difficulties. Olive oil was largely used by the monasteries for ritual purposes, in particular in lamps. Most of it was received in payment of *livelli* and bequests or produced on monastic estates. The monasteries' dealing in oil is sporadic: much of the traffic took place through the sacrestan of the monastery, rather than the kitchen or other accounts, and in most cases the *Sacrestia* accounts are much less full and much less complete than the main accounts.

Wine, on the other hand, was a major element in the monastic economy, both for consumption and for sale. Wine purchases and sales became much less frequent in the accounts after the mid-eighteenth century, but until that point, purchases and sales of wine in small as well as large quantities are almost as common as purchases and sales of wheat. There is then no lack of information on the price paid for wine, particularly in the seventeenth century. The problem is to interpret those figures. Grapes (*uva*) were as frequent a purchase as wine: there were taxation advantages in buying grapes and producing your own wine. Furthermore, the young and almost certainly weak wines which were consumed probably travelled very badly: it was much better, if possible, to produce and store them at the point of consumption. The idea that in the seventeenth and eighteenth centuries in Italy and elsewhere in southern Europe, wine was just wine, with no distinction of quality or kind, certainly does not hold for the Veronese. Wine, and its price, was clearly graded. Red wine (*vino nero*) was usually cheaper than white wine, in particular the sweet white wine made from dried grapes (*vino santo*) which was greatly in demand from the monastic houses for the celebration of mass. *Vino santo* was graded by quality and also by age; young wine, wine of the present harvest year or of the one immediately past, was of greater value than older wine. The wines of some regions, the Valpolicella amongst them, commanded a premium in the market. By the later eighteenth century, the accounts of S. Maria in Organo distinguish clearly between a wide range of differing qualities of wine – *vino lambrusco*, *vino grosso*, *vino picolo*, for instance. Furthermore there was also a considerable market in 'near-wine' products – *mezzo vino*, *aquarolo* and so forth – the results of greater and greater dilution of the grape juice before fermentation and in 're-constructed' old wines:

Table 12   Prices of wheat, rye, millet, maize and wine, 1630–1797.
(Decade averages in *troni*; grains per *sacco*; wine per *botta*)

	Wheat	Rye	Millet	Maize	Wine
1630–9	26.0	7.2	—	—	156.4
1640–9	27.6	—	—	—	141.8
1650–9	24.26	11.2	—	—	128.7
1660–9	19.73	10.3	11.1	11.0	112.7
1670–9	20.93	11.4	10.6	10.0	110.0
1680–9	17.54	9.7	8.75	10.6	84.1
1690–9	22.71	13.6	10.8	14.6	99.0
1700–9	24.20	14.7	11.7	14.3	224.0
1710–9	22.08	—	—	—	—
1720–9	17.60	10.8	—	11.8	—
1730–9	22.19	13.2	11.9	13.5	
1740–9	23.65	15.3	12.1	15.1	238.5
1750–9	23.95	15.1	13.1	15.6	210.5
1760–9	27.63	16.6	13.0	19.6	
1770–9	33.27	20.0	19.6	23.6	
1780–9	34.36	—	—	25.2	
1790–9	37.87	—	—	29.0	

Sources:
ASVR
S. Bartolomeo della Levata: 39.
S. Cattarina Martire: 34, 35, 36, 37, 43, 44, 46, 47, 48, 49, 54, 56, 59, 62,
67, 71, 75, 78, 84, 85, 87, 88, 92, 93, 94, 95, 97, 102, 106, 108.
S. Croce: 24.
S. Daniele: 127, 131, 138, 141, 144.
S. Fermo Maggiore: 67, 68, 69, 70, 71, 72, 72bis, 74, 74II, 75, 76, 77, 78,
79, 80, 81, 83, 84, 85, 86, 87, 88, 89, 90, 91, 123.
S. Fermo in Braida: 65, 81.
S. Giorgio Maggiore: 92, 94.
S. Giorgio sopra Garda: 104, 109.
SS. Giuseppe e Fidenzio: 118, 123, 130, 133, 134, 138, 140, 141, 143, 145.
S. Lucia: 20, 24, 25, 46, 48, 52, 53, 57, 62, 66, 68, 72, 74, 75, 77, 79, 80,
81, 82, 83, 84, 85, 86, 87, 88, 90, 91, 93, 94, 95, 96, 98, 99, 100, 101,
103, 104, 105, 106, 107, 108, 110, 111, 114, 116, 118, 119, 120, 121, 122,
124, 125, 127.
S. Maria degli Angeli: 19, 62, 63, 64, 66, 69, 72, 73, 74, 76, 77, 79, 80, 85.
S. Maria in Organo: 222, 251, 273, 274, 288, 293, 298, 299, 315, 322, 324,
326, 329, 336, 337, 348, 350, 359, 369, 380, 383, 395.
S. Maria della Scala: 49, 53, 56.
S. Martino d'Avesa: 19.
S. Michele in Campagna: 107, 108, 110, 112, 114, 116, 119, 121, 123, 124,
125, 126, 127, 142, 144, 146, 148, 150, 152, 154, 157, 161, 163, 165, 167,
171, 179, 183, 185, 189, 191, 193, 195, 196, 198, 199, 200, 201, 202, 203,
204, 205, 206, 207, 208, 209, 211, 213, 214, 215, 217, 218, 221, 225, 229.
Redentore: 133.
S. Spirito: 28, 29.

wine was usually sold within a year of its production, as is clear from
the large number of discounted sales of *vino vecchio* or *vino del anno
passato* which occurred in most autumns after the vintage. Old wine
could, however, be revitalized either by mixing it with the new or, as
was the frequent practice on the estates of S. Maria in Organo, by
filtering the old wine through the grape debris left after the current
year's wine had been pressed. The *vino ripassato* was sold at a
premium over the price of old wine, but more cheaply than new wine.
The bewildering variety of types, qualities and situations of wine
makes the calculation of a price index for wine peculiarly dangerous
and the figures presented in Table 12 should be seen as no more than
an indication of a central point around which wine prices fluctuated.

Table 12, as a result of the way it is compiled, hides one very significant factor in the whole price history: the longer-term trends conceal
very sharp variations between years. For instance, the price of wheat
rose from 20 *troni* per *sacco* in May 1677 to 32 *troni* 10 *marchetti*
in February 1678. Falls could be as sharp and as sudden; short term
fluctuations of prices were an inevitable and inescapable factor of life
for both producers and consumers, and an element in almost any
economic strategy which could never be ignored. Even the attempts
of the state to stabilize prices only served to reduce somewhat the
most spectacular upward fluctuations. It must also be emphasized that
prices also fluctuated between seasons within the same year; in
particular rumours and reports about the coming harvest could send
spring and early summer prices rocketing.

This fluctuation within and between years was, obviously, a feature
common to most pre-modern agrarian economies: only those regions
like the United Provinces which had access to varied and wide-ranging
sources of grain could escape even partially from the problem.
Equally, to some extent at least, the patterns of crises in prices in the
Veronese replicate the general European crises, inevitably perhaps
given the importance of both imports and exports of grain in the
Veronese economy.

The most enduring impression which comes from these figures is of
a long period of relatively stable food prices running from the mid-
1650s to the 1770s. Within this century of stability, of course, there
are fluctuations; both the annual fluctuations discussed above and
longer runs, such as the rise in the first decade of the eighteenth
century. Fluctuations were not merely upward, and the century saw
periods of lower than average food prices, above all in the 1680s and
the 1720s; indeed these downward fluctuations, about 20 per cent of
the average for the whole period, were numerically more significant
than the upward, which never exceeded 12 per cent of the average.

It is at the beginning and, even more strikingly, at the end of the
period that price fluctuations are at their greatest. The 1630s and
1640s saw prices, for wine as well as for wheat, which reflect the

severe economic and population crisis of those years, a crisis which
was European as well as Veronese. The price history of this period
clearly belongs, in one sense, to the pre-1630 period when prices,
particularly of wheat, were high and, despite the best efforts of the
city officials, supplies were subject to disruption. The crisis of the
1630s and the 1640s can perhaps best be seen in terms of a combination of an economy adjusting to changed economic and social circumstances, and a series of pressures – some political, some climatic –
coming from outside. Even more severe and long-run was the inflation
of the late eighteenth century, an inflation which continued and
indeed grew disastrously worse in the aftermath of the fall of the
Republic. Compared with the average of the previous century, wheat
prices slightly less than doubled by the 1790s. There is clear evidence
from other sources of the problems which this rise caused for many
consumers.

The run of wheat prices is by far the most complete and there is
sufficient evidence of diet to suggest that, until the mid-eighteenth
century at the earliest, wheat and wheat mixtures were the major
cereal components of the diet of most, if not all, consumers in the
Valpolicella. The prices for other food grains, however, do indicate a
number of points of significance. Prices for the minor grains tended
to show greater fluctuations, both between years and within years,
than did wheat. This can be explained in part by the fact that the
minor food grains do not seem to have been bought in bulk by the
monastic purchasers upon whose records these figures depend. It may
be that smaller consumers bought minor grains in a more consistent
sort of way, but it seems unlikely. In addition, the fluctuations of the
minor grains, in particular their tendency to increase in price in spring
and early summer, reflects their role as the 'fall-back' of diet – covering, to some extent at least, the crucial few months before the arrival
of the new harvest on the market.

Table 13 demonstrates a number of important features of the
relative prices of wheat and the minor grains. (The figures for minor
grains before 1660 are too fragmentary to be used in this table.)

Two things are very clear from this table. First, reflected in changing
relative prices is the shift in patterns of consumption within the minor
grains. Millet and above all rye had been the chief 'secondary' grains:
the newcomer, maize, began as a much cheaper grain, reflecting its
early use as animal and poultry food, but it soon pushed its way
forward, as its price begins to show. The triumph of maize was not,
however, as total in the eighteenth century as some commentators
have suggested; rye falls decisively behind only in the crisis of the late
eighteenth century. Secondly, again particularly in the later eighteenth
century, the price of the minor grains increases relative to the price
of wheat, again suggesting the growing importance of the minor grains
in the nutrition of the population in the second half of the eighteenth

Table 13 Relative prices of wheat, rye, millet and maize, 1660–1797.
(Decade average prices of rye, millet and maize as percentage of decade average prices of wheat)

	Rye	Millet	Maize
1660–9	52	56	—
1670–9	54	51	48
1680–9	55	50	60
1690–9	60	48	64
1700–9	61	48	59
1710–9	—	—	—
1720–9	61	—	67
1730–9	59	53	61
1740–9	65	51	64
1750–9	63	55	65
1760–9	60	47	71
1770–9	60	59	71
1780–9	—	—	73
1790–7	—	—	76

Sources: As Table 12.

century. It must again be emphasized that a major but inevitable weakness in the figures presented here is the lack of any information on the price of 'grain-mixtures'. These seem to have played a major role in the agriculture of the Valpolicella and much of the Veronese and to be a major element in consumption. Furthermore, even where 'pure' grains were traded, it seems to be the case that consumption was very frequently of mixed grain flour. This obviously allowed variations of the mixtures in response to prices and hence is an element in price movements, and certainly indicates the effects of price movements on consumers. It also, of course, emphasizes again the flexibility and sophistication of the economic mechanisms of this pre-modern economy – and presents an insurmountable barrier to the price historian.

The price history of Verona does not suggest, until the 1760s or possibly the 1770s, an economy in profound crisis. The hundred years after 1660 display a long period of price stability; furthermore, that stability was at a level markedly lower than that which had obtained in the preceding half-century. During this period of price stability there were, of course, years of crisis and high prices, but it is remarkable that only eight of the 46 worst years for prices between 1630 and 1797 fell between 1660 and 1760. Those bad years – 1735, 1751, 1709, 1759, 1677, 1749, and 1693 – rank as twenty-sixth, thirty-third, thirty-fourth, equal thirty-eighth (1709 and 1759), fortieth, forty-second and forty-fourth in the period. What is equally striking is how well the Veronese survived, in price terms at least, the great European crises of the 1690s and the 1700s.

The great price crises came at the beginning of the period – in the double aftermath of the economic crisis of the 1620s and of the demographic crisis of the 1630s, and against the background of the last stages of the Thirty Years War – and, more seriously still, at the end of the period, from the mid-1760s onwards. In some senses the earlier crisis was more severe, coming as it did at the end of a long-run economic crisis: three of the four most expensive years of the whole period (1648, 1631, 1649) fall into these two decades. On the other hand, although the late eighteenth century crisis had some remissions, albeit relative ones, the later crisis ran on for much longer and included a high proportion of the most expensive years (28 out of 46). Furthermore, the period 1772–4 saw three consecutive years of disaster, mirroring similar problems elsewhere in Europe. The ability of the Veronese economy to deal with general crises in this later period is strikingly less than its ability to do so in the prosperous century which preceded it.

V

The three indicators of performance considered in this chapter are only partial and to some extent they must be treated with scepticism. A consistent pattern, however, does emerge from them. After the crises of the 1630s and 1640s in which population and production fell, and prices were at very high levels, the Valpolicella economy seems to have settled down to a century of stable and relatively low prices, expanding production and, particularly in the eighteenth century, growing population. Towards the end of this period, however, strains are beginning to show: prices begin to rise, production increasingly moves over to lower grade food grains and population growth begins to slow. The last years of the eighteenth century seem to have been years of difficulty, with population still growing, production still increasing, but steadily falling behind population, and prices rising steeply. This late eighteenth century crisis was no more than the prelude to the disasters of the Napoleonic era, but nonetheless presented major problems for consumers, producers and the state together. The late eighteenth century crisis was part of a general European crisis, the 'Crisis of the Early Industrial Revolution', which the Valpolicella weathered much less successfully than it had weathered earlier crises. The causes of this lack of resilience in the later eighteenth century will be discussed in later chapters, but it must again be emphasized that international problems played a large part in the crisis. Undoubtedly local factors such as the flight of capital from the countryside to Verona, the decline of the silk industry and growing soil exhaustion and erosion played their part, but the European climatic and other crises of these years must take a large part of the blame. What must be answered is not why did the crisis of the late eighteenth century occur, but why it was that an economy and society which had weathered earlier crises so well, and which, if the figures for production can be believed, was able to respond to rising prices at times of crisis by increasing production, was less and less able to respond positively to this new crisis.

This pattern of a relatively prosperous late seventeenth and early eighteenth century fits the Valpolicella clearly into the southern European pattern which is appearing from the work of Emmanuel Le Roy Ladurie on Languedoc, of Henry Kamen on eastern Spain and of Domenico Sella on Lombardy.[18] It is increasingly clear that, although the great commercial cities of the Mediterranean lost their supremacy to the new commercial giants of the Atlantic in the early seventeenth century, that decline emphatically did not mean long centuries of economic depression for their hinterlands and land empires. In many ways, it could be argued, this Baroque century was in many sections of the rural Mediterranean world perhaps the most prosperous of their recent history. It is equally clear that most of the great crises of the seventeenth and early eighteenth centuries hit the 'prosperous' and 'advanced' north of Europe much more severely, and the northern European economies, particularly their rural sectors, were much less able to survive them than were the 'backward' and 'depressed' rural economies of the Mediterranean.

Imperfect as they are, the performance indicators suggest a Valpolicella economy which was growing strongly after the crisis of the early seventeenth century. Furthermore, this was an economy which was changing its patterns of production and apparently concentrating rather more on market production, particularly of grapes and wine, without at the same time reducing its food production – an economy, that is to say, which was able to respond to the problems and challenges presented by a changing world without evidently changing its social or economic structure in a revolutionary sort of way. Like many of the other economies of the Mediterranean, the Valpolicella was able to deal with the crises of the late seventeenth and early eighteenth centuries in ways which were at least as effective as the ways the economies of the north reacted to them. The means the South adopted were different and, since they did not involve fundamental restructuring of societies and economies, must be judged by eighteenth century criteria to have been both more efficient and more beneficial than those adopted by the North.

4
The system of agricultural production

To say that this was an agricultural or an agrarian society and economy is a mere beginning. In any agricultural society the system of agricultural production is, of course, of crucial importance. The dependence of the society on agricultural production and output inevitably has a series of consequences for, for instance, the economy's response to certain types of external and internal pressures, but it is rather the detail of the systems which are employed to provide that agricultural production which are crucial to the patterns of society and of economic organization which develop. Not merely is the system of agricultural production central to the prosperity of an agricultural economy but also to the social system of that economy. The ownership and management of land helps to determine social status and social roles in the economy as a whole; the agricultural system also helps to determine the annual and daily calendar of an economy; not merely the calendar of tasks, of harvesting, ploughing and so forth, but also the annual calendar of prosperity and distress – even of life and death. The timing of harvests, itself in part dependent upon choices of crops, rotations and methods of cultivation, can dictate not merely hunger or plenty, but also the timing of marriages, purchases or journeys. It must be emphasized that it is not simply the old question of 'land-ownership' which is important, but the much wider questions of land-exploitation, land occupancy, tenancy, cropping and the employment of labour – questions of the totality of the agricultural system, and indeed of the total rural system, if it can be called that – that are significant.

I

It is as difficult to adopt a '*totaliste*' approach to an agricultural system as it is to look at the totality of any social or political system. In many ways, indeed, the study of agricultural systems or of rural systems, is even more difficult than the study of the totality of a political system. Above all, agricultural and rural life in general are so much taken for granted and, for much of the past, have been so completely insignificant and so ill-regarded, that evidence for any rural system is very difficult to come by and even more difficult to interpret.

The general problems of the student of rural systems affect the historian of the Valpolicella. Above all, the realities of the agricultural system were both too familiar and too vulgar to attract the attention of the Veronese *literati* until the very end of the Republic when the Academy of Arts, Sciences, Literature and Agriculture was established.[1] Until that point, perhaps inevitably in the native region of Vergil and Catullus, rural life had been seen as above all a classical background to pictures or to the life of 'rural simplicity' of the *villegiatura*. Above all then, the real problem is, as so often, one of sources.

Literary sources for rural life, and in particular for the systems of agriculture practised, are in Verona as elsewhere in Italy, few in number and heavily influenced by classical tradition. This is perhaps surprising in an area and a region which was in many ways in advance of much of Europe in its agricultural technique, certainly until the eighteenth century. It is only at the very end of the Republic and in the first years of the nineteenth century that the first of the newer, more practical agricultural manuals begin to appear. Even the most famous of these, Lorenzi's *Coltivazione dei Monti*, published in 1778, is above all a literary production – in fact a lengthy poem without the pithy good sense of Thomas Tusser.[2] Furthermore, Lorenzi's concern is with the improvement of agriculture rather than with any form of description of the processes involved. Since it seems to be clear that the late eighteenth and the first decades of the nineteenth centuries saw a very clear change and deterioration in the agricultural system, Lorenzi's information is doubly suspect. The same must be said of the collections of recollections of rural life in the later nineteenth and early twentieth centuries which have enjoyed a certain popularity amongst Veronese historians in the last two decades.[3] Interesting though these are, and although they are of very great significance for the more modern rural history of the Veronese, it is quite clear that the bitter experiences of the nineteenth and early twentieth centuries – which have a very real claim to be the true Dark Ages of north Italian rural life – so completely overlie any recollection of earlier periods and earlier systems that it is fair to say that, far from representing a source of information on the distant past, they represent no more than information on almost the most recent period of Italian history.

As so often, our chief source must be a series of documents and other records whose major concern was not the agricultural system, but other things, to which the agricultural system was no more than the background. Of course, this distant concern with the agricultural system has its advantages: the authors of such documents had no direct case to make about the way in which the land was cultivated, but in general saw it as merely background to their more immediate and pressing concerns. This gives this sort of evidence a very real advantage over other sorts; as the agricultural background is no more than background, its reporting is entirely unselfconscious. On the other hand, the way in which such evidence arises brings with it the whole question of just how representative the detail it describes is.

The most immediately obvious of such records are the surviving records of the major estates. Much of what we know about agricultural and rural systems in, for instance, France or Spain has come from the surviving mass of estate records. Unfortunately two factors mean that estate records are less useful in the Veronese than they might be. First, as has been discussed earlier,[4] estate records in the Veronese have been subjected to even greater loss and dispersal than have other records; second, as will be discussed later, during the seventeenth and eighteenth centuries most Veronese estates were administered in such a way that the estate bureaucracy, and certainly the central estate bureaucracy whose records are the chief survival, were only very indirectly concerned with actual agricultural practice – practice was the concern of the tenants and not of the owner. Even the records of demesne farms, where they exist, are incomplete and ultimately unhelpful for the details of the system. A case in point is the surviving archive of the dal Bene family, whose main Valpolicella estates lay in Volargne. Although the earliest material in the archive dates from the middle of the sixteenth century, and although there is a scatter of administrative material from the seventeenth and early eighteenth centuries, it is not really until the 1770s and 1780s that the estate records become any more than sketchy. Even then, and this is also true of the earlier material, what is recorded is basically the financial relationship between landlord and agents – the *gastaldo*, the *lavorenti*, and the wage labourers – rather than details of agricultural activities as such. Even a document like the *Giornali*, the daily records of payments to labourers and of the activities undertaken, record not the pattern of daily agricultural activity, but rather the operation of what was, in the case of the Volargne estate, an important industrial and timber producer.[5]

A second major source, as elsewhere in Europe, is taxation records. One of the major sources of income of the Veronese state was, and had been for centuries, a tax on the capital value of land, the *estimo*. More will be said subsequently about the *estimo* and the ways in which it was assessed; in principle it was tax assessed each year on the demands presented to Verona by Venice and assessed on the basis of a periodic valuation of the capital value of the land in each owner's possession. Like the old English rating system, which it resembles in many ways, the *estimo*, relied upon a periodic revaluation of the capital value of the land. The records of the *estimo* are particularly valuable as a source for the ownership of land and for the transfer of land,[6] but one peculiarity of the system makes them also valuable for the study of agricultural systems and agricultural management, and that arises from one of the two differing systems of assessment which were adopted. In the communes of the Territorio outside Verona, the assessment of the value of land held in the communes by natives of the communes and of others who were not citizens of Verona, was in the hands of the *stimadori* of the communes themselves. Those assessments, which were made relatively regularly in the seventeenth century[7] and much less so in the eighteenth,[8] were recorded in the volumes which, in the form of the copies submitted to the central authorities, form the basis of the section *Estimo Territoriale* in the Archive *Antichi Estimi Provvisori* in the *Archivio di Stato* in Verona. In terms of information on agricultural practice and estate management these records are, if not silent, at least very laconic.

However, the method of assessment of the *estimo* of the citizens of Verona, on the land they held, whether in the city or the Territorio, was very different. Rather than being assessed by sworn communal officials, the citizens were required to submit their own statements, not merely of the land they held but also of the value of it, any factors which, in their opinion, reduced the value of the land, and details of how the land was managed. Inevitably, given the lack of any standard formula for these submissions, and the requirement to state any problems which the land suffered, these returns by individuals – the *Polizze Citta* – are an important, if at times frustrating, source of agricultural and other information. They do, however, present a number of major problems in interpretation and use. First, the reassessment of the *estimo* of the city was undertaken at infrequent and irregular intervals: there were major reassessments in 1653, 1682, 1696 and 1745. Even these dates are misleading in that they represent no more than the dates at which the reassessments were brought into use; in particular, the reassessment of 1745 represents information submitted and collected over a period of nearly twenty years[9] and, in some cases, corrected and updated by the landowners themselves long before the new assessment came into force. On the other hand considerable numbers of potential tax payers 'forgot' to submit *polizze* and only submitted them, if at all, long after the main assessment.[10]

Secondly, the method of determining whether land was to be assessed under the city or under the Territorio meant that the *polizze* often refer to only parts of holdings: in theory, the *polizze* record the land held by citizens of Verona but, as a result of the transfer of land from the inhabitants of the Territorio to those of the city, particularly in the aftermath of the Plague of 1630, and the reduction of the paying capacity of the Territorio, which was not matched by a reduction in

the total sum demanded, land transferred to citizens after 1633
continued to be assessed under the communes and hence does not
form part of the *polizze* assessment.[11]

Thirdly, there was a great tendency, particularly in the later seventeenth century reassessments for tax-payers or their agents to repeat
verbatim the previous returns and it is frequently difficult to be sure
whether an apparent lack of change is a consequence of this or of a
genuine lack of change. The *polizze* are, perhaps inevitably,
incomplete. Also, like so much else of the taxation record, they have
been very badly damaged by water on a number of occasions and are,
in many cases, in a very brittle state, to the extent that many of them
have lost their edges – the edges on which the final sums of, for
instance, value or area were recorded. Their lack of any standard form
means that while many are loquacious, others are totally laconic; in
particular many fail to detail areas, or even places. Above all, the
polizze are tax returns, with all that implies about the truth of their
contents. Admittedly the *polizze* were submitted by the proprietors or
their agents on oath, but there can be little doubt that their contents
present only a version of the truth; Prof. Borelli has elegantly
demonstrated the extent of evasion and open misinformation that the
polizze contain.[12] Like tax-payers everywhere, the Veronese sought
to minimize the returns from their estates and to emphasize the
difficulties and problems; to judge from the returns from some
landholders, the effects of land-erosion and flash-flooding in many
communes was so great as to render the exploitation of the land
pointless.

If the taxation returns suffer from their use to argue cases and,
above all to reduce the liability of the compiler to taxation, litigation
records are suspect in the same ways and for the same reason. Records
of litigation in the Veronese courts survive in two forms. The first, and
the most complete, are the records maintained by the *Uffizi*, the
notaries of the courts themselves, preserved in the series *Uffizi Veneti*
in the collection *Rettori Veneti* in the *Archivio di Stato* in Verona.[13]
These are, strictly, the records of the judicial process, tracing each
action from its original submission through to the final decision (final
that is to say as far as the Veronese court was concerned; many actions
were also filed simultaneously in the Venetian courts), and including
the issue of summonses, orders for the examination of witnesses and
so forth. The records of the actual hearing of the case before the judge
play only a small part in these records and are frequently very cursory.
The structuring of the records presents a large number of major
problems: first, most, although not all, of the notaries separated
different types of business into different books – writs in one, hearings
in another, examinations of witnesses in a third, and so forth[14] – thus
making the process of following a case through the records extremely
difficult. Again, the records were kept, inevitably given their nature,

in chronological order; until the very end of the eighteenth century, the records have no internal indexing. Litigation in the Veronese courts could drag on for years, even decades, and the gaps between 'events' in a case could be a few days or a few years. The use of the *Uffizi*, then, is full of problems and goes a long way to explaining the lack of any real study of the Veronese legal system in action. The problem is further compounded by the lack of any clear division of jurisdiction between the several courts – for instance, litigation involving tenancy contracts could, and did, find its way before any of the judges in Verona – so the historian cannot rely on finding all agrarian cases in any one court.

Hence the records of the Veronese courts, although they remain a potentially important source, and a potentially significant study on their own account, do not really offer the historian of Veronese agriculture a usable source of information. The litigation sources which do offer a real and available source are the *Processi*, the filed records of law suits which form so large a part (in some cases all) of the archive of many Veronese families. The *processi* have been one of the major sources which have been used in the past by Veronese historians and are one of the few parts of the *Archivio di Stato* which are relatively well-catalogued. They are, indeed, a very major source of vital information, but they do present a series of major problems. The first, as always, is the question of survival and availability. The *processi* in the *Archivio di Stato* are made up, disproportionately, of those involving the Commune of Verona and the suppressed religious houses; the private archives contain a large number of *processi*, albeit with a very large preponderance of nineteenth century cases, but they represent only a small selection of the total litigation. Furthermore, although they do contain a number of non-noble archives, such as those of the Bonvicini family, the greatest bulk of them by far are noble archives. The form of the *processi* also makes them more difficult to use and there was a natural tendency for families to retain, chiefly, the records of their successful litigation. In addition, the Veronese adversarial system of litigation means that each family's collection of litigation contains a very high proportion of impassioned and biased pleading by advocates and *causadichi*, and relatively little balanced reporting. In the vast majority of cases, agriculture, and the agricultural system is no more than the background to other issues.

The Veronese legal system provides a further problem and difficulty, which may best be illustrated by the problem of sharecropping and *lavorencia* contracts. *Lavorencia* was, without a doubt, the chief form of estate exploitation for much of the seventeenth and eighteenth centuries and, to judge from the frequent complaints advanced by landlords against their *lavorenti* in the *polizze* and elsewhere, it was a fruitful source of conflict and litigation. It is clear too that the relationship between landlord and *lavorente* was usually regulated by some form of written contract. What is, however, startlingly clear, is that very few of those contracts seem to have survived in the notarial record, and that very few – relatively – cases about *lavorencia* came before the courts. This does not signify an unsuspected peace in landlord–tenant relationships, but rather the existence in the Veronese – and almost certainly elsewhere in early modern northern Italy – of a whole world of quasi-legal and quasi-judicial relationships existing beyond the world of the notaries and the official law-courts. It is clear that the contracts upon which *lavorencia* was based were not formal notarial documents, but rather *scritture private*, contracts drawn up in legal form and frequently following the appropriate notarial formulae but not registered with a notary unless, as happened in some cases, one of the parties wished to litigate over it. Equally, there existed what can only be called an unofficial judicial system for the resolution of disputes by privately appointed arbitrators. Almost certainly, only a small proportion of rural disputes came for decision to the courts in Verona. Pretty certainly, too, the unofficial judicial system was used rather more by the smaller landowners and the rural landowners, the inhabitants of the rural communes, than by the well-to-do and noble landlords of the city; after all, the costs of litigation in Verona were relatively high, and the judges of the Communal courts, and increasingly of the Rectorial courts, were drawn from the ranks of the city nobility. The picture of rural relations and of the agricultural system which comes from the *processi* is, hence, slanted and probably incomplete.

The same is true of the other major 'official' legal source for the rural and agricultural history of the Veronese, the notarial record. From the beginning of Venetian rule in the Veronese, all registered notaries in the Veronese had been required to maintain records (*protocolli*) of all documents they prepared. When a notary or his family ceased to practice, and hence to have any use for these records, they were, in theory, deposited in the notarial archive in Verona, where they were consultable (and were consulted) by other notaries and interested parties.[15] This huge mass of day-to-day legal documentation constitutes one of the major unexploited treasure-troves of the Veronese. Nothing, however, is that simple: the notarial archive was largely destroyed by fire in 1724; any material from before that date for most of the Veronese has only survived because it was still in the hands of the notaries or their families in 1724. Furthermore, there seems to have been little concept of a long-standing link between individuals or families and notaries: the notarial record of a family or an estate may be spread over the records of a large number of notarial firms and archives. In addition, as has been pointed out above, most agricultural contracts and many agricultural disputes almost certainly never went anywhere near a notary.

In many ways the most useful legal sources for agriculture and the agricultural system are not cases and disputes directly concerning agriculture or tenancy contracts, but rather cases in which details of agriculture and agricultural practice form the background, the supporting details, to other things. Two major sources of this sort are the records of the courts of the Vicar of the Valpolicella and of the major criminal court of the city, the office of the *Maleficio*. In both cases, the litigation which came before them was not directly concerned with agriculture, but agriculture and agricultural activities play a major role in the depositions of accusers and witnesses. This incidental detail has, at least, the advantage of not being material to the issue being tried by the court and hence of being likely to be less manipulated than evidence in other situations.

The legal sources for the agricultural system are, then, important, but they cannot be treated as being wholly trustworthy nor yet complete. Even for that area of agricultural operation, the tenancy system, into which the legal system might reasonably be expected to intrude most clearly and most constantly, legal sources seem likely to give only a partial and potentially distorted picture. The picture which comes from the legal sources is one which must be incorporated in an overall picture, but it must not be mistaken for that overall picture. Indeed, the problems of use of legal sources for the study of the rural and agricultural sector in the Valpolicella leads to another, vitally important point about the society and the economy. It is clear that alongside the state, and in some ways paralleling its activities and functions, there existed a whole separate system of jurisdiction, a sort of autonomous structure of self-regulation. It was not really a state within a state, since there is little sign of any conflict between them, nor yet a counter-state, as was found in some colonies – a system to which the 'natives' went to gain traditional justice and traditional adjudication in contrast to the foreign or 'false' justice of the colonial legal system – since individuals had recourse to both systems, but rather a locally-developed and locally-controlled system. In a sense, the existence of this system may be said to be one of the major differences between the modern and the early modern state and between modern and early modern societies; certainly one element in the Napoleonic and post-Napoleonic centralization of power and administration in Italy was the discouragement of this parallel system. Equally, it is possible to point to the existence and survival of this system in the Veronese, and elsewhere in the Venetian Terra Firma Empire, as a symptom of the survival under the 'imperial yoke' of a vital and flourishing autonomous local and particular culture and society: the Age of Absolutism in the Venetian Empire did not mean the disappearance of local autonomy or local social systems. That may well have been one of the great strengths of the Venetian Empire, as well as one of its major weaknesses.

In such a society, where the state and its legal and administrative institutions did not monopolize social and legal relationships, it is hardly surprising that the legal record is only a partial reflection of agricultural practice and the agricultural system. The historian of the agriculture of the Valpolicella has, then, to rely on other, rather less likely sources of information, sources whose intention and prime concern is not with agriculture, but with other things, and for which agriculture is merely secondary. One of the major sources used in this study, the collection *Patrimonium Ecclesiasticorum* in the Archivio of the Curia Vescovile, falls firmly into this category.

The fathers of the Council of Trent, in attempting to reduce if not solve the problem of over-ordination – the creation of large numbers of unbeneficed, and indeed indigent priests, which had been a major scandal in the later Middle Ages – successfully required (at least in well-administered Dioceses such as Verona) that ordinands should produce clear evidence of their financial standing and security. This requirement meant that the episcopal chancery would collect and keep sworn statements as to the financial position of the candidates, their families and sponsors. The canon enjoined on bishops the duty of ensuring, before they admitted any candidate to the priesthood, that the candidate, following his ordination would have a capital sum, secured either in land or the income of benefices, sufficient to maintain him. Venetian legislation fixed this sum at a capital of 1000 ducats, which by the conventional calculation, (used, for instance in estimating the value of land for the *estimo*) which treated a normal return as being six per cent, would produce an income of almost one lira per day, equivalent to the summer daily wage of a farm labourer (*bracente*).[16] This sum had to be the candidate's own, either by inheritance or by gift, and had to be secured on real property; to estimate the value of any piece of land, it was necessary to know its area, its type and the cropping patterns involved. In addition, the bishop was required to satisfy himself that in giving the ordinand the capital sum, the donor, usually either a relative, a group of relatives, or a noble patron, was not depriving himself or the rest of his family of the means to live or, indeed of the means to marry. Hence, the Chancellor had to enquire into the economic and social position of the donor and his family.

The form of the records is determined by these concerns. The standard form of the 'file' in the curia is, first a notarial document declaring the candidates wish to proceed to the priesthood (no equivalent requirement was imposed in Verona on candidates for minor orders), and setting out the canon and the ways in which the candidate believed he could meet the conditions. The Chancellor or the Vicar General then summoned witnesses to testify to the value of the land, and to the social and economic status of the candidate or the donor; it is these examinations of witnesses which are such an important and valuable source. The questions follow a formulary established by the late sixteenth century and are recorded in Latin; the responses are anything but formulaic, especially in the seventeenth century, and are recorded in the Veronese vernacular in which they were delivered. Farmhands, shopkeepers and others from the rural communes were summoned and gave their views on land they had personally cultivated, and on people and families they had known all their lives. At this point, too, the families of candidates on some occasions submitted sworn statements of their total wealth and income. Having heard the witnesses, the Chancellor declared himself satisfied or not with the patrimony offered by the candidate; if the patrimony was adequate, the Curia issued a mandate permitting the ordination while, if the patrimony was not adequate, the candidate was allowed to seek further sponsors and further security.

The *Patrimonio* records are a major – and as yet unexploited – source, not merely for the agricultural history of the Veronese but for the whole social history of northern Italy. Their use for the history of the agriculture of the Valpolicella presents a number of problems. As always with the Curial records, practical problems of conservation and access loom large. The *Patrimonio* records are relatively well-preserved, although some are in a very fragile state. They are organized chronologically, being bundled together in years; within years they are (or were) organized in alphabetical order of the Latin form of the christian name of the ordinand; the file itself usually has no external indication of the place of origin of the ordinand.[17] It is the nature of the process which reduces their potential value for the historian of the Valpolicella, however. First, as is usually the case with the ecclesiastical bureaucracy, in the eighteenth century the enquiries become more and more cursory, and the recorded answers more and more conventional and formulaic. Secondly, in the Valpolicella as elsewhere, the effects of the canon and of the patrimony system was to limit the social and economic catchment area of the priesthood (and of the regular orders male and female, to which the canon also applied). The priesthood, and in particular the parochial clergy, became increasingly the preserve of well-to-do, non-noble families, in many cases of local origin; peasant families were too poor to be able to place their sons in the priesthood without the patronage and sponsorship of the well-to-do or the nobility, while the nobility were more concerned with placing their sons in the higher reaches of the hierarchy. This capture of the church (and of much of its wealth) at its local level by the local leadership is one of the major elements of social change in many areas of the Veronese in the seventeenth and eighteenth centuries, but its immediate effect is to limit very severely the social range of the information in the *Patrimonio*. Furthermore, the Valpolicella was not a particularly fertile field for ordinations; a comparison with the number of ordinations from other areas of the Veronese, even close to the Valpolicella such as the Val d'Adige, indicate that Valpolicella families were much less likely to put their children into the Church than were their neighbours. Even within the Valpolicella the distribution of ordinations was not constant; some communes such as Pescantina, and some groups, like the *Parons*, were much more likely to seek the ordination of their sons than were others. As a result, the *Patrimonio* is rather slanted towards particular communes and particular types of economy.[18] Unlike the *Estimo* and other taxation records, the *Patrimonio* tends to over-value land and the economic standing of families, for very obvious reasons.

The sources for the history of the agriculture and agricultural system of the Valpolicella are copious if flawed. They provide both wide insights and very real problems in interpretation. The other major problem of interpretation comes from the central fact of the system itself, its extreme variety and flexibility.

It has already been made clear that the Valpolicella was an extremely varied region geographically and economically.[19] That variety means that evidence from one commune cannot be used necessarily as an indication of what was happening, or what the system was, in any other commune. Equally, as will become clear, the system was far from static, even during these years of 'decline' and 'stagnation'; evidence from one decade cannot be used, therefore, as conclusive for any other decade without strong corroborating evidence.

Above all, though, it is the very complexity of the system which makes it difficult to interpret. This was in no sense a monocultural system, or indeed a mono-anything system, for any region or for any individual. No individual, and certainly no family (or very few), could rely on a single crop or a single employment for survival. Patterns of agriculture and of management varied from place to place and from time to time. Equally very few individuals fulfilled a single function in the system; few were merely landlords, merely tenants or merely wage labourers. Individuals moved from category to category with enviable ease. Furthermore, at any one time they could and did fulfil more than one economic and social function; the small landowner was likely also to be a tenant of some kind and also to earn money as a wage labourer as the opportunity offered, while noble landowners were not averse to renting land if it was more convenient to do so. Individuals, and even more families, were not mono-local; the level of personal mobility, both long- and short-term, in this economy is striking. Equally, purchase, inheritance and dowry inevitably spread the landholdings of even the most minor landholders over a range of communes and regions. This was, then, a highly complex, and at times highly confusing system. It would be tempting to simplify it for ease of analysis, to treat it, as it has usually been treated before, as if it were – as the agriculture of the Veronese was to become in the nineteenth century – basically a monoculture. It would be dangerously wrong to do so, however, since the key to this system, and to its survival and prosperity in the so-called Age of Decline, was exactly that complexity and flexibility which makes it so bewildering and which makes it appear so perverse to modern economic theory.

Most obviously this variety appears in the variety of crops grown. Cereals were the basis of the economy, as they formed the bulk of the diet of the people of the Valpolicella as of the rest of early modern Europe. They were, however, intermingled with other crops: vegetables, legumes, fruit, not merely grapes, tree crops, hay, all of which were much more than by-crops or weird exceptions. Nor were the broad types dominated by single crops; although wheat was the predominant food grain, at least until the later eighteenth century, it was by no means the only one: rye, oats, barley, and a wide range of millets, and mixtures of all these were grown. Equally, though the vine was the main fruiting plant cultivated, olives, apples, pears, cherries and a number of others were widely grown and widely sold. The leaves of the mulberry were also one of the major industrial crops of the Valpolicella and the mulberry shared with the olive the honour of being the most widely cultivated tree in the Valpolicella. Even within individual species there is clear evidence of the existence of defined and appreciated varieties: the difference between winter and spring wheat and the differing varieties of maize and millet were widely recognized, while there is considerable evidence of the existence of distinct varieties of apples, pears and grapes. This pattern of widely differing varieties and species is further confused by the changes through time which affected cropping patterns; hopefully the idea of a stagnant and unchanging pre-modern agriculture has long been laid to rest, but it is important to emphasize again that in the Valpolicella, as elsewhere in Europe, the seventeenth and eighteenth centuries saw a continual and continuing process of change in the crops grown.

This wide chronological variety, as well as the biological variety of the crops grown, makes any assessment of overall cropping patterns very difficult. Certain points can be made; the geographical and climatic patterns of the Valpolicella meant that the balance between crops, and in extreme cases the presence or absence of some crops, varied. The hill-tops – Cavalo, Breonio for instance – were less suited to grapes than were the lower communes: a combination of colder winters, later and damper springs, and fierce storms, often with hail and storm-force winds, in August and September meant that returns were lower and less secure. Again, the colder winters in the higher hills meant that olives were much more marginal in the higher communes than lower down. At the other extreme, the dampness of the valley floor lands of Ponton and Pescantina meant that rye rather than wheat was the favoured grain crop. It was not merely climate which affected the pattern of cropping: wheat was markedly less popular in communes like Corrubio in which most of the land was terraced than it was in more level areas where plough rather than hoe cultivation was the rule. It must be emphasized that, in apparent disregard of the law of comparative advantage, these variations did not mean that grapes disappeared from the highest communes nor that the valley bottom communes became rye monocultures, but merely that the part that grapes or rye played in the overall productive balance differed by a greater or lesser extent from the norm.

The complexity and variety of the system did not end with the variety of arable crops since this was an agricultural economy in which animals and animal husbandry played a significant role. The conventional wisdom, both in the seventeenth and in particular the eighteenth centuries[20] and amongst modern Veronese historians[21] is that the early modern period saw a sharp and serious fall in the number of animals, in particular cattle, but also sheep and horses in the Veronese economy, with all the consequences that implied for the prosperity and fertility of the land. It is certainly the case that the Veronese, which had been during the Middle Ages and the Renaissance, a major sheep-farming and horse-raising region, did slip back during the early modern period from its pre-eminence in pastoral farming; it may even be that the number of draught and plough cattle declined, though that must be rather more dubious. Again, there must be a major suspicion that the great decline in pastoral farming and in the imput of animals into the mixed economy came in the later eighteenth century, and, above all, as part of the disaster associated with the Napoleonic and immediately post-Napoleonic period. Certainly the picture which appears through, for instance, the Valpolicella law suits, is of a countryside still relatively densely populated with animals, not merely cattle and bullocks, but also sheep and goats, pigs, horses, asses and mules. Agriculture still found most of its motive power in its animals rather than in human labour; although hoe cultivation was common, it was mostly to be found in terraced areas, where it was sheer practicality rather than shortage of animals which forced hand-cultivation. It must be emphasized that it was as much the economic and technological context as poverty or decline which determined particular agricultural patterns and practices: no matter how wealthy or how well-provided with draught and plough animals their inhabitants were, most of the terraced fields of communes such as Corrubio or Mazzurega had to be hand-cultivated if they were to be cultivated at all. Animals were, of course, a valuable asset; his plough team or teams was the greatest capital investment of any *lavorente* and the one which made him most attractive to potential employers. The number of animals may have been in decline, and there certainly is evidence, particularly in the middle and late eighteenth century, of growing difficulty in finding grazing for the animals, but it would certainly be wrong to see the Valpolicella (and probably the rest of the Veronese) as being denuded of animals by 1800.

Other factors, too, increased the variety and complexity of the agrarian system. The wide geographical variation of the Valpolicella has already been mentioned, but to this must also be added the wide variety of patterns of landholding and land management which appertained even in relatively consistent geographical areas; it is not possible, except in the very crudest and broadest terms, to characterize the Valpolicella as an area of 'landlord' or 'peasant' ownership, nor as one of 'direct' or 'indirect' management. Leaving aside the whole question of change through time, the pattern of tenure and exploitation was far too complex and varied to allow such generalizations to be made. It is above all, variety and flexibility, in social and economic terms, which made the Valpolicella economy so prosperous through the late seventeenth and eighteenth centuries.

II

Central to the whole question of the operation of the system and to its rationale is some consideration of the issue of what was the perceived unit of economic and social activity – of what was the unit which was seen as being in profit or loss. This is, of course, perhaps the central issue of all pre-modern economic history, and the one which plays most havoc with perceptions of the operation of the economy and of agricultural systems; it is also the one which is of all the complex issues of pre-modern economic history the most difficult to come to terms with, in part at least because it has been one of the most controversial of issues and one of the issues into which modern concerns, and modern mythologies about the decline of the family and the rise of alienation, have become most deeply entangled.[22] Despite all the complexities, it is vital to make at least some attempt to tackle this issue, since any discussion of economic or social rationality, or any attempt to assess how successfully the economy achieved its aims would be largely meaningless without it.

The conventional wisdom is that the unit of economic and social activity was the 'family' or the 'household'; both are terms of such elasticity and broadness – vagueness – of definition as to make such a statement at the same time a truism and of meaningless imprecision. It is surprisingly difficult, in the case of the Valpolicella to say very much concrete about either unit. Certainly 'family' and 'household' were in no way coterminous. Despite another piece of age-old wisdom, still repeated, the typical pattern of cohabiting family in the early modern Veronese, rural or urban, was not a large extended one, but rather a small nuclear one; the accidents of mortality and migration, if nothing more profound in social or cultural terms, ensured that the large majority of families would be small – less than six people – and bi- or at the most tri-generational. It is also clearly the case that a very major element in the 'decision' or rather 'accident' of extension or nuclearity of individual families was circumstance; there was no clear and simple movement in the history of individual families from the extended to the nuclear. Some families moved in that direction, others moved as births, death, age or economic circumstance dictated, from the 'modern' nuclear family to the 'pre-modern' extended one. If there was a shift from the extended to the nuclear, and there may have been one before the nineteenth century, it was the movement on balance of a society in which families were moving in both directions and in which the numerical advantage, certainly since the late sixteenth century, had clearly lain with the nuclear family.

It is, however, not enough to say that this was an economy dominated by the nuclear family, in which the nuclear family was the basic unit of economic activity. Sufficient examples exist to indicate that this broad generalization, although it may hold good in most cases, requires some modification and qualification if it is to explain the situation more fully. What may well have been a major housing shortage in the mid and late eighteenth centuries intensified a tendency which was present earlier towards the cohabitation of a number of (usually) related families in the same large house; it is very tempting to see in this a form of extension, of the creation or continuation of a large family or kin unit. In some cases this may have been so, but from the internal history and internal organization of many of these households, it is clear that, far from being integrated family units they were frequently feuding and, even more frequently, that the sharing of a house between the members of a family involved the physical division of the house in some cases in the most inconvenient and impractical ways. Cohabitation did not necessarily, even for brothers, imply co-activity. If this pattern moves the situation even further away from the idea of the extended family or kin as an economic unit, there is a major element which shifts the balance back the other way. The legal regime of Communion of Goods – or the joint ownership of land by the whole body of general heirs, rather than its several divisions between them – was a common device in the Veronese to avoid the problems generated by the partible inheritance of land. Living in communion of goods did not necessarily mean cohabiting, merely some kind of agreement, usually unwritten or at least unregistered, between the heirs over the management of property and over the rights of individuals to be consulted over alienations.

The advantages of the common regime were not simply those of protection from division and morcellement – indeed, as will be argued later, morcellement was not seen as, necessarily, the disaster it is regarded as by modern agricultural economists and economic historians – but rather that the common regime gave management advantages. In particular, community of goods between brothers or cousins, allowed some of the co-sharers to abandon their local residence and seek employment elsewhere, either in other rural communities, or in the city or, indeed, beyond the Veronese. The extent to which this framework actually permitted a formal *frereche* type of organization or indeed a conscious management approach to the total economy of the extended group is open to question; little evidence exists, but it does seem possible to suggest that the family in communion of goods may well have operated its internal economy on a rather different basis to the way in which a single family unit operated.

It is clear, too, that the system of communion was a system of management; it would be very easy to fall into the trap of believing that communion of goods represented some kind of emotional or social attachment to the idea of the family as a wider extended unit. Such attachment did, to some extent exist, but it seems clear that that attachment was emotional rather than practical. Strong evidence for that comes from the frequency with which families dissolved their communal organization after one generation; basically a common regime involving more than a single generation produced internal complexities which made efficient management impractical: above all, the calculation of shares and the problems of gaining the necessary unanimity for legal action, for alienation in particular, which was a normal part of agricultural management and not a final desperate throw, made communal regimes involving large numbers of shares and sub-sharers almost impossible to work.

Large communal families were inefficient, whatever their emotional value, and hence large communal families did not, in general, exist. Above all, communion of goods made possible a family in which individuals carried on other economic or social activities and at the same time retained a share in the family landholdings. This type of arrangement was of most obvious value to those 'middle-class' families in which one or more of a number of brothers sought professional employment – in the law or the church, for instance, at a distance, perhaps in Verona – but retained their full rights and share in the family land back in their home commune. It is not fully clear whether this relationship involved any flow-back of income or profits from their urban or outside employment to the family back in the home commune; certainly there is some evidence for the provision of capital by the urban member for his rural relatives. Communion of goods was not, it must be emphasized, anything more than a business arrangement judged on its efficiency and profitability; it should not be taken to be anything more than that. It was certainly not a result of any mystical or emotional attachment to the family unit as such nor to the idea of the indivisible oneness of the family lands; one of the things which broke up communions was the great difficulty experienced in gaining the necessary approval from all the members of the communion for the frequent alienation of land which was an important part of economic management.

The regime of the communion of goods illustrates also a further crucial point about the management and organization of the Valpoli-cella – and Veronese – family and estate. Even at the 'peasant' level this was a highly sophisticated and complex society, in its economic as well as social organization; the communion of goods regime can be seen as an attempt, and in very many cases a successful attempt, to organize the family as a corporate unit, with a division of functions and, to some extent at least, with a specialization of functions. It is important to point out that communion of goods did not exhaust the complexities of the legal structure of families and family holdings; in many cases family holdings existed as a complex mixture of individual and communion holding, of alienable and inalienable land and so forth. The family as business corporation was powerful and varied, and the concept of the family as an economic unit stretched well beyond the simple nuclear family or beyond the single cohabiting household; after all, the co-owners and co-members of a family communion could live at a distance of twenty or more miles from each other.

The tendency so far has been to reduce or deny the importance of wider units of kinship, above all of the extended kinship or *casa*. In strictly economic terms this is entirely correct. There is no evidence whatsoever of a wider kin group acting as any sort of economic unit, for the management of assets or in any other way. The *casa* did, undoubtedly, have an emotional and social role to play; relationships, both by blood and by marriage were important, and it certainly seems to have been the case that individuals went to their kinsfolk for, for instance, credit and for the use of influence. The negotiations and operations which resulted seem, however, on the basis of the small amount of information we have, to have been on a strictly business footing.

The second element in any such discussion must be a discussion of, or rather a reference to, the aims of such groups in the management of their estates and assets. The codification of economics in the twen-tieth century has left this central issue of the economic systems of the past too much neglected. Economic and social historians are, rightly, concerned to insist that the laws of modern economics do not, neces-sarily, apply to non-modern economies, but as Marshall Sahlins[23] has pointed out, the most apparently-irrational behaviour in past economies and past societies can and should be explained, not by the over-easy assumption of the stupidity or 'primitiveness' of the past but by searching for the underlying rationality of that behaviour as a way of understanding the relationship of behaviour and context. Again, of course, it is necessary to avoid as far as possible the opposite distor-tion: the idea that the behaviour of the past was in some way more 'natural' or 'wholesome' than the behaviour of the present, and that in some way it represents a model to which the present should, or even could, return. Both the reduction of the past to stupidity and the elevation of the past to the status of role model are fundamentally wrong.

The search for the economic rationalities of the past – a branch of the search for *mentalites* – is one of extreme difficulty and one fraught with pitfalls. Above all, it is necessary to reject any idea of reconstructing economic rationalities and economic strategies on the basis of 'official' sources, be they religious or secular. In most cases the rationalities on which individuals and families proceeded were, to them at least, so obvious as not to need, or indeed to be capable of, formal expression. All that the economic and social historian can do is, starting from the assumption that the behaviour of individuals and groups in any period of history is both rational and functional within their rationale, to seek to elucidate some kind of system inherent in that behaviour; the only test of such a construct can be the success with which it explains patterns of activity. This process is, of course and inevitably, circular; it relies on the historian using the construct built up on the basis of observation of a system to explain that system. Though such a process is philosophically dubious, it is a necessary one if the history of past economic systems is not to be crippled by the lack of a crucial element. Because of the circular nature of this structure it is necessary to discuss some of the apparent principles of the economic system at this stage and also to return to the discussion at a later stage.

How did the economic world look to a cultivator in the early modern period? The first element in any attempt to answer this question must be, in a sense a negative one. One of the major things, perhaps *the* major thing, which separates the early modern period from the modern period is, as every schoolboy knows, that collection of economic and social events which, rather inadequately, we link together as the Industrial Revolution and its aftermath. Economic historians, being essentially earth-bound, have tended to see the Industrial Revolution in terms of a series of technological and sociological changes in the organization first of production and then of society as a whole; the effects of the Industrial Revolution on economic perceptions, in particular the economic perceptions of the mass of the people, have been largely ignored – or, even worse, abandoned to the concern of social historians and sociologists concerned above all with the post-Industrial Revolution changes in society.

In many ways to do so is to ignore the central element of the Industrial Revolution, to turn it into no more than a more or less interesting set of changes in the eighteenth and nineteenth centuries, rather than a fundamental turning point in history. It is, of course, much easier to insist upon the effects of the Industrial Revolution on perceptions than it is to indicate what those changes were with any degree of certainty. One point, though, is clear; a 'Revolution of

Rising Expectation' occurred following and related to the technological changes of the Industrial Revolution. That revolution was
not simply an expectation of improvement and growth; it was also,
and much more significantly, an expectation of continuing improvement and growth. W. W. Rostow's conception of the Industrial
Revolution as the take-off into self-sustained growth,[24] whatever its
failings as an economic definition, is absolutely right as a definition of
the Industrial Revolution as a turning-point in perceptions of the
economy. Slowly in the nineteenth century and more rapidly in the
middle and late twentieth century, the mass of people began to accept
and act upon the notion that next year, on balance, would be better
and more prosperous than this year, and that the next decade would
be better and more prosperous than the last decade. By the 1960s
economists themselves began to talk of continuous, exponential
growth; economic disaster was defined in terms of a slow-down of
growth, of a deceleration in the rate of improvement. Even the
prophets of doom talked in terms of world disasters caused by over-
development, by over-expansion. In such circumstances, perceptions
of the risk and the problems involved in economic activity were
bound to change, and with them the strategies which individuals and
families would follow.

Risk, and the response to risk, lies at the heart of the change in
economic rationality which is being discussed. It is necessary to abandon the idea of risk as good or beneficial, of change as almost
inevitably a good thing and for the better, if we are to understand how
early modern men and women saw the central issues of economic life.
It is perhaps a truism to point out that the line which separated
success from catastrophe in the pre-modern world was a very fine
one; the psalmist's warning that 'in the midst of life we are in death'
was, for all ages before the twentieth century, not merely a striking
poetic image but a practical reality. The idea of the transience and
imperfection of the sublunary world, and of the longing for the
immutability of the empyrean came, not from philosophical ideals but
from a very practical perception of the real – earthly –world. Life in
the pre-modern world was not a question of a constant and unchanging world, in which day followed day and generation generation in a
regular and stable course, but rather a constant and unremitting struggle against fates who were frequently unkind and always arbitrary.

Demographers and social historians have frequently and rightly
pointed out some of the consequences of the insecurity of life on
demographic patterns and on social relationships, and it would be
wrong to suggest that what applied to human life did not also apply
to economic activity. The performance indicators assembled in
Chapter 3 already suggest that, even in the long-term, the performance
of this relatively successful and prosperous early modern economy
was not constant in its direction of development; for lengthy periods,

'growth' went into reverse, even without the effects of catastrophic plague or famine. In the long-term, of course, we are all dead: for individuals and families in the early modern period what was in many ways more significant than the long-term fluctuations and trends of the economy certainly in terms of their own day-to-day or year-to-year strategy – were the shorter-term fluctuations. Such fluctuations could be, and particularly in the seventeenth century were, much more severe than the long term changes: plague, famine, war, or even the less apparently dramatic events such as harvest shortfall or trade recession made a much more real mark on the livelihood of individuals or families than did the long-term trends of the economy. The crises, the set-backs, of the pre-modern economy were real; that is to say, they represented a real and often substantial decline in production, prosperity and food supply. Furthermore, they affected a population which started in general from a lower level, from a point nearer to the poverty line – better perhaps to say to the survival line – than did, or do, post-Industrial Revolution populations: not merely were crises more severe, but in addition more of the population spent more of their time hovering around the edges of catastrophe.

Nor were the insecurities limited to those of general economic or political crisis; even in times of plenty and peace, the fluctuations and crises of the family cycle – illness, old age, the birth of children and so forth – could, and did produce crises for individual units. Some of those crises could, to some extent, be foreseen, but by no means all; this was an economy and a society in which unexpected crisis was always potentially lurking around the next corner; Job was, understandably, a popular character in early modern popular literature and popular preaching. Furthermore, it is as well to remember that the physical, biological and economic context meant that, in particular for the less well-to-do units in the economy, each year was a series of potential crises. Above all, what could perhaps be called the Merchant of Venice syndrome made life and housekeeping a constant struggle. Antonio, the Merchant of Venice, falls into the hands of Shylock because, although he is a rich man, the delayed arrival of his ships meant that, at a crucial time, he was without money; in modern terms, a cash-flow problem arose since major expenditure arose at a time when income, although expected, was not yet available. In the rural context, the Merchant of Venice syndrome was more, for some people at least, the Merchant of Venice trap; the agriculturalist's equivalent of Antonio's ships was the income from the land, or to put it another way the gathering of the harvest. Until the harvest was gathered, payments could not be made, even if they fell due, unless by recourse to providers of credit. This, of course, was a sufficiently serious problem in a commercialized agriculture; in a system in which at least part of the production was for autoconsumption, the Merchant of Venice shortfall represented not economic difficulty and recourse to moneylenders, but hunger and possible starvation. In a very real sense, stress was a problem of the pre-modern period rather than of the present day world.

The certainty or at least the expectation of growth was, then, replaced by the equal certainty of crisis and catastrophe. The prudent manager, of a family or indeed of a commercial organization in the early modern period, had to develop a strategy, or series of strategies, to deal with this instability. The Victorian stand-by, of saying that early modern Europeans dealt with these problems in the way that Arabs or 'natives' did, by a fatalistic acceptance of the Will of God, by resignation, humility or apathy, will do no more for the seventeenth century European than it will do for the modern African or Egyptian. The early modern Europeans' strategies were based upon a series of clearly defined, if not expressed, priorities and concerns.

The first element in that structure seems to have been survival, both of the individual and the group; zoomorphic suggestions that what was involved was the defence of the gene-pool are incorrect and individual survival occupied as large a place as did that of the group. That individuals and groups should be able to face whatever crisis fate should produce with some certainty of survival was absolutely central. Survival meant, above all, the avoidance of risk; only the foolhardy would take on more risk than was absolutely necessary. Risk in an agricultural context meant, in part at least, the risk of crop failure; crop failure could not be avoided, but it could be minimized, above all by spreading the risk. Monoculture was dangerous, it meant putting all the eggs in a single, fragile basket and hence the rationale suggested mixed farming, the more mixed the better, with a wide range of crops to ensure some kind of success in all but the most absolutely disastrous of years. Again, over-dependence on a single soil type placed too great a strain on a single element and, therefore, what was significant was not concentration of holdings and economies of scale, but a variety of soil types and a spreading of risks. Specialization and concentration, two of the watchwords of modern agriculture, were rejected, wherever possible, not through conservatism but through a real and lively appreciation of their dangers.

The principle of risk-spreading went much wider than simple agricultural technique. After all, agriculture was itself one of the major sources of the instability of the system; therefore, diversification into industrial employment, into the production of industrial raw materials, into wage labour, into migrant labour further spread the risk. The family operating under the communion of goods had, of course, a great advantage here too; the more the members of a group, the greater the diversity they could add to their structure – the greater their insurance against catastrophe. The principle of insurance and risk-spreading lay at the very centre of the economic strategies of cultivators and landowners in the Valpolicella, and indeed in the whole Veronese, and informed all of their economic decisions. The principle of insurance, however, in the Italian context and indeed elsewhere in early modern Europe, ran clean counter to the dictates of modern economics; insurance implied diversity rather than specialization, dispersal rather than concentration, and the maximization of stability rather than the maximization of output and income through change. One of the advantages of the Valpolicella was that it was able, through a combination of climatic, geographical and social factors, to make the strategy of insurance work over a long period. It is only necessary to contrast the relative prosperity of the Valpolicella in the later seventeenth century with the disasters which befell the wheat monoculture areas of northern France[25] to realize the appropriateness of the strategy, albeit a strategy which, in modern terms, makes the Valpolicella look backward.

Two central themes, then, coincide in any attempt to explain or interpret the economic rationale and the economic structure of the agricultural system of the Valpolicella. The first is the importance of the household or the family group – and no clearer terminology can be, or perhaps should be evolved to categorize the basic unit – as a unit not merely of social belonging but also of economic activity, as the basic unit of economic planning and economic strategy. The second is the importance of survival and of planning for survival in this context. Any explanation of this society which sees the individual as the sole element, or which gives 'growth' the primacy over survival or insurance in its economic make-up, will fail. It also follows that the measure of economic success or failure, the level of discontent – potential or actual – with the economic system, was very different to similar measures in a modern context, for, if we are to reject the idea of a fatalistic acceptance of circumstances, we must also explain why there was so little pressure to change within the system. The only realistic explanation, in a political structure in which the state lacked the mechanisms and coercive force to impose a particular economic or social system on an unwilling subject population, is that for most of the people and for most of the time, the agricultural system delivered what they wanted with some degree of efficiency. In few areas of mental activity is the gulf between the pre-modern and the modern world so complete as in this perception of the economic system and of what it was required to deliver. Without at least some understanding of and sympathy for this very different mental system, it is impossible to appreciate fully the complexities and efficiencies of the pre-modern system or to approach it in anything other than a mood of frustrated pity for the idiocies of our ancestors.

III

Classically, Mediterranean agriculture has been categorized as a mixed system without any great level of specialization. The climate of the Valpolicella is not truly Mediterranean in that its summers, though dry, are not as arid as those of areas further south and also that its winters are much more continental than the mild and wet Mediterranean. The Alpine foothills attract rain and rain-bearing clouds, and the altitude of much of the Valpolicella also mitigates the worst of the summer heat. Nonetheless, as has been emphasized before, the agriculture of the region is essentially mixed; arable and pastoral, commercial and subsistence farming were mixed in a balance which varied from commune to commune and from year to year. Like all other pre-modern agricultures, the Valpolicella was dominated by grains, but not to the exclusion of other crops; after all, a grain monoculture, where it was not inevitable, represented a failing in the terms of the principle of insurance. It is, in fact, extremely difficult to assess the importance of grains in anything other than an impressionistic sort of way. The whole question of cropping patterns is an extremely difficult one; what is available is basically a record of production rather than of areas under particular crops. In any case, such figures would be of dubious value; first because of the role of fallow in the rotational systems of the Valpolicella and secondly because of the intermixing of crops on the same land. Any view as to the actual cropping pattern, either the balance between arable or pastoral farming on the one hand, or the balance between grains and other crops, or indeed that between types of grain, can be no more than an impression, or based on the indirect evidence of harvests. Equally, any hard and fast answer to the question involves a dangerous imposition on the way in which the agricultural system worked.

It is clear, however, from such estate and tithe records as we possess, that wheat (*formento*) was the major food grain produced in virtually all the Valpolicella communes throughout the period. Although the climatic and other difficulties of the seventeenth century may have caused some kind of shift away from wheat towards other food grains and also towards the growing of mixture-grains, including wheat mixtures, wheat clearly remained the predominant grain. On the estates of San Fermo Maggiore in Bure and S. Pietro, the proportion of the monastery's share of the production of the (sharecropped) estates represented by wheat fell from 75.6 per cent by volume in the 1740s to 65.5 per cent in the 1780s;[26] even after the decline is taken into account, wheat still represented approximately two-thirds of the grain production of these estates. A similar picture, and one which holds for the seventeenth century as well as for the eighteenth, comes from the S. Giorgio tithe returns;[27] despite all the differing vicissitudes of the two centuries, wheat was and remained, certainly in volume and almost certainly in value terms, by far the largest single item in the production of the Valpolicella.

Wheat was the major grain crop, but it was not the sole one by any means. As has been suggested previously, the Valpolicella produced a bewildering range of other food grains. The mixture was not, it must be emphasized a result of the specialization by particular cultivators in particular grains; all cultivators grew a wide variety of grains and, indeed, one of the reasons why maize became such an important element in the cropping pattern of the Valpolicella in the eighteenth century was that at least one variety, *cinquantin*, which got its name from its fifty-day growing period from sowing to harvest, could be grown as a catch crop following winter wheat. Possibly some others could be added to the rotation system after the harvesting of winter wheat, thus adding another crop and another element to the agricultural system, an element which offered a further insurance in that it could be used to rescue something from a bad season for winter wheat.

Grain, despite its dominance, was not the only field crop grown. One striking feature of the system, both economically and ecologically, was the importance of leguminous crops in all the rotation systems, a factor which may go some way to mitigate the growing lack of animal manure in the system. Beans of several different sorts – peas, vetches and lentils – were a major component of the production of most farms. This had been so for a very long time: the traditional distribution of beans and bean soup to the population of S. Giorgio at Martinmas has its origins in the early Middle Ages.[28] Beans were an element of both human and animal food and it is, of course, difficult to be sure whether, at any one time, the beans and other pulses were being fed to the cattle or used for human food or flour. There is little conclusive evidence of the proportion of the land growing pulses and other nitrogen fixing-crops during this period; it may be, and there is some evidence from Breonio to suggest this, that growing population pressure in the eighteenth century increasingly pushed the pulses out of the rotation systems, or reduced the frequency with which they appeared – a shift which may well have contributed to falling yields in the medium and longer term.

In commercial terms the most important crop of the Valpolicella was the vine. Virtually everywhere in the Valpolicella, from the highest levels down to the plains and the river valley, grapes were grown and wine produced. Grapes, of course, had a number of agricultural advantages over wheat. In particular, vines were much more conveniently grown and tended on terraced land than wheat or indeed other cereal crops. The olive was also a major element in the economy, and in particular in the commercial economy of many holdings and estates, especially in the seventeenth century. Despite the claim of Alessio Besi of Isola di Sopra in Verona in his *polizza* that 'il torcolo nella casa di Santa Sophia o Semonte del quale ne cavo quasi niente perche e piu la spesa che l'utile',[29] olives and olive oil seem to have represented a major element in the commercial income of many land-owners. In their *polizza* of 1745 Francesco and Paolo Fattori claimed that the dryness (*secca*) of the olives on their estates at Novare had resulted in an annual loss of income of 200 ducats from an estate whose total net return to them after the loss was no more than D900,[30] while Ferdinand and Agostino Montenari of S. Benedetto drew attention in their declaration of their estate in Bure to their 'torcolo infrutuoso per la seca ben nota di tutti li olivi che facevano una volta circa la 3ª parte di entrata'.[31] Other landlords were to complain that the loss of the olives meant a loss of up to two-thirds in the profits of their estates.

Perhaps not quite so important as olives, especially in the seventeenth century, were the leaves of the mulberry tree (*moraro*). The mulberry was one of the major industrial raw materials of the Veronese, upon which its extensive and important raw silk industry was dependent. Mulberry trees were taxable as a valuable asset, although, as with all taxable assets, the number of trees is only very imperfectly known. It is clear, however, that the number of mulberries was high and that many, or most, agriculturalists had at least one tree. Although, within the normal strategy of most households, some part at least of the production of these trees would be used to support household production of silk, there was also a large-scale market in leaves, the leaves either being sold by the sackful or, equally commonly, the production of individual trees being rented out for a whole season.

The importance of pastoral farming in this structure has already been discussed. It is important, however, to indicate the lack of specialization in pastoral farming. Even in the high communes, where the availability of extensive grazing rights through the period might lead to the expectation of pastoral specialization, and where indeed during the later Middle Ages the *Fattoria Scaligiera* had established sheep ranches and sheep breeding stations, farming was still essentially mixed. If there was specialization it was not in the production of individual units but in the occupational patterns of individuals, usually employees or agents; shepherding was, when it was anything more than a part-time task for the younger children, a specialized employment. In part this may have been a consequence of the migration of the sheep and other flocks to the higher pastures in the summer, and of the specialized nature of the shepherd's other major task, cheesemaking. Whatever may have been the case in, for instance, the communes of Monte Baldo or of the Vicarate of the Mountains further to the east,[32] there does not seem to have been any large-scale transhumance of flocks either from the lower communes to the higher within the Valpolicella or from the communes of the plain into the area. The division between arable and pastoral farmers, and between arable and pastoral farming, was not a clear one or a particularly significant one; as with so many other things in the agricultural system of the Valpolicella, the distinction was no more than a question of balance within an individual's situation and, as such, varied through time.

The question of mixture and balance, then, is absolutely crucial to the understanding of this agricultural system. It was even more significant than the mere question of the balance between crops and systems over a holding as a whole. As with most other Mediterranean agricultural systems, there was a great deal of multiple use of land, not merely through the rotation systems, but also and even more significantly through the multiple use of land for several crops at once. Classically, in every sense of that word, the most significant of those multiple uses was the growing of vines not in vineyards but as boundary and shade crops between arable cultivation. This mixture was in fact a double one, since, in the Valpolicella at least, the vines were supported on trees grown along field edges, sometimes olive trees, but more usually mulberries or willows; hence a plot of land might well be providing three commercially or internally useful crops in a single year. Again, it was not merely arable land that was used in this way. Pasture land, and land for hay production, was in short supply throughout the early modern period, but even pasture land was not so valuable as to be allowed to produce a single crop; very frequently, pasture land and hay fields doubled as olive groves (or possibly the other way around). This double use was particularly important in view of the irrigation of hay land – it was often the only land which was irrigated – and of the need of olive trees for irrigation if they are to produce large crops as far north as the Valpolicella.

The physical and climatic variations of the Valpolicella involved, also, a very mixed series of geographical types of cultivation. Unlike the plains of the Veronese, where soils were generally uniform and where land was normally suitable for plough cultivation, usually, given the heavy clay nature of the soil, with large ox teams, the Valpolicella has a wide range of soil types – from deep heavy alluvial clays and light moraine soils to the thin limestone soils of the uplands and the valley sides. Again, although the lower communes have large, relatively flat fields which could be cultivated in much the same ways as the plain fields, albeit with smaller ploughs and teams, the higher and foothill communes also had much terraced land, with the terraces varying from the relatively broad which could still be cultivated with an ox-drawn plough, to the very narrow and steep, on which hoe cultivation (*zappa*) was the only effective means of cultivation. Terrace land, too, was extremely expensive to maintain and to develop: the terrace walls (*marogne*) were often massive, reaching twenty feet in height in places, requiring the movement of large quantities of rock.

Even though there is little evidence of large-scale terrace building after the 1620s, the cost of maintenance of the *marogne* was also extremely high, given the prevalence of flash-flooding which led to the collapse and even washing-away of terraces. Gian-Matteo Padoani, for instance, complained in the *polizza* he submitted for the *estimo* of 1745 on behalf of his wife Flavia Boldiera for her dowry land in Torbe that the land was:

> continuamente deteriorando a causa di piovali a causa che l'aqua conduce via la terra con vigne piantate sopra le marogne che sono di continua e grave spesa a mantenirle.[33]

Terraced agriculture was certainly more cost intensive and more heavily dependent upon labour than plain land agriculture.

The whole question of land purchases and the shifting ownership patterns of land is, as Chapter 6 will discuss, an extremely difficult and complex one, particularly for the seventeenth century, but it seems reasonably clear that, in neither the seventeenth nor the eighteenth century was there any real movement towards either the consolidation of landholdings into coherent blocks for any reason other than aristocratic prestige, or of the abandonment of terraced land in favour of plain land. It is true that in the aftermath of the disasters of the 1630s, in the Valpolicella as elsewhere, there is considerable evidence of the abandonment of high land, some of which, but by no means all, was terraced; but this was in fact the abandonment of marginal land rather than of terraced land, and indeed, in some regions, the abandonment of cultivation on the relatively flat hill tops and the movement downwards of cultivation meant an increase rather than a decrease in the proportion of terraced and hoe-cultivated land.

Here again it is important to see this pattern as being not a symptom of the incurably uneconomic or perverse reaction of the cultivators and landlords to their economic context, but rather a clear and entirely rational response within their economic system. In terms of risk-spreading and insurance, a concentrated holding – with one type of land, dependent on a single pattern of crops, upon specific patterns of labour, capital and context – is, far from being an economically sound investment, a dangerous concentration of risk. It is much better to have and to maintain a mixed pattern of holdings, even better a mixed and scattered pattern of holdings, since that way the frequently very local effects of storms, particularly in the summer pre-harvest period, may be reduced. Far from being a sign of the economic primitiveness of the Valpolicella system, the dispersion and *morcellement* of holdings fits very clearly into the rationale of the system and can be seen as a very real attempt at a solution to the problem of insecurity in the system.

A further element in the mixture was woodland. The whole of the

Venetian land empire was desperately short of wood, not merely for ship-building, which was the major concern of the Venetian state, but also of wood for building and firewood. Fortunes were to be made in the shipping of wood down the Adige from Trento and beyond, and the wood merchants of the Riva San Lorenzo were amongst the wealthiest and most important of the commercial groups of the city: from them at least one of the major noble families of the Veronese, the Bevilacqua of San Michele alla Porta, had sprung.[34] Fortunes continued to be made throughout the period, and the ownership of forest land (*terra boschiva*) was a valuable asset to any landowner. Even the smallest patches of wood could and did produce important returns; the management and exploitation of woodland was an important element in the economic mix for many landholders, and many more would gratefully have taken on woods if they had been available.

The picture of the agriculture of the Valpolicella which begins to appear from this pattern is one of an agriculture which was immensely diversified, with a wide range of crops and a wide range of sources of income: an economy, then, which lacked the regional and commercial specialization which, in modern economic terms is equated with efficiency and progress. In fact, the pattern which had developed in the Valpolicella, which is not unique in the Veronese hills, was one which was especially and peculiarly fitted to the requirements of the population on the one hand and to the constraints of the economic and physical system on the other. The context in which this system had to operate was one of uncertainty and potential disaster, in which the most immediate and lively concern was for survival and for a reasonable guarantee of income, albeit not necessarily the maximum income for the producer.

As has been pointed out before, the system had to produce in addition something else; it had to produce some kind of cover against the Merchant of Venice trap. In other words, it had, to be geared as far as possible to a reasonably constant flow of income, rather than to the production of a single block of income, no matter how great, at one point in the year. The Valpolicella system did this admirably; the spread and variety of crops, to say nothing of the other, non-agricultural sources of income, meant that if a family or household could work the system properly, they were not dependent on a single source of income on a single block of income at, say, the time of the wheat harvest but could rely on some kind of income spread over a number of months, from the time of the sale of the silk 'harvest' in May and June, through the grain harvests in the mid-summer and on to the vintage in the autumn. Such a spread had many important advantages, and was an important bonus for the cultivators of the Valpolicella and elsewhere in the Veneto hills, compared with other cultivators in the plains, in northern France or in Germany who were, inevitably, constrained by climate and social circumstances to depend much more heavily on single crops and hence on single sources of income. The social and economic consequences of this were many; credit, and the role of credit brokers, which is so important in many agricultural systems and which leads to so many problems in those societies, were of a very different hue in the Valpolicella than in other areas of Europe: debtors were not so completely in the hands of their creditors; debts could be paid, in part or in full, at more than one point in the year; the old problem of the agricultural debtor, borrowing at a time of shortage and settling at a time of glut, was not abolished but certainly reduced. Again, a single trader or merchant was much less likely to gain a stranglehold over an individual, leaving aside the whole question of the greater competition which arose from the closeness of so many major centres of commerce and consumption.

All in all, the Valpolicella system achieved what it set out to do; it produced a stable and relatively secure system of agricultural production, which in most years and under most circumstances guaranteed, as far as any pre-modern system could, the survival of those involved in it. Indeed, it is possible to go further; the system also managed, until the crises of the later eighteenth century and, in particular, until the disasters of the Napoleonic years, to provide a level of prosperity for much of the population based not upon growth and change, but upon stability. Stability was what the system offered, and since the system was able to deliver stability – and to do so, it would seem, rather better than conflicting systems elsewhere in Europe – pressure for change was unlikely to build up inside it. Change could only come either from a change in the context or from external shock, and it was chiefly the latter which was responsible for the collapse of the system in disaster. It was not backwardness or primitiveness or even conservatism *per se* which seemingly stopped the Valpolicella moving on to an agricultural revolution in the eighteenth century, but a very real and very realistic unwillingness to move from a system which worked and which delivered the benefits the population required to one which palpably was based on a series of lunatic gambles. What we must remember is that to seventeenth and eighteenth century Veronese, it is the modern world's obsession with change and with risk which would appear perverse and indeed lunatic.

IV

An unwillingness to change, or rather an unwillingness to see change as necessarily good, does not mean either an unwillingness to accept change, and in particular to accept new crops or new practices, nor does it mean simplicity or a lack of sophistication. The importance of new crops and new technologies in the pattern of Italian agriculture is relatively well-known. Many of the 'improvements' in agriculture which were introduced in England as part of the Agricultural Revolution owed their origins to northern Italy and their use was no less widespread in the Valpolicella than in England. The history of the spread of maize, even though the conquest of north Italian agriculture by this crop in the course of the eighteenth century has almost certainly been over-emphasized, reveals the willingness of cultivators to adopt a new crop which fitted into the accepted and reliable system: maize was a very useful addition to the mix of crops produced, to some extent replacing the older millets and to some extent marking a major advance on them in yields; it was only when it began to be a new monoculture that it began to threaten the system, and with it the security and modest prosperity of the Valpolicella and indeed of the whole Veneto. The development of the Veronese silk industry, the planting of mulberries and their inclusion in the system again, indicates that this system was capable of encapsulating change and indeed accepting change enthusiastically if, and only if, it fitted into the overall logic of the system.

Technological change in agriculture in Italy in the seventeenth and eighteenth centuries was relatively limited and concerned above all with water supply and control. In so far as major advances were made, they were made in the drainage and watering of the fields of the plains and, in particular, related to the flooding and drainage of rice-fields.[35] Although there is some evidence of the use of the new irrigation technology in the lower communes of the Valpolicella, the area was, inevitably, little affected by the new developments, and its agricultural technology seems to have remained little changed throughout the period. The major piece of technology most in use was still the plough. The plough in use in the Valpolicella, the *versor*, seems to have been a relatively light one, again consonant with the lightness of much of the soil. The usual motive power for the plough was a pair of oxen (*boi, bovi*); there are a few references to ploughs with larger teams, but they are very rare and are treated as such by the sources.[36] The area which such a team could plough in a season of course depended to some extent on the geography and geology of particular holdings. For the calculation of such a figure the only source is the *Polizze Citta*. Unfortunately, their recording of the numbers of ploughs needed to cultivate estates is totally erratic, and had virtually ceased by 1745; furthermore, there is a circularity in such an argument, since the number of ploughs employed was, to some extent dependent upon the number of *lavorencia* and other holdings into which the estates were divided, one plough team being the usual capital of one *lavorente*. Since this was only one of many factors which determined the size of units of exploitation, these figures cannot be used as any more than a rough indication. On this basis the average area which was ploughed by single teams in the seventeenth century seems to have been about 38.5 Veronese campi, though, as might be expected, that figure is larger in the lower and flatter communes.[37] The very small amount of eighteenth century evidence suggests a similar figure.

The other major technological elements in the agriculture of the Valpolicella, the flour mill (*molino*) and the olive press (*torcolo*) were both considerable capital investments. Corn mills were essentially water-driven, chiefly dependent upon the Adige or upon the flow of water in the streams and *torrenti* of the hills. As a result they were liable to destruction by flooding, in particular of course, the floating mills (*molini terragni*) of the Adige itself and were also subject to interruptions due to lack of water. Gian-Matteo Padoani (again) possessed in Torbe: 'due rode de molini terragni posti in que monti che lavorano lentamente . . . per la poca aqua che discende da que monti'.[38] Gironimo Badili of Pigna in Verona and his brothers possessed, in 1653: 'un molino in Mazurega qual per la scarzesa delle acque lavora due o tre mesi all'anno'.[39] The *torcolo* was, again, a major capital item, usually the property of the larger and richer land owners, usually powered by oxen or by mules. The decline of olive production – although, as suggested earlier it was not perhaps as great as many of the taxpayers would have wished the government to believe[40] – reduced the value of the olive presses and led to their abandonment and ruin.

If the technology of agriculture was and remained essentially simple, the rotation systems of the Valpolicella were highly complex and highly sophisticated. It is well to remember that, in a situation where artificial fertilizers and pesticides were not available, rotation systems were virtually the only way, outside costly systems of irrigation, that farmers and cultivators had of influencing levels of production and productivity. The study of rotation systems in operation, rather than in theory, is highly complex and difficult, above all because in the Valpolicella, as almost certainly elsewhere, it is impossible to talk of a 'system' as such. What is clear from the information which is available is that patterns of rotation were developed which were suited to individual plots of land, rather than involving the universal application of fixed systems. Furthermore, the importance of fixed crops – vines, olives, mulberries for instance, which, because of the long periods necessary for them to come to maturity (five years in the case of vines, ten or more in the case of olives) had to remain in position – meant that rotational systems had to be developed which took them and their needs into consideration.

Information on the rotational systems is extremely sparse. Occasionally the *Estimo* or the *Polizze Citta* contain some reference to the seeding and rotation of land,[41] but it is reasonable to conclude, given the nature of those documents, that when such references occur, they are included to indicate the unusual nature – and usually the less-than-good practice – of the rotations they describe. The one major source used in this study which deals, albeit in passing, with rotations is *Patrimonio Ecclesiastico*, and in particular the *verbali* of the Chancellor's examination of witnesses as to the value of land being submitted as the *patrimonio* of the ordinand. Unfortunately, *Patrimonio* does not give a full picture: the questioning of witnesses is somewhat erratic, and the recording of details of agricultural practice covers only a short period. Furthermore, the wide regional disparities of ordinations within the Valpolicella means that certain regions, in particular the high hills, are over-represented and others are not represented at all. Unfortunately, much of this evidence comes from the period before 1630, but there is little to show that the crisis of 1630 led to a simplification of the systems of rotation, nor to the abandoning of the matching of systems of rotation to particular pieces of land.

The evidence, such as it is, in fact precludes any discussion of a system, or systems of rotation. What is very striking, however, is that the patterns of cultivation of individual fields and individual blocks seems to have been matched to soil types and contexts. To take just a few examples, Donise *f.* (= son of) Guglielmo Testoni of Santa Sofia, summoned as a witness in 1603 to the value of land in San Pietro being offered as *patrimonio* on behalf of Girolamo Benassuti of San Pietro in Cariano, described it as being: 'delli migliori campi che siano in Valpolisella',[42] a judgement which was supported by Luca Copi of Bure, *gastaldo* of Andrea Poeta of Verona:

> si semina ogni anno tre campi di formento e doi di fave et tagliato il formento vi si semina il miglio et l'anno seguenti si mette il formento in quelli doi campi dove le fave et si sestrepolo poi uno de quelli del formento.[43]

The role of beans as both a fodder, and in some cases, a food crop and as a nitrogen-fixer, was widely known and widely used in the Valpolicella systems. Again, fallow was used, sometimes in association with beans or other legumes. In 1605, for instance Bartolomeo Marchioretti of Breonio described the system used on one and a half campi of land in Breonio being donated as *patrimonio* to Bernardino Maragi of Breonio by his uncle Bartolomeo Maragi:

> doi anni di grani e l'altro ano si fa a coltura ma se li scode anco trar deli liomi l'anno della cultura che ghi ne tuole seminar.[44]

Continuous cropping of good land was also possible: on the lands in Mazurega donated by don Matteo Borchia, rector of Cavalo, but a member of a well-known Monte family as *patrimonio* to Antonio di

Vico of Mazurega 'per longa servitudine quam dixit habuisse et habere a Don Antonio', in the words of Bartolomeo fq (= son of the late) Biasio Vico: 'si semina doi anni continui di formento et l'altro anno di marzolo'.[45] Such patterns of intensive cultivation were not uncommon. In Bure, on lands forming part of the *patrimonio* of Agostino di Zocca of Fane, a three-course rotation, two years of wheat and then one of beans, was in use.[46]

None of this constitutes any very clear pattern, and it seems clear that, although it may be possible to detect more patterns than have been demonstrated here, the important fact about this structure is that, given the complexity of physical and climatic types, a variety of systems of rotation and of cropping were in use and continued in use. Two consequences are related to this. The first is that a variety of patterns once again gave a broader range of security; individual pieces of land would be at different stages in their rotations and hence would respond in differing ways to weather and other patterns. The second, reinforcing the first and, indeed the whole system, is that a well-balanced, and hence more secure, holding would include a range of rotation patterns. Therefore, since the rotation patterns were dependent in large part on soil type and climate, a wide range of geographical locations was advisable; again the idea of insurance and security involved dispersal and division rather than concentration.

V

The extremely mixed and complex farming of the Valpolicella looks, in some ways, like an agricultural economist's nightmare; a diffusion of effort, a waste of energy and precious little seeking after economies of scale or comparative advantage. Even the central question of commercialization and of market production was not clearly solved. Much of the production of the Valpolicella farms, of their grain as well as their wine and grapes, was sold, and was destined to be sold from the first. On the other hand, most of the production could, if the need arose, be diverted to local consumption and to subsistence. Certainly the effect of the market on Valpolicella agriculture was much less than might be expected. The demand for wine and market gardening crops from the city, which the Valpolicella was peculiarly well positioned to supply and which to some extent encouraged the expansion of cherry production, did not, it would seem, produce a commercial revolution in agriculture, and certainly nothing to parallel the effects produced by city markets in England, France or the Netherlands. Commercialization also involved the development of domestic industry and, above all, the development of the raw silk industry, rather than the exploitation of what should have been clear-cut advantages of position and climate. At first sight, this was no more than a backward and conservative economy, an economy in terminal decline because it had lost the will or the ability to respond to market forces and to the imperatives of economic change: if the trading cities died through stagnation and ossification, so too, and inevitably, did the rural sector – and for the same reasons. What a moral tale for the Victorian moralist or the modern economist!

The Valpolicella agricultural system was not, however, so half-witted or so backward as all this suggests. By not taking the risks which change involved, by not becoming trapped in a situation in which a single crop, a single market, or indeed a single employment could decide success or failure, survival or otherwise, the early modern farmers and producers of the Valpolicella, and by extension of much of the rest of the Mediterranean, sought to guarantee – and to some considerable extent seem to have succeeded in guaranteeing – the security and survival of their families and households. Insurance, rather than risk or change, stability rather than growth, were the watchwords; the rationale behind these aims ensured that the reaction of this agricultural system would appear perverse to modern society, but just because it appears perverse, it does not follow that it was in any way inefficient or primitive.

5
Units of exploitation

I

The technology of agriculture was only one, and perhaps one of the less significant, factors in this system. Of much greater significance, in particular in view of what has been said about the mixed nature of holdings and the importance of mixed economies, is the way in which land was held and exploited. This chapter will be concerned not with the legal ownership of land which, whatever its undoubted importance for the structure of society and the overall wealth of the economy, was, in a sense, at one remove from the real economy, but with the working of land and the organization of holdings.

This was, it must be made clear, not in any sense a peasant economy, with small owners cultivating their own holdings simply with the labour of their own families, nor renting similar sized holdings from a largely absentee body of landlords. Holdings of both sorts did exist, of course, scattered all across the Valpolicella, but they were by no means typical, even in communes like Breonio where the absence of large-scale external landowners might, at first sight suggest such a structure.[1] The legal status of land within a holding was not particularly significant: a farmer might well be operating a holding made up of land he owned, coupled with land rented from others, either local or outsiders, for cash or kind rents and, although this was rather less common, sharecropped land. There seems to have been very little social status attached to the ownership of land rather than renting, nor, as will be clear from Chapter 6, was there any real question of any kind of 'mystical' connection between landowner and land. Some land stayed in the same hands for many years and indeed, by the system of *fidei commessum*, some land was inalienably linked to certain families, but the liveliness of the land market, and the ease with which individuals bought and sold land, makes it very clear that for the most part land was a commodity to be bought and sold and not something to be retained in particular hands at all costs. Equally, the distinction between the 'land-holding peasant' and the wage labourer was, in this society, an entirely meaningless one; at different stages in their lives individuals fulfilled both roles and, indeed, many wage labourers were also small, and in some cases not so small land owners as well. The whole weight of the legal distinctions associated with ownership is irretrievably blurred in this society and economy, and any attempt to discuss the management and exploitation of land simply in terms of ownership or rental seriously misrepresents its structure and its flexibility.

It must equally be emphasized at this point that this was in no sense a feudal system dominated by a few territorial landlords. As Chapter 6 will make clear, the pattern of landownership in the Valpolicella was by no means a simple one; few communes were dominated by single landlords or indeed by a group of landlords to the exclusion of all other landholders; in most communes the ownership of land was shared between noble and non-noble absentee landlords, large-scale resident local landlords and smaller scale landholders. The geography of settlement meant that the lands of individual communes marched together and in many cases the boundaries between communes represented no real break in agriculture or landownership; many noble *possessioni* spread over two or three communes, while the landholdings of even the smallest landowners could, and did, lie in more than their home commune. It is also the case that, unlike, for instance the situation in many French villages, individual cultivators, and indeed individual sharecroppers, might well be working the lands of a number of landlords rather than just one.

This extreme complexity makes the study of the Valpolicella farm particularly difficult; equally, the very mixed nature of the cultivation which has been suggested in earlier chapters makes those holdings and their nature even more elusive. The estate of Ottavian and Fulvio Suttori, described in their *Polizza* of 1745:

> Una possessione con casa colombara forno e cortivo stalla fenile et con una muraglia et orto in diversi corpi di pezze di terra prativa arativa vegra boschiva prativa con vigne alberi fruttiferi et non olivi et morari con tenda da uccellare in Negrar e Valgatara,[2]

is in many ways typical of the sort of mixed and complex holdings which were to be found in the Valpolicella, both as owned units and as units rented as farms or as sharecropping tenancies. Far from being a single, simple agricultural unit, the holding or the farm, was a complex and varied unit of production. In fact the Suttori holding also had an important semi-industrial sector, as a producer of raw silk, making the mixture even more complex.

The lack of a single pattern of landholding and of land exploitation makes the study of the basic unit of production extremely difficult. It also means that source material is sparse and very sporadic. Even amongst the most obvious types of holding to have left records – the

holdings of the nobility and of the institutions such as the monasteries
– information is very rare. Most estate management was indirect,
through sharecroppers or farmers, and hence estate records, where
they survive, are largely the records of dealings with *lavorenti* or
farmers, and such records are basically the records of annual account
settling or of emergency loans: the dal Bene account books of the
sixteenth and seventeenth centuries are no more than that.[3] Records
of estates managed directly and of home farms are rare indeed, and the
few that exist[4] unfortunately are concerned with atypical estates and
in particular with management of their industrial activities. The
problems are even worse, inevitably, for the smaller 'bourgeois' and
'peasant' holdings, for which virtually nothing has survived. Even the
most central of all the features of estate management, sharecropping
contracts, tended to be one of the areas which were dealt with by
private written agreement rather than by the formality of a registered
notarial contract, and hence their survival has been entirely piecemeal
and haphazard. In many cases, survival has only occurred where an
owner has drawn up a separate collection of his contracts, either for
his own information or as a formulary for future contracts.[5] This
haphazard nature of survival makes the surviving contracts all the
more valuable, but at the same time it makes the whole question of
their typicality even more difficult than usual. Few, if any, sharecropping contracts have survived from the estates of locally, as distinct from
city-based landlords.

The sporadic nature of the records would be less significant if it
were not clear that the nature and terms of contracts fluctuated, in
some cases significantly. In the Valpolicella at least, it was not the case
that the terms and nature of contracts remained fixed, by custom and
usage; just because a holding had been let out to sharecroppers it did
not necessarily follow that the land would remain sharecropped land
indefinitely. It follows then, that any discussion of the system of
exploitation and of land-occupation can only at this stage, and
probably in any case, be tentative and indirect.

II

The agricultural system of the Valpolicella encompassed all sizes of
holdings from micro-holdings – little more than the gardens of houses
– through to large-scale estates. It is fair to say that no Valpolicella
estate, and indeed no Valpolicella holding of a noble or citizen family,
reached the scale of the great *podere* of Tuscany[6] or Piedmont,[7] or
indeed of the noble estates of the Basso Veronese. The economic role
which these holdings played in the total strategy of individuals also
varied, from being (rarely) the sole source of support of an individual
or family, to being no more than a picturesque rural setting for

pastoral idyll and for the life of the villa. Particularly for some of the nobility, their Valpolicella estates were no more than an elegant side-show to the much more economically significant activity of their other estates.[8] Size, too, is inevitably somewhat misleading. The very varied land types of the Valpolicella involved very wide variations in the productive capacity and hence value of land. The *estimo* recognized this in the sense that land was valued for taxation purposes not directly by area but by a (conventional) measure of the value of land based upon an estimate of the income produced by the land.[9] The mixed nature of the economy of each holding, too, makes area pure and simple a very misleading measure of the effective size of any holding. In particular, pasture land and land for the production of hay was a vital element in the economy of any holding of more than the absolute minimum size, and the balance between pasture and arable was similarly crucial. A larger holding, in terms of area, might be less valuable and less usable than a somewhat smaller one, if the smaller one included pasture and the larger one did not. Certainly, many landlords were effectively forced to rent pasture land for their tenants' plough teams, and at considerable cost, if they were to be able to attract tenants for their land.[10]

The yield of the land, too, is a major element in the value of land. The system of agriculture practised, and the nature of the sources, makes the calculation of yields per hectare extremely difficult. It must be emphasized also that there is even less information on the return from seed. There is precious little evidence even as to the proportion of crops retained as seed or as to the amounts of seed provided by landlords to their tenants under *lavorencia* and other contracts. The differing yields of land are also reflected in the value ascribed to land both in the *Estimo* and in private land sales. Such evidence as there is points to very clear differences in yields. In the 1670s and 1680s, for instance, plain land in the estates of Giovanni fq (= son of the late) Pietro Barzisa in Negrar and S. Vito yielded between 1 and 1.5 *minali* of wheat per *campo* and mountain land 0.5 *minali* or less.[11] These figures are of the landlord's share of the production (*parte dominicale*) and, therefore, the actual yield of the land is dependent upon the terms of the *lavorencia* contracts under which the land was farmed. In broad terms it is reasonable to assume that the real yield of this land was twice these figures. *Patrimonio* gives very similar figures for Negrar land for the seventeenth century: they range from 2.5 *minali* to 5.5 *minali*.[12] The same source gives yields of between 2.25 and 6 *minali* per *campo* in the lower level communes of Maran and Fumane and between 2.5 and 4 in Breonio.[13] It must be remembered that these are not yields from particular years, but averages worked out by whoever was valuing the land; it must also be remembered that a greater or lesser proportion of the area of the pieces of land involved was taken up with other crops and that the actual production in any given year would be related to the rotation system used. Furthermore, of course, it is clearly the case that the purposes for which the record was made influences the level of return recorded. The *Estimo* figures are underestimates, and usually seem to be returns of the net profit from the land – the production less all the landlord's expenses, converted into their grain equivalents; on the other hand, the *Patrimonio* figures are likely to be exaggerated since the purpose of the Chancellor's enquiries was to establish that the land donated was of sufficient value.

Despite all the variations which have been discussed earlier, there seems to have been a generally accepted optimum size of holding. Taking the few figures which are given in the *Polizze* for the size of *lavorencia* holdings, and they are so scattered it is not possible to say, for instance, whether the size of *lavorencia* holdings changed in the eighteenth century, those holdings average 62.75 *campi*; the smallest recorded – although it must be emphasized that they were not necessarily the smallest in reality – were about 36 *campi*,[14] although in most cases holdings as small as this lacked the necessary pasture for the draught animals, as was the case with the estates of the brothers Giovanni and Giuseppe Mosconi in Settimo di Castelrotto[15] and usually the landlord had to rent pasture land for his tenants. Possessions smaller than this size were usually rented out piecemeal[16] or, and this was usually noted in the *Polizze* as a major cause of financial loss, cultivated directly by the owner (*in casa*).[17] To some extent custom dictated the size of these holdings and tenurial units, although units could be split, as were for instance the S. Pietro in Cariano holdings of the monastery of S. Fermo Maggiore in 1739,[18] or, more rarely, united to form larger units. In general, holdings were of a size to be cultivated using a single plough team, although in some cases two were used.[19]

It is also very clear that the holdings of tenants, including sharecroppers, were not simply made up necessarily of land rented from a single landowner. *Lavorenti* took sharecropped land from a number of different landlords. Santo Zardin, the *lavorente* of the Maran lands of Scipione Stagnoli in 1745 worked his rented land in addition to his own;[20] Bastian Marchesini of Cerna worked the land of both Mario Benedetti of Prun and Count Antonio Medici[21] while the two possessions of Giovanni and Alberto Bon in Negrar and Mazan were: 'lavorate da para otto bovi che servono anco a benefico di altre terre contigue di raggione di altri particolari'.[22]

The size of the better *lavorente* holdings seems also to have been roughly the size of the average home farm, although there is some evidence, which has been discussed by Viviani,[23] that the later eighteenth century saw some increase in the size of home farms. By no means all holdings, of course, came to this level, and, just as the great numerical bulk of owned holdings were below this level,[24] so too the great mass of rented holdings fell below this level.

How much, in terms of income was this optimum holding worth? The valuations of the landlord's share in the *Polizze* and the values put on similar estates by the estimators of the *Patrimonio* provide some indication, but they are only indications, albeit ones which may serve as the parameters of a spread between the conscious under-valuation of the *Polizze* and the conscious over-valuation of the *Patrimonio*. Calculations of this sort are, of course, always very difficult and, as has frequently been pointed out already, particularly misleading in this economy in which it was rarely the case that income from cultivation was the sole income of a household – but they do have some value in indicating the base income of some households. In 1745 Giovanni Battista Campeti declared the value of his two posses-sions in Gargagnago and S. Ambrogio, both of 60 *campi* of arable and pasture land, with vines and a few young olives, farmed by Nicolo Richel and by Vicenzo Richel and his brothers, as being 230 ducats *parte dominicale*.[25] Of course, Campeti was attempting to underestimate the value of his land, and would have deducted any expenses he could think of, legitimately or otherwise, before arriving at this figure, but a conservative estimate would suggest that the gross income of the *lavorenti* from their holdings would be in the region of 300 ducats. Barbara Lombari, the widow of Count Romolo Giona, in her *polizza* of 14 June 1740, values a possession in Castelrotto:

> spiantata di vigne et altre alberi dalle frequenti sutte et altre disgrazie che accadono senza la soventione di palli et stroppe che con molta spesa convengono comprare annualmente essendo morte in avantaggio nell'inverno passato molte quantita di vigne si puo ricavar l'entrata soggieta a mantenimento di Fabriche et infortunie disgrazie

at 350 ducats, *parte dominicale*.[26] Unfortunately, she does not say how many *lavorencie* the possession was divided into, but if it were divided into two that would again produce a gross figure of at least three hundred ducats.

Perhaps surprisingly, the *Polizze* for the earlier *Estimi*, produce a very similar figure. Those 1653 *polizze* which permit such a calcula-tion suggest that the landlord's return from single holdings of the size being discussed was between 125 ducats and 250 ducats, depending on location and size of holding, in turn hinting at a gross income for the *lavorente* of 200 to 300 ducats.[27] The *Estimi* of 1682 and 1696 offer less by way of information and also some useful confirmation. Both *Estimi* are full of complaints from landlords about the deteriora-tion of their land and their income since 1653. In 1692 Angelo Sigismondi Paletta complained that all his land in Negrar and Torbe had deteriorated seriously even since his last *polizza* in 1679:

per le tempeste et innondacioni dell'acque che ogn'anno nella Valpolicella
sono venute ch'hanno ruinate vigne e fruttari e particularmente le innondacioni dell'acque che per essere tutti li miei beni in collina e in monte le
hanno condotta via la terra e lasciati in mal stato siche e impossibile il
riddurli fertili come prima erano

so that on one of them he had been forced to reduce his share of the
production of the land from the *lavorencia* to one-third.[28] Other
landlords such as Ottaviano and Giuseppe Roveretti made similar
complaints of erosion and other deterioration, in addition to the loss
of vines, olives and other crops.[29] The late seventeenth century too
saw an expansion of the renting of land for fixed annual payments,
rather than for a share of the production, although even here the
apparent problems of agriculture, or at least of landlords, in the 1680s
and 1690s, could lead to a return to sharecropping, as was the case
on the Negrar lands of Gasparo Giusti.[30] Such information as these
polizze contain indicates a similar range of incomes, from 100 ducats
(on the Barzisa estates in 1696[31]) to 250 ducats (on the Manfredi
estates in Bure also in 1696[32]). Given that, if the landlords are to be
believed, most of the costs of dealing with erosion fell on them rather
than on their tenants, the implication of these figures is that the
income of the *lavorente* or other types of tenant from such a holding
remained at roughly the 1653 levels. This is borne out, to some extent,
by the cash rents which were paid for land in the late seventeenth
century. For instance, Benedetto della Torre rented 81 *campi* of land,
including 11 *campi* of woods, in S. Vito to Pietro Poli for an annual
rental of 250 ducats[33] and Carlo Barzisa rented 70 *campi* of land in
Arbizzano to Francesco dal Ferro for 160 ducats.[34] Since there is no
evidence of critical land shortage or land hunger, and indeed rather
more evidence of problems for landlords in recruiting tenants,[35] it
seems unlikely that these rents represented rack-rents or that they left
the tenants in financial difficulties. A rough estimate then of the
income value of an average sized *lavorencia*, throughout this period,
suggests that the *lavorente* of such a holding would expect a gross
income – in cash and in kind – from his holding, of about 300 ducats
per annum. Using the conventional Veronese method of converting
income into capital worth, this would make the average seventeenth
and eighteenth century *lavorente* worth 5000 ducats, a figure which
corresponds quite closely with the assessment of the total capital of
the families of ordinands in the *Patrimonio*.[36]

It is clear then that the largest and, in some ways, most typical of
the tenurial units – of the units of exploitation – were good-sized
units, and their renters and cultivators were not deprived and
oppressed peasants on the pattern of the French *metayer* or the
Tuscan *mezzadro*, but, in some ways, nearer in scale and in wealth to
the tenant farmers of eighteenth century England.

Again, the caveat must be entered that, for virtually every tenant, as well as for virtually every landlord, the agricultural production of the land was only one element in their total income. As will be indicated in Chapter 7, large as well as small operators in the agrarian system supplemented – although the implications of that word are perhaps wrong – their income from cultivation with other forms of income, in particular industrial and extractive operations or service employment, both in agriculture and outside. Such employments could be very valuable indeed: Carlo Orlandi of Pescantina, who provided the *patrimonio* of Bartolomeo Moraia in 1675, possessed, in addition to the land worth 1500 ducats put up as *patrimonio*, other land worth at least the same and:

il trafico della fornasa che le dara . . . cento ducati di utili ogni volta che cuoce e cuoce dieci in dodici volte all'anno.[37]

Paron Giacopin Giacopini, also of Pescantina, would have been able to live comfortably on his income as a '*paron di barche*' but had in addition a considerable land holding.[38] The figures for income above must, then, be treated as the bases upon which other income was added, rather than a final overall figure. The same holds true for smaller holders and smaller tenants: land represented only a proportion of their total income, greater or lesser depending on circumstances and also upon the time of the year.

III

Neither feudal nor customary tenures played any major role in the structure of the Valpolicella agricultural system. Full-blown feudalism, even if it had ever existed in the Veronese,[39] had (as elsewhere in Italy) long ceased to have any real role in the organization of agriculture or society by the seventeenth century.[40] All that remained of feudalism were the *regalie*, the traditional payments to the overlord, which were still collected on many estates: most were nominal, and all were fixed. Gieronimo Beghin, the tenant of an estate in Negrar belonging to the Olivieri family paid the landlords 2 botte of grapes, 8 pesi of pork, 2 pairs of capons, 2 pairs of hens and 50 eggs a year.[41] The tenant of the Pellegrini lands in Prun and Torbe made an annual payment of:

un animal di pesi 5, botter di pesi 4, formaggio di pecora pesi 2, porcine pesi 4, minalli 4 castagne, minalli 4 noci.[42]

The other remnants were the *Giurisdictioni* or *Iures*: the right, originally of feudal origin, to control water supplies, to license shops

or inns – or the right to monopolize those services. Bartolomeo
Sartorari reported in 1696 that 'posedo in Mazan tre fontane con la sua
investitura'.[43] Giovanni Barbieri and his nephew Giovanni Battista
possessed: 'una casa con ius facolta e liberta di far osteria, magacin et
bettola in Ceraino'.[44]

Such feudal dues and rights were relatively uncommon in the
Valpolicella, certainly much less common than in some areas of the
Basso Veronese where, in communes such as Erbe or Villa Bartolomea,
virtually all land was held subject to the payment of feudal *regalie*.[45]
The extension of the power of the commune of Verona in the Middle
Ages and the establishment of the Vicarate had as a parallel the disappearance of the jurisdiction of the seigneurs; with the very minor
exception of the private jurisdiction of the Bishop of Verona at Pol,
all judicial functions, and virtually all licensing functions in the
Valpolicella were in public rather than private hands.[46] The power of
the landlord in the Valpolicella was economic and social rather than
judicial and administrative.

If the tenure of land was not feudal, neither was land held on
customary tenures. Even where the same tenant or family rented a
particular piece of land from the same landlord over a long period,
that tenure was renewed periodically by formal, written agreements,
rather than being continued on a customary basis. The terms of such
tenures changed from contract to contract, and hence the element of
feudal dues as the variable factor in a basically fixed or slow moving
system of rents and tenures which played such a major role in the
development of fiscal feudalism in France, for instance, had little place
in the Valpolicella system. This was in essence an economic system
well into the stage of contract rather than custom, and one in which,
above all, written contracts were not merely the norm but virtually
universal. Most of those contracts have not survived, either in their
original form or in registered notarial copies, and where they have,
the very fact of their survival makes them, in a sense, unrepresen-
tative. It is clear that the contracts or copies of them were an important part of the documentation, not merely of the larger estates but
also of families and individuals. Each household kept, to some extent
at least its own small family business archive; virtually all of these have
now regrettably disappeared and it is only a few noble and bourgeois
families which have retained even parts of these archives.[47]

If contracts were not fixed by custom neither were they
stereotyped; inevitably of course, since they dealt with similar issues,
their basic outlines tended to be pretty constant, but within that basic
similarity they seem to have exhibited considerable flexibility in
meeting the complexities of the agricultural and economic situation.

As with so much in the Valpolicella economy, what is striking is, in
a sense, the modernity of the situation – especially when compared
with the usual idea of the inflexibility of pre-modern systems and in

particular with the received idea of the growing conservatism of a decadent seventeenth and eighteenth century Italy in contrast to the thrusting and changing North. In striking contrast to much of France, for instance, the Valpolicella was able, through its tenurial system, to respond to changing economic situations without too great a stress on its legal or traditional agricultural system.

No 'noble reaction' or 'revival of feudalism' such as may have occurred in eighteenth century France was possible or indeed necessary in the Veronese, since the legal as well as the economic and social situation allowed a very different type of response. If the tenant was exposed to the full force of market conditions, without the cushioning protection of feudal custom, equally the landlord had no more than his economic power over his tenants; he could not use other methods and other functions to coerce them and, as will be explained later, until the late eighteenth century, the balance of power frequently seems to have lain with the tenant, in particular the larger tenant, rather than with the landlord.

Not all land, of course, nor even all the land on the great estates of the nobility, was rented out. A considerable portion of the land was cultivated directly by the landlord or their salaried employees. The fluidity of the legal situation allowed landlords to make the shift from renting to direct exploitation and back again on the basis of essentially economic criteria. There was little fear on the part of the landlord that to rent land out would involve some permanent commitment to its continuing as rented land, or that to do so would fix its rent for all time. The management of estates, too, could be varied almost at will, since there was no effective 'freehold' for estate officials or estate bureaucracies. Above all then, this was a system in which flexibility and the ability to respond to economic circumstances was high, certainly as high as in the more 'progressive' agricultural societies of England or the Netherlands.

Two major patterns of rental of land dominated the Valpolicella: fixed cash rental (*affitto*) and sharecropping, (*lavorencia*). During the seventeenth and eighteenth centuries, even during the period from the 1680s to the 1720s and 1730s when *affitto* became much more common than previously and many *lavorencia* estates were handed over to cash-paying tenants, the great majority of rented estates were rented on a sharecropping basis. Sharecropping has, of course, got a bad name; whether in the American South and West or in Languedoc or Tuscany, the sharecropper has become a byword for oppression and exploitation, while the nineteenth century collapse of the northern Italian economy turned the northern *lavorente* into another Tuscan *mezzadro*. However, for the seventeenth and eighteenth centuries in the Valpolicella it is necessary to abandon this picture of a smallholder, completely without capital of his own and continually sinking deeper and deeper into debt. It is clear that the large-scale

Valpolicella *lavorente* was, to some extent at least, a capitalist farmer, farming land on the basis of a written and closely negotiated contract which was reviewed on each side from time to time, and not automatically renewed by either landlord or tenant.

The principles of the *lavorencia* system are relatively straightforward and also well suited to the type of farming and the types of risk involved. Uncertainty ruled, for the large producer as well as for the small, and for the landlord as much as for the tenant. The *lavorencia* system spreads the risks of agriculture between the tenant and the landlord, each side of the bargain drawing from the land a share of the production of the land in any particular year, and hence being insulated to some extent from the problems which crop failure or glut involve for both sides. The disasters of climate or, more rarely in the Valpolicella, of destruction by military action, were spread – although it is significant that in most Valpolicella contracts from the seventeenth and eighteenth centuries the landlord takes, what is, in effect, a disproportionate share of the risk by allowing his tenant the same abatements of his share of production to compensate for the destruction of crops as were allowed by landlords to tenants holding their land under fixed *affitti*. The *lavorente* contributed not merely the labour and the expertise to work the land, but also part of the capital in the form of the draught animals and equipment.

The most typical form of *lavorencia* contract was an agreement, normally not registered as a notarial instrument but rather as a private document, between a landlord who was usually, although not inevitably, a resident of Verona and a tenant who, as will be demonstrated later, was not necessarily a native of the village or even the region in which the lands he farmed were to be found. Unlike the Tuscan *mezzadria* contracts studied by McArdle,[48] Valpolicella *lavorencia* contracts were usually for a period of three or five years. This in itself is significant; a longer period of tenure gave the *lavorente* a much greater ability to deal with single bad years, or indeed with a run of bad years, a problem which the annual contracts of Tuscany exacerbated. Perhaps as a consequence, there is much less evidence in the seventeenth and eighteenth centuries of the difficulties which arose for both tenants and landlords at the point of the ending of an old tenure and the beginning of a new one.

The details of each contract were, as has already been suggested, varied to fit the particular context of the land involved in the contract and the particular economic circumstances. The outlines were roughly the same in most contracts: the final production of the land was divided between the landlord and the tenant, sometimes on a half-and-half basis, sometimes on the basis of the landlord taking only one-third. The total production of some crops remained with the tenant: these were usually lower grade crops or fodder crops. The landlord also retained the whole production of certain crops, most notably mulberry leaves, which were frequently rented separately from the land, most often on an annual basis. The tenant agreed to provide the draught animals for the land, although in many cases the landlord found himself bound to assist his tenant should the tenant's draught animals die or be stolen during his tenure of the land. The tenant also agreed to raise pigs for the landlord and, with increasing frequency, to raise silkworms for him under the *soceda* system. *Soceda* can perhaps be described as the livestock equivalent of *lavorencia*: the landlord provided the pig or the silk-worm eggs (*semenza*), the tenant undertook the often unpleasant task of raising the pigs or the worms and received a share of the final proceeds, either in cash or in kind. *Soceda* was also the usual way in which the fattening and grazing of sheep and cattle was organized. The raising of the landlord's pigs and of his silkworms, both of which were activities any prudent farmer or indeed any prudent organization[49] would undertake, need not necessarily be any real hardship and the *soceda* system meant that the *lavorente* had at least the advantage of a start with someone else's capital.

Capital was, of course, what the nineteenth century sharecropper lacked: he was dependent upon the landlord both for seed, which frequently formed a major part of his debts to the landlord, and for the basic working capital of the land, his plough teams. Indeed, much of the evidence from the nineteenth century suggests that the *lavorente* had no plough team and that sharecropping land was basically cultivated by hand; plough teams were in essence a feature of the great home farms, cultivated by direct, wage-labour, rather than sharecropping. The seventeenth and eighteenth century sharecropper was a very different proposition in this respect. The *lavorente* of any estate was expected, indeed required, to provide his own plough team if he was to gain the tenancy; many had two or more.

In many cases *lavorenti* had other animals too: not merely the sheep and goats which were part of the normal equipment of any farm, but also mules, asses and even horses. The pasturage for these animals was a major concern: in most contracts the landlord was required to provide pasture land for the *lavorente*'s animals, either from the estate itself or, if necessary, by renting it from other landlords – or even, *in extremis*, buying hay for the *lavorente*.

The only remains of feudalism in these contracts is, occasionally the duty of the *lavorente* to cart the landlord's goods free of charge. This applied not merely to the produce of his own *lavorencia*, which it was understood would be delivered to the landlord's store house (either on his rural estates or, more usually in Verona), but also, the produce of the landlord's own estates. This duty was one which did not appear in every contract by any means; the number, and frequently the nature, of the loads to be carried was clearly defined in the contract and additional loads were paid for at the market rate. By tradition, and it seems to have been a tradition widely observed, the landlord was responsible for feeding the *lavorente* or his men both on their journey to Verona and in Verona: the costs of this food supply could be large.[50] The real problem, of course, was likely to be that the landlord would require his cart-loads at times of pressure in the agricultural year, when the *lavorente* too would be in need of all the draught power he could get hold of.

Much the most contentious part of *lavorencia* contracts, and certainly the one about which most of the recorded litigation seems to have centred, was the question of the maintenance of the property, the restoration of damage to fields, buildings and crops caused by storms or other reasons, and the planting of new trees or vines to replace ones at the end of their productive lives. Pretty obviously this was a matter of very considerable concern to the landlord, but rather less to the tenant. As a result the contract set out, often in some detail, the duties of the tenant with regard to maintenance and the planting of new vines and trees. Even this level of specification was not enough to avoid disputes and a frequent complaint about tenants at the end of their tenure was that they had, particularly in the last years of their tenure, neglected these duties.[51] The contract (*scrittura*) of *lavorencia* between the fathers of the monastery of S. Fermo Maggiore and the *lavorente* of their land in S. Pietro on March 1685 dictates:

> come devono eser partite   l'Entrate
> L'uva et tutti li grani includendosi anco le fave va partito per mitta
> Li altri legumi et milio delli 5, 2 al Patron
> La legna grossa et le fassine di muraro per metta et le sarmente di vigna tutte del lavorente
> L'uva tutta per mitta et la seda ma se li deve dare meza la semenza
> Oblighi
> Piantar una bina di vigne a l'anno a loro spese
> Condur tutta l'entrata nell'Arra, Granaro et Caneva del Monastero
> Far carezzi 18 all'anno
> Regalie
> alla Pasqua ovi 250
> al Natale Caponi para 5
> A Tutti li Santi Polastri para 5[52]

The other major element of concern to the landlord was, of course, the good cultivation of the land. Unlike some *lavorencia* contracts from the Basso Veronese,[53] the surviving Valpolicella contracts do not specify in detail just what 'good cultivation' means: perhaps they should have, since a great deal of litigation seems to have followed from the allegations of landlords that their tenants had failed to cultivate the lands to the best of their ability – or more strictly to the best of the capacity of the land. The causes of these disputes were disagreements over times or methods of ploughing, over times of sowing and of the crops to be sown, over harvesting times, the maintenance of terraces and drains and the use or otherwise of irrigation.[54] One of the duties of the *gastaldo* or *fattor* of any estate was to oversee the operations of the *lavorenti* and to ensure that they did not delapidate or neglect the landlord's interest in the cultivation of the land.

The *lavorente* also expected to be housed; a *lavorencia* without a house was virtually unlettable and where there was no house, the landlord was, on occasions, forced to rent one for his tenant or, in some cases, to allow the *lavorente* to live in a house more suitable for the landlord – with all the loss that that might involve in terms of rent for the landlord.[55] Very few inventories or descriptions of the *case rusticali* which were regarded as appropriate for *lavorenti* seem to have survived, although a number of drawings of them appear on contemporary maps and plans.[56] Such material as exists suggests that the house and farmyard of a seventeenth and eighteenth century *lavorencia*, although they did not normally reach the standards of the houses of the landlords, were nonetheless amongst the more substantial houses in the village, sometimes on a par with the houses of the wealthier local landowners.

It is increasingly clear that the Valpolicella *lavorente* was far from being a down-trodden peasant, certainly in the seventeenth and eighteenth century. It seems pretty clear that his economic and social standing was relatively strong; it is also reasonably clear from the nature of the contracts which have survived that he was in a relatively strong economic position *vis à vis* the landlord. Certainly, to get tenants, landlords had to make concessions – over the proportion of production which the landlord took, over the supply of pasturage, over the demands for cartage to name but a few. In no sense does the landlord seem to have been in a position, as it is quite clear they were in the middle and late nineteenth century, to dictate terms to their *lavorenti*.

In many cases, *lavorenti* worked land for a number of masters, including themselves, and in many cases not merely for outsiders but also for other well-to-do village families. The social and regional origins of the *lavorenti* are complex. A large proportion of them seem to have been of local origin, although not necessarily from the same commune as the land they held; many of them came from relatively well-to-do families, although it must be said that since many *lavorenti* invested in local land and local marriages, this is something of a circular process. *Lavorenti*, however, did move considerable distances from their home bases in search of tenure and landlords were willing to attract *lavorenti* over quite large distances: a number of the *lavorenti* on the dal Bene estates in Volargne came from Soave to the east of Verona where, it is true, the dal Bene had other estates. A large number of *lavorenti* seem to have migrated from the higher communes of the Valpolicella to farm estates on the lower levels.

Lavorencia tenure was not hereditary, but contractual: when a *lavorente* died in harness, in mid-contract, his heirs (or widow) were expected, even if they were minors, to carry out the remainder of the contract. The heirs might then be offered next tenure of the lands, but there was no expectation that they should be, and the decision to rent land to individuals remained an entirely business one. That having been said, in many cases *lavorenti* retained the tenure of lands for very lengthy periods, and their heirs succeeded them in the lands. There are a number of instances of dynasties of *lavorenti* which ran for many years. Unfortunately, the *polizze* for 1653 identify very few *lavorenti* by name but in 1682, part of the lands of Tomasini in Arbizzano and S. Vito were being worked by Zuanne Righetto[57] while in 1745 the lands, transferred in 1722 to Antonio Maria Perez, were being worked by his descendant, Gian Maria,[58] and other relatives were working the land of Counts Innocenzio and Giuseppe Tomasini Soardi.[59] In many cases the continuity of tenure was not in fact interrupted by the shift to cash rents in the later seventeenth century, since some at least of the renters of land were the old *lavorenti*.

While the picture of the Valpolicella *lavorente* as a north Italian equivalent of the eighteenth century English tenant farmer may be a little exaggerated, it does have more than a grain of truth in it. It is very clear, not merely from the calculations of the worth of holdings made earlier but also from their purchases of land, particularly in the eighteenth century, that the *lavorenti* were anything but a downtrodden class of impoverished peasants as they were to become in the nineteenth century. They were, in fact rather a well-to-do and prosperous section of society and the economic structure, in many cases pushing themselves and their families up the scale into quite considerable landownership.

Equally, it is clear from the surviving *lavorencia* contracts that the economic power in the relationship with their landlords did not lie exclusively on one side. The desperate land-hunger which characterized the nineteenth century and which was to drive tenants to take land on almost any terms did not exist even in the late eighteenth century; landlords had also to struggle to obtain good tenants for their land and, since the capitalization of agriculture was much higher in the eighteenth century than in the nineteenth, the cost to the landlord of having to take on the cultivation of land himself, and to provide the draught cattle and to pay the labour force involved, made failure to get a tenant a major economic problem. Consequently, *lavorenti* seem to have been able to drive reasonably hard bargains over the terms of their contracts: on poor land, the landlord, for instance, had to accept a smaller proportion of the production than a half[60] or, and this was relatively common, to accept a large share of the costs of storm and weather damage. Equally, and this was a major complaint in those areas of the Valpolicella where soil erosion and flash-flooding were (or were reputed to be) serious, the landlord had, in the landlords' own estimation at least, to bear a large and at times crushing burden of costs for the clearing of land, and the construction of terraces and flood protection works – work which in the very different conditions of the nineteenth century would have fallen much more heavily on the *lavorente* than on the landlord.

Lavorencia had, of course, its problems and inconvenience for both sides; the landlord was as subject as the tenant to a fluctuating income, while the tenant only gained a share of any improvement he may have made to the land or its productivity. The landlord was also expected to act, in effect, as a banker to the *lavorente*, a function which, in the nineteenth century (and in the eighteenth century in Tuscany and elsewhere), was to be one of the mechanisms by which the landlord tied his sharecroppers more and more tightly to him in what could almost become a form of debt peonage. In the seventeenth and eighteenth centuries in the Valpolicella, although there were, inevitably, some feckless *lavorenti* who ran up debts they could not pay and were either evicted or sold up for debt, in most cases, and there are large numbers of them recorded in the surviving estate account books, the transactions between landlord and tenant were relatively small, and the final balances usually relatively minor and paid off without too much difficulty: the *lavorente* could afford to move on should a better chance offer itself, while on the other hand the landlord could afford to change his tenants without having to write off large sums owed to him as accumulated debt.

In a sense though, both the central problem and the central strength of *lavorencia* was the sharing of the risks of agriculture between landlord and tenant. What *lavorencia* certainly did not allow to the landlord was a constant and certain income; good and bad harvests, storms and wars, prices and the condition of trade all affected the scale of his income. Of course, *lavorencia*, with its virtual guarantee of an income in kind if needed, had its advantages in an economic situation in which food supplies were uncertain; better to have a supply of grain and wine coming in, even if it were an uncertain and unpredictable one, than to be left completely without and hence forced on to the market at times of dearth. *Lavorencia* was, then, admirably fitted to the sort of economy which has been described earlier, and to the sorts of economic and social strategies which, it has been argued, formed the centre of the rationality of this economy.

A considerable literature has developed around the nature and effects of sharecropping in Italy. In particular sharecropping on the pattern of the Tuscan *mezzadro* or the sharecroppers of southern Italy has been seen as a form of feudal survival or again as a re-feudalization – in many ways paralleling the seventeenth and eighteenth century re-feudalization of Central and Eastern Europe or the effective reinforcement of feudal economic ties in Russia after the Emancipation of the

Serfs. Furthermore, sharecropping has been seen as one of the major factors which held back the agricultural sector, particularly in the Centre and the Mezzogiorno in the nineteenth and early twentieth centuries, and which as a consequence played a major role in the slowness and uncertainty of Italy's economic development. The literature and the debate in a sense centres around Central and Southern Italy and, in direct terms, has apparently very little to do with the North which tends to be praised as progressive (or at least relatively so), and as providing the engine for growth which was being held back by the slowness of the rest of the Peninsula. The history of *lavorencia* in the Valpolicella does, however, provide a number of significant comments upon the whole debate. First, the dichotomy between a sharecropping Centre and South and a 'farmed' (for want of a better word), North, is certainly for the seventeenth and eighteenth centuries a completely false one: much of the land of the North was farmed using tenures which in law and economics are sharecropping tenures. Admittedly in the nineteenth century, for reasons discussed here, sharecropping became less significant in the North, but this was not as a consequence of economic advance but exactly the opposite – the result of economic decline and grinding poverty. Second, it is clear that sharecropping as such was not, in itself, a system of unequal economic exploitation, of the dominance of a desperately poor sharecropper by a rich, powerful and avaricious landlord. That it could and indeed did become so is beyond doubt, but that process is a consequence of economic, social and political factors, not because of the nature of sharecropping. The *lavorencia* system of the seventeenth and eighteenth century Veneto demonstrates a totally different pattern: to deny that it is sharecropping because it does not correspond to received ideas of what sharecropping should be, seems at best an evasion. Finally, the north Italian experience surely indicates very clearly that the institution of sharecropping in itself is not a cause or only a subordinate cause of economic decline or failure to grow. Given the right context, sharecropping can be progressive. It was, as in the post-Bellum South, Latin America or the *Mezzogiorno*, economic decline which caused the degradation of sharecropping, rather than sharecropping which caused economic decline.[61]

The late seventeenth and early eighteenth century saw a swing to another form of land exploitation. Again, it is not a question of the appearance of a new system nor the replacement of one system by another, but rather a swing of balance between two systems which already existed. Alongside *lavorencia* since the Middle Ages had existed the system of *affitanza*, basically the renting of land for a fixed period of years at a fixed annual cash rent.[62] The advantages of *affittanza* to landlords is in one sense clear; in good theory, by renting out their land to an *affituale* rather than to a *lavorente* they gained a clear and fixed cash income for a given number of years. So long as what was important was a fixed income, and so long as the movement of prices and agricultural production was not such as to threaten the value of the fixed rental or to make their payments uncertain, the *affittanza* had the advantage of transferring much of the risk of the system to the renter. In fact, the contracts which have survived move *affittanza* away from the purity of the ideal; as in *lavorencia*, the landlord had to agree to bear some part of the risk of storm and other damage and to contribute the major part of the costs of improvements.

From the 1670s and 1680s onwards the *polizze* and other sources suggest a major shift towards renting, a movement which can be seen on both ecclesiastical[63] and lay estates. Large numbers of estates which had previously been let on *lavorencia* terms were shifted over to fixed cash rentals. To some extent this seems to have been in the hope of gaining better, and certainly more secure, returns. One element, too, seems to have been the willingness of some renters to take on much larger single holdings than a *lavorente* would have been able to work: in the early 1680s, for instance, Angelo Sigismondi Paletta was able to rent the whole of his Valpolicella land to a single tenant, Francesco Magiol, rather than to five or six separate *lavorenti*[64] and obviously this relative simplicity of organization had many management advantages. Even where there was not this advantage, land was increasingly rented rather than sharecropped.

Evidence as to the identity and origins of the new renters is extremely limited, but what is striking is that many of them, like Magiol, came not from traditional land-working families but from commercial and service families in the city: Magiol, for instance, was: 'a quel tempo hoste all'insegna della Stella in Verona'[65] and many of the other, identifiable renters were of similar origins. Some, it is true, were the former *lavorenti* shifting over to the new system, but it must remain likely that the new renters in many cases retained the old *lavorenti*, or employed new *lavorenti* to work the land for them; it seems unlikely that many of the new renters worked the land themselves or employed direct labour forces to do so.

This growing involvement of the commercial classes of the city in agriculture, which is to some extent mirrored also by a growth of purchases of land either in the form of whole estates or of small pieces of land,[66] raises a number of questions about the Veronese economy in the seventeenth century – in particular since such a movement by the 'bourgeois' out of commerce into land[67] can be seen as being in some ways parallel to the shift in capital by the Venetian nobility at the end of the sixteenth century.[68] It seems to be clear that, by the 1670s and the 1680s there was a supply of capital in the city which was available for investment in land and which, furthermore, saw investment in the working of land, or at least in the receipt of kind income from land, as being economically worthwhile. What is also clear is that this phenomenon was occurring at a time when the nobility saw constant income and a removal from the direct risks of cultivation and agriculture as being in their interests. The first implication of all this must be that, as far as some groups in the city at least were concerned, the mid-seventeenth century, far from being the period of deep decline which some of the sources suggest, was a period of some prosperity, and one in which liquid capital was relatively easily obtained – since the fixed cash rents were to be paid in coin at fixed dates each year. The second implication is that, in the 1670s and 1680s, and possibly until the late 1730s (although by that date the large-scale return to *lavorencia* was fully under way) investment in agriculture seemed more profitable, or at least more secure, than other forms of investment. This again gives a rather different view of the difficulties of Veronese agriculture in the late seventeenth century to that which the *polizze* suggest.

To what extent these rentings and the rentals paid were speculative is not at all clear. Unfortunately records such as those of S. Fermo Maggiore do not permit any very clear judgement as to whether the landlord gained any very considerable direct cash advantage over the rental they had been accustomed to receive from the *lavorenti*. What is clear, however, from the *polizze* and elsewhere is that, if both sides had hoped to find in the expansion of *affittanza* some more profitable form of organization, those hopes were soon dashed and many of the new renters were driven into serious financial difficulties by the new rents. The landlords, in their turn, found their income from their estates falling and, after a few attempts to resolve the problem by reducing the rentals, most landlords by the mid-1740s at the latest had returned to *lavorencia*. The history of the S. Fermo estates which were rented out in the early 1700s shows a clear fall in the return to the landlords. The estates at S. Pietro in Cariano were first rented in 1710 to Steffano Proci of Fumane and Gironimo Benassuti of S. Pietro for three years at an annual rent of 500 ducats, payable in three instalments each year.[69] Subsequent payments were made, but were frequently late and when the agreement was renewed in 1714, the rent was reduced to 450 ducats per annum.[70] Even at this reduced rate, the pattern of payments was extremely erratic, and in 1716, Proci was replaced by Giovanni Battista Guardini (or Zardin) of Maran and his brothers; the final payment of the rent for 1716 was not made until August 1717.[71] By November 1719 Guardini and Benassuti had had enough and were replaced by two more distant figures, Giovanni Giacomo Ludrini and his brothers and Giovanni Saleti of S. Michele in Campagna; payments still continued to be erratic.[72] When, in November 1722, Ludrini abandoned his tenure, the new contract, with Francesco Mascanzon, for the first time and possibly ominously, also names his *piezi*, securities for the payments due to the monastery.[73] Mascanzon was no more regular or certain in his payments than any of the earlier *affituali* had been and, in November 1726, the managers of the monastery's land returned to *lavorencia*.[74] In 1729 they made another attempt to rent the land, on this occasion to Antonio Zillotto for 450 scudi, equivalent to about 435 ducats.[75] When Zillotto's contract was renewed in November 1732 for three years, the annual rent had fallen to 410 scudi, roughly equivalent to 395 ducats.[76] Finally, in November 1735, the estates were returned to *lavorencia*, which remained their tenure until after 1797.[77] The S. Fermo estates were perhaps unusual in the persistence of their managers' attempts to rent them, but the story of falling income and more and more uncertain returns from the land was repeated frequently.

Why did the renting of land fail in this way? Two explanations were offered by landlords in the seventeenth and eighteenth centuries, although it is of course important to bear in mind that they were seeking to establish that their land had seriously deteriorated and that, therefore, their tax assessments should be reduced. The most popular explanation was that the period of renting coincided with particularly bad climatic conditions, in particular that the late seventeenth and early eighteenth centuries saw cold winters, summer droughts and heavy rains which led to erosion and soil damage. Angelo Sigismondi Paletta complained that his Valpolicella estates were:

> molto deteriorato . . . per le tempeste et innondacioni dell'acque che ogn'anno nella Valpolicella venute ch'hanno ruinate vigne et fruttari e particolarmente le innondacioni dell'acque che per essere tutti li miei beni in collina et in monte le hanno condotta via la terra e lasciati in mal stato siche e impossibile il vi riddurli fertili come prima erano.[78]

Many other landlords repeated the same complaints: that the land was deteriorating naturally and that returns on *affitanza* land was falling as was the return on all land. This may well be true, but the production figures discussed in Chapter 3 suggest that this deterioration may well have been much less than the landlords wished the tax office to believe; it is worth pointing out that similar complaints had been made in the 1653 *polizze*[79] and probably earlier.

Interestingly, the other explanation was the inexperience and, possibly, criminality of the *affituali*. Sigismondi Paletta, for instance, was forced to take action against his tenant Francesco Magiol:

> persona inesperta della rendita delli beni . . . che pero l'affitanza stesa li fu di danno tale che lo fece fallire ne continuo la locatione medema che solo circa anni 2½ tutto che fosse fatto per anni 6 e l'affitto del terzo anno furono fatte per li piezi che si constituirono nella locatione medema come del tuto se ne puo vedere chiaramente del processo sopra di cio seguito.[80]

In 1696, Gasparo Giusti complained that he had been forced to abandon renting his Negrar lands and return them to *lavorencia* on account of the 'deterioramenti fatti dalli affituali'.[81]

It may well be, then, that the cause of the failure of renting lay as much in the greed of the landlords in attempting to wring as high a rent as possible out of the land, as in the inexperience and possibly downright ignorance of the city and commercial renters of land in the management of estates and in the assessment of a reasonable expectation of return from the land. Of course, climatic and other problems in the 1690s and 1700s would make such a problem much worse; one thing that *affitanza* was not good at was responding quickly and flexibly to rapidly changing conditions, which was one of the strengths of *lavorencia*. The failure of *affitanza* may be seen in some ways as a moral tale, revealing the dangers of letting urban investors take over farming, but it does raise important questions about the nature and the functioning of the urban economy in the later seventeenth and eighteenth centuries. The picture it seems to imply is, first of all, of an urban sector with some prosperity and some surplus capital; and secondly of an urban 'middling' group, willing and able to see and to seize a perceived opportunity for investment beyond the city walls and beyond their traditional employments. Altogether the picture which this offers of the Veronese economy at this time of crisis and decline is a thrusting and dynamic one, far removed from the stagnant backwater the north Italian cities are supposed to have become by that date.

IV

Not all land was rented out by its owners, local or noble. Much land, in particular the smaller holdings, was cultivated directly by its owners, on occasions in addition to the land they rented from others. These self-farmed holdings range from the micro-holdings which in many cases are effectively no more than gardens, to holdings as large as the best *lavorencia* holdings, on which the owner not merely used his own labour and that of his family but, in addition, bought in labour as and when it was necessary. If the owners of such land could be employers they could also be employees, and the smaller their own holdings were, the more likely they were to be employed on the land of others. Equally, and like the *lavorenti*, the small owners drew income from a number of other sources, and their holdings have to be seen rather in terms of a complex family pattern of employment and income rather than as simply landholdings. As such, a consideration of them, their organization and rationale belongs to a later chapter.

It is to the organization of the great estates and their home farms to which the discussion must now turn. As has already been indicated, by no means all of the land of the great estates was rented out to *lavorenti* or *affituali*. Some land was kept under the direct management and exploitation of the landlord and his or her agents, above all to provide a supply of food and income for the noble household itself. This land, the home farm as it were of the estate, provided the central core of the day-to-day supplies of the household and frequently lay around the country house of the landlord, so that, during the period of the *villegiatura*, the landlord and his family should have fresh food on hand. The other reason for keeping land in the direct exploitation of the landlord was that it was too poor or deteriorated, or in too small pieces, to be rented out economically – in itself an interesting comment on the land market and on Malthusian pressure.

Direct management and cultivation was always seen as less efficient and certainly as less profitable than renting the land; since for land cultivated *in casa* the landlord, although he drew all the production from the land rather than merely a share, had to provide the labour and the capital for the exploitation of the land and this was regarded as a major expense, certainly a greater expense than the *lavorente*'s share of the production. This suggests, although no more, that this was in effect a high wage, high labour cost economy and hence one which would have been ripe for mechanization had it not been for the efficiency of the *lavorencia* system. Even at the height of the problems with the *affituali* in the early eighteenth century there seems to have been little economic or social pressure towards demesne farming and direct cultivation, again in great contrast to what seems to have been the case in the nineteenth century.

The organization of the home farms was, in fact, a part of the larger system of management of the estates; the local manager being responsible for the operation of the home farms as well as for the oversight of the estate's other activities in a neighbourhood. The local estate manager was very much the local personification of the estate and the immediate representative of the landlord, and seems to have had a social status to match.

The internal organization of estates seems to have been as varied as the many different estates and, indeed, as various as the many differing landlords. Equally it has to be pointed out at this stage, although it will be discussed in more detail in Chapter 6, that the complexities of sale, inheritance and dowry meant that, in many cases the ownership of estates in any given locality might well be impossibly entangled, and that, as a consequence in some cases at least, one manager might well serve as the manager for a series of owners managing their intermingled lands together and dividing the proceeds amongst them. This produces the familiar problem that only very rarely do detailed estate records survive and that family papers, which in other regions might be expected to include detailed material on the operation of the estates, frequently contain no more than annual statements of accounts from the agents of the final balances due to the landlord. Unfortunately, although some landlords do seem to have

taken a more direct interest in the operation of their estates, the tradition of, or fashion for, the farmer-nobleman was largely absent from
the Veronese; in most cases the management of the estates was left in
the hands of the agents and only became of concern to the landlord
either when the income from land was not sufficient to maintain the
noble life-style or when the agents proved dishonest or incapable.

Virtually without exception, the landlords of the Valpolicella owned
estates scattered widely across the Veronese and their Valpolicella
estates represented only a small part of their total holdings. In general
landholdings in the plains of the Basso Veronese were larger and more
profitable, certainly in terms of grain production, than were the
Valpolicella estates. As a result, in most cases the Valpolicella estates
tended to be organized and managed as an offshoot of the other
estates rather than as separate entities. It must also be remembered
that, just as the *lavorencia* holding or the smaller self-cultivated
holding was far more than simply a producer of agricultural products,
but often an industrial producer as well, so too the estate manager was
responsible for the industrial as well as for the agricultural operations
of the estate. The *fattor* or *gastaldo* of the estate also acted as revenue
collector and superintendent of the landlord's rented land in his area
and also collected the rents of the landlord's houses, shops and
workshops.

The structure and nomenclature of this estate organization should
have been clear, but in fact could be extremely confusing.
Theoretically the central manager of the estates was the *fattor*, responsible directly to the landlord for the overall management of the
estates, and the channel through which orders and information came
from the landlord to the lower levels of management in the estate. The
fattor, theoretically at least, was usually responsible for the Verona
revenues of the estate and for the central sales of produce; in many
cases the *fattor* also had direct responsibility for the day-to-day
management of the most important estates or those closest to Verona.
The local official was the *gastaldo*, who was in effect the local
manager, and the farmer and operator of the lands farmed *in casa*.
The *gastaldo*, in theory, reported to the *fattor* and received his orders
from him. In fact, the reality was much more complex and much less
clear cut. In a number of estates the landlord acted in effect as his own
fattor – as was for instance the case on the dal Bene estates in the late
eighteenth century where Gerolamo dal Bene kept direct control.[82] In
other cases there was no formal *fattor* and one of the *gastaldi* acted
as effective general manager; in yet other cases, despite the existence
of a *fattor*, the *gastaldi* reported directly to the landlord.

Both *fattori* and *gastaldi* were salaried officials of the estate; like all
officials in the early modern Veronese they were paid in a mixture of
cash payments, food, housing and, almost certainly of considerable
importance to them but equally certainly unquantifiable, the

inducements, tips, gifts and straightforward bribes which oiled all wheels in this system. The cash payments seem relatively small – say 20 ducats per annum for a *gastaldo* in the seventeenth century[83] – although it is always worth remembering that in a partially subsistence economy the possession of even a limited income in ready cash can give the appearance, and the social status of considerable wealth. But to those cash payments must be added free housing, often in the landlord's own village house, virtually free food, often free clothing for the *gastaldo* and his family[84] and all the potential income from bribes and inducements. In many cases *fattori* and *gastaldi* went on to become landowners in their own right and to become important in commerce in Verona and elsewhere. Certainly many of the identifiable Valpolicella *gastaldi* came from important and well-to-do families within the region. It must again be stated that the Valpolicella estates were often marginal to the main economic structure of the great noble holdings and that the main holdings of many landlords lay elsewhere. The most ambitious of *gastaldi* had to leave the Valpolicella to gain preferment, and equally *gastaldi* from other estates and other regions were imported into the Valpolicella. There was also a tradition of dynasties of *gastaldi*, son following father or brother following brother in the management of the same estate.

Of the education of the *fattori* and *gastaldi* unfortunately little is known. Virtually all of them were literate and some of them show signs in their official papers of some kind of legal training. Their agricultural and management training was almost certainly practical rather than theoretical and may well have been gained while acting as *fameio* to an older man. One of the weaknesses of the system may well have been the lack of education of the estate managers and their unwillingness to take risks with their employer's property, a property upon which their own prosperity and income directly depended. It is, significantly, the case that many of the *gastaldi* were of local origin or married into local families and became, in many cases an important part of the local community, not separated from it as they were to be in the nineteenth century both by their economic status and by their being the representative of an increasingly oppressive and grasping estate system. This picture of the *gastaldo* integrated into the village community may appear idyllic, but as a member of local society it is not hard to believe that the *gastaldo* would become increasingly unwilling to introduce change into that village society.

The bottom rung of the estate ladder was occupied by the labourers, the *braccenti*. On most estates there was a distinction between those *braccenti* who were permanently employed and who lived in estate houses and those who were employed on a daily basis. The distinction was one which had its importance, in particular where the landlord moved *braccenti* from estate to estate,[85] but in fact the 'permanently' employed *braccenti* were only paid on days on which there was work for them, although they do seem by convention to have had first call on any work that was going.[86] The economics of a *braccente* household, as of the smaller 'peasant' holdings, did not revolve around a single employment or a single source of income, which would have been far too risky; they involved the balancing and mingling of a complex mixture of sources of income, and it is not really possible to look at the position of the *braccente* purely as a day labourer.

V

Very strikingly, the Valpolicella in the seventeenth and eighteenth centuries was an economy dominated by large rather than small holdings. It is, of course, true that, as will be clear from Chapter 6, the numerical majority of landholdings and certainly of parcels of landownership were smaller than the optimum size *lavorencia* holdings and home farms which have been discussed in this chapter and that, looked at purely in terms of their landholdings, the typical Valpolicella family was one of small-scale, even peasant cultivators. In fact, that picture is in some ways very misleading: few, if any of the 'peasants' relied on their landholdings and nothing else for their income; renting of land and wage labour were also important elements in that mix. It was the larger holdings, both the *lavorenti* and the estates, which provided much, although not all, of the additional employment available to them.

Whatever the nature of the smaller holdings, both estates and larger *lavorencia* were in essence commercial undertakings, producing for a market economy; the production of a *lavorencia* had to be sold, at least in part, to allow for the upkeep of the capital on which the *lavorente* depended. Indeed the success of many *lavorenti* in buying land and houses for themselves and their families, and in marrying into some of the better local families, all argue for large cash surpluses in their hands and for some considerable commercialization of the larger holdings. Increasingly the picture of the sharecropper as downtrodden and tied to subsistence has to be abandoned; arguably, and more than arguably, the Valpolicella sharecroppers were in one of the best positions in this society to be 'progressive' and to modify agricultural practice.

While to some extent this holds true and while there is some evidence of agricultural innovation amongst the sharecroppers, as indeed on the larger estates, it is necessary to return again to the principle of insurance and of risk-spreading. As has been pointed out earlier, risk, and the avoidance of the consequences of risk, was as important a part of the strategy of large landholders as it was of small; the same fears and the same problems held as good for the large-scale *lavorente* as they did for the smallest peasant. Hence, although some landlords did complain about the scattered nature of some of their holdings – for instance there seems to have been little attempt to construct the sort of consolidated holdings which were to be so popular in the nineteenth century, nor was there any real attempt to concentrate on the production of single crops for market – it was the result of a deliberate risk-reducing philosophy. This was no failure of initiative nor the result of blind conservatism, but the working out of a clear and rational economic and social strategy, a strategy which, in seventeenth and eighteenth century eyes, had much to commend it over the mad-cap activities of English and Dutch farmers.

The system, however, failed. By the middle and late nineteenth century the whole map of the agricultural system had changed. The great *lavorenti*, the rising rural class of the seventeenth and eighteenth century, had disappeared, in part reversing the route which the city *affituali* had followed in the late seventeenth century moving into the city and taking up professional and commercial employment. But, above all, it occurred because an agrarian revolution every bit as great as that which had occurred in eighteenth century Britain had wiped away the landscape of large tenures and relatively rich tenants and replaced it with large directly-farmed holdings, tiny peasant micro-holdings and sharecropping holdings more on the pattern of Tuscan *mezzadria* than Venetian *lavorencia*. The reasons for that dire revolution were many: the hyperinflation of the Napoleonic and post-Napoleonic years made anything other than direct cultivation a major mistake for the landlords; taxation and hyperinflation wiped out the capital of the *lavorente* families and cattle disease destroyed their plough teams, famine in 1815–7 reduced their financial independence and burdened them with debt from which, in the depressed agricultural economy of the nineteenth century, they had no hope of freeing themselves; and finally, the success of the old system and the population growth it encouraged in the late eighteenth century, which was continued into the nineteenth, increased pressure on land until human labour became cheap and draught animals expensive.

In the final analysis, although the Valpolicella system failed, it did so after providing the population of the area with at least two centuries of prosperity and reasonable stability. In a Europe in which many regions were suffering disastrous famines, to say nothing of the effects of war, the Valpolicella and indeed the Veronese as a whole, enjoyed a period of stability and relative prosperity. It must be emphasized that that stability was not the same as stagnation, nor was it the consequence of a purblind refusal to see the advantages of agricultural and economic advance as practised elsewhere. Rather it was a consequence of the pursuit of a clear and logical strategy which emphasized differing goals to those of modern economies and, indeed, apparently to those of other seventeenth and eighteenth century economies. Within the stability of the economic system, a great deal was changing, and those changes can be very clearly seen in the changing patterns of landownership.

6

The ownership of the land and its vicissitudes

I

In the Valpolicella, as in all economies and societies dominated by agriculture, the ownership and control of land lay at the very centre of most social and economic relationships. Land provided not merely the major source of income and the major source and store of wealth, but in addition its control and distribution also constituted one of the most potent, perhaps *the* most potent, forms of patronage available in the society – in particular for the control and influence of the great mass of the population. Equally, the ownership of land and the income from land, was one of the major indicators of economic, if not necessarily of social rank, in a society in which rank and hierarchy were of crucial importance. No study of the society or the economy of the Valpolicella in the early modern period can be complete without an examination of the system of land ownership, the patterns of that landownership, and the way in which they changed through time and from region to region, and that this chapter sets out to provide.

Land and landownership was central to the economic and social structure of the Valpolicella, but it must be made clear from the outset that this did not imply a static or even a stable pattern of landowner-ship. Equally, it did not imply, nor should it be taken to imply, that any 'mystical' connection existed between landowners –large or small – and individual pieces of land, nor indeed between individuals and the status of landowner. From at least the fifteenth century and almost certainly long before that, the Valpolicella, in common with the whole of the Veronese, had had a lively and extensive land market which saw large numbers of deals each year and deals involving large quan-tities of land. Noblemen, peasants and others all bought and sold land as the opportunity presented itself or as the need arose. At the lowest levels of landownership, and not only there, owners moved from the 'proprietor' to the 'tenant' category and back again, seemingly easily and without regrets. Legal devices such as the *fidei commesum* did, of course in theory and (in most cases) in practice, prevent the free transfer of land, but even amongst the noble and well-to-do families where it was chiefly practised, its effects were not such as to constitute a permanent tie to a total holding: *fidei commesum* usually only applied to part of a family's total holding and the evidence suggests they were frequently, if illegally, broken.

The fluidity of landholding and the speed with which land changed hands indicates, as few other things could, the fluidity and dynamism of this society and economy, particularly since it is clear that the movements of landholding were by no means simply and straightforwardly a transfer of land from 'peasant' to 'noble' hands nor yet from 'feudalist' to 'capitalist'. It follows, too, that as in so many things in the Valpolicella, the keynote of any discussion of landholding must be change rather than stability, of variety rather than simple structures, of extreme regional variations as much as of a single simple pattern.

II

Compared with the great complexity of land law and landholding systems elsewhere in pre-modern Europe, the Veronese system was simple. The early disappearance of feudalism, the long and continuous Roman Law tradition and the traditions of the communal state all tended to emphasize a free land market and a situation in which intermediary and overlord rights were first subordinated, and finally almost completely extinguished, by clearly defined individual and absolute rights in land. There is little sign of the multiple levels of rights, nor of the central if residual role of the state in tenure which is to be found in other European states, where the survivals of feudalism were of great significance.

The ownership and transfer of land was very largely regulated and controlled by contract rather than by custom. The transfer of land in particular was, throughout the period of this study, based upon written and registered contracts. The transfer of land between individuals, families and corporations was not, in general terms, restricted: land passed from noble to commoner, commoner to noble, individual to corporation and vice versa with little, if any, constraint other than price and the availability of land for sale. The contracts were virtually universally and at all levels of society, formally recorded in notarial documents, although it has to be said that in many cases the formal recording only took place at some distance after the actual transfer – in some cases private transfers of land were only formally registered twenty years after they had taken place and only then because of imminent litigation.

The restraints which existed on transfer and on the absolute individual ownership of property were few. Land transfers, more strictly land sales, were largely restricted by voluntarily imposed constraints. The most important by far of these was the *fidei commesum*, a form of entail. The Common Law of the Veronese permitted individuals to impose, usually in a will but also by a separate and special contract, a form of family trust on land, which in effect made the land inalienable, except by a complex process involving the consent of all potentially interested parties. *Fidei commesum* was undoubtedly a factor in fixing some elements of some estates both large and – since it was used by relatively poor families – small. However, its use was, as far as it is possible to say, less than the use of entail in eighteenth and nineteenth century Britain. Above all, the twin features of multiple inheritance and dowry meant that whole estates could not effectively be placed under the provisions of *fidei commesum*. Again, it must be emphasized that the transfer and alienation of land was not, and was not seen as being, a disaster to be avoided, but rather a perfectly normal and neutral part of the economic structure of landholding.

Intermediate and seigneurial rights, too, were few and insignificant. The few seigneurial rights surviving were rights to control aspects of the agricultural economy – such as the supply of water for irrigation – or of the commercial aspects of rural life – such as the right to license or run mills or inns. These feudal rights – *Iures* or *Giurisdictioni* – were, legally and in fact, separate from any particular land or indeed any land at all and, like rights to tithe, were alienable – and, theoretically at least, taxable.

Much more important, certainly in numerical and, probably financial terms than these feudal remains, were a series of traditional or contractual payments imposed on specific pieces of land, and transferred and alienated with them. In essence they were of two kinds: regalian rights and *livello*. Regalian rights, the remnants of feudal dues for a long time limited and formalized, affected by no means all land and were largely in the form of kind payments. The regalian rights attached to any piece of land did not necessarily imply any claim to ownership but were merely a recognition of former ownership or former seigneurial right. The new owner of land over which regalian rights applied was responsible for the continued payment of those rights: the rights themselves were alienable and transferrable separately from the land to which they applied. The rights could be extinguished, usually by their purchase from the holder by the owner of the land: apparently they could not be, or were not, created. In general, too, the regalian rights tended to be of small value – a couple of hens, some eggs for example – and of relatively small importance. Unlike the plains region of the Veronese, where large estates were a much more significant feature and where feudal tenures had been more widespread, little land in the Valpolicella was subject to regalian payments.

Much more significant than these payments are the monetary rights over the production of land which came from the institution of *livello*. The usual dictionary translation of *livello* is 'lease' but, in the Valpolicella at least, this translation is misleading. *Livello* was not, in any sense a 'lease' payment paid to an owner or even a ground rent paid to a ground landlord. The historical origins of particular *livelli* were complex and varied. Probably the commonest form of *livello* was a donation of produce from land for pious purposes to a church, monastery or other ecclesiastical body, either specifically tied to, for instance, the saying of masses, or even a general bequest. Such a donation was a perpetual charge on land which continued after the transfer of the land to another owner. Not all *livelli* were pious in origin or paid to religious bodies. The origins of lay *livelli* are rather less clear than those of ecclesiastical ones. Some undoubtedly represented a commutation and transformation of surviving feudal rights; others may well have had their origins in transfers from ecclesiastical bodies: *livelli* were also alienable.

The level of *livello* payments was usually fixed in cash or kind and seems to have remained fixed. It is impossible to calculate the proportion of production or income of individuals or of pieces of land, but impression suggests that they were relatively low, certainly compared with the *fitti* – annual payments which formed, in effect, repayments on mortgage debts and which could on occasion take up almost all of the revenue of plots of land. It is perhaps significant that when, in the eighteenth century, the state, increasingly concerned about the large amounts of revenue being lost by the offsetting of *livelli* and *fitti* against *estimo* valuations, sought to control growing abuse, it was the *livelli* they allowed to remain virtually untouched, while the *fitti* were, as far as taxation returns were concerned, obliterated.

In the main, landownership was uncluttered by any real level above that of direct ownership. In any study of the Valpolicella system it is not necessary to consider except briefly these other levels. *Livello* and regalian right gave their owners no say in the management of land or in its disposal; they were *de facto* purely monetary and fiscal rights, whatever their legal or historical origins. There is no real level of seigneurial right nor yet any complex structure of multiple rights to cloud or confuse the picture of landholding.

III

Landholding in the early modern Valpolicella was neither stable nor static. Despite its crucial role in the social structure, land was in essence an economic commodity, certainly not an object to be held on to desperately nor to be hoarded without question. Any study of land-holding in the Valpolicella has then to take into consideration not merely the statics of the situation, but also the dynamic and often rapid changes in landholding which continually went on.

The movement of land between individuals, families and groups was a standard and normal feature of the rural system. It is very easy to fall into the error of seeing land transfer, particularly rapid land transfer, as being in some way a sign of social or economic change, even of breakdown. Obviously, large-scale transfer which results in a permanent and long-term shift of land from the hands of one social group or sector to another does constitute a major social and economic change of possibly profound significance, but a level of land transfer, a kind of 'Brownian motion' of landownership is both natural and inevitable. One problem in any study of this sort is to separate this Brownian motion from apparently more significant changes in patterns of landholding.

The level of Brownian motion in any economy varies with the general economic and social context: in some areas and circumstances it is, and always will be, much lower than in others. In particular, commercialized and monetarized economies are likely to have a higher underlying rate of transfer than less commercialized ones. All the evidence suggests that this underlying rate in the Veronese in general and in the Valpolicella in particular was high; it is, of course, impossible to deal with this problem practically on anything other than an impressionistic basis, but the very clear impression must be that the underlying rate in northern Italy was high compared to that of many other parts of Europe at a similar period: certainly the numerous volumes of the *notarelle* of the *Cancellaria* of the *Estimo* point to a high rate of the movement of land and landed rights.

The Brownian motion of land transfer in the Veronese can be seen as being largely the result of three processes: inheritance, dowry and sale. Other causes, such as the lapse of mortgage or transfer forced by the non-payment of taxation, confiscation and litigation played a part, and could at times be spectacular in their effects, but in terms of the overall level of transfer they were relatively insignificant.

Inheritance law in the Veronese was complex, but based on the Roman Law principle of partible inheritance. In most cases real property was divided equally amongst the male heirs general of the deceased; testamentary disposal and the law of *fidei commesum* affected the distribution of portions between heirs but the basic pattern – that inheritance produced land transfer, often on a large scale – remains the same. Partible inheritance also produced complex patterns of transfer, some land passing into individual hands, some into joint ownership. The break-up of joint ownership also resulted in effective transfers.

Dowry also provided a major element of transfer, not merely at the highest social levels but all the way down the landholding scale. The size of dowries became a major concern for the state which was worried that escalating levels of dowry, the consequence of competitive conspicuous expenditure, were leading to the impoverishment of already weakened noble families. To some extent, and surely significantly, this escalation of dowry took the form not of land but of goods – furniture, pictures, jewels – or of cash. In part this was a consequence of the problems which dowry transfers of land could cause both for the receiving family and also for the women involved. Dowry land was joined to the land of the husband's family; on his death it returned to the control of the dowager; by tradition mothers passed on their dower land as dowries for their daughters.[1]

The land market in the Veronese and the Valpolicella was an active and a large one; all available evidence suggests that this had been so for many centuries. Even the registered sales of land, which were a fraction of the total sales, were considerable. Land was sold for a large number of reasons – social and political as well as economic. The consolidation or improvement of holdings, the consequences of transfer of location and habitation, investment, and the need to raise capital for investment in other sectors and in other forms of consumption all played a part, in addition to sales for reasons of debt or necessity. Equally, purchases of land, although they were usually economically determined, should not be seen purely in terms of land hunger nor of greed on the part of purchasers. Land *qua* land was not, in itself, a valued commodity: rather it was the productivity and investment value of land which determined its saleability. The difficulties which the *Magistratura ai Beni Inculti* had in getting purchasers, and in particular local purchasers, to buy marginal or uncultivated land, and the lengths they had to go to to subsidize improvements to it, indicate that, even amongst the Venetian aristocracy who were as far as the Valpolicella was concerned the leading group involved in the *Beni Inculti*, acres were not enough: it was the value of land which was significant.

It must be emphasized that not all sales were genuine sales. In particular the *Emptio cum Locatione* – *locazione* in the vulgar – produced sales which were not, nor were intended, at least at their origins, to be actual or permanent transfers. The Civil Law provided a number of means by which land could be mortgaged, or rather by which loans could be secured against land. Although these forms continued in occasional use, the Church's absolute interdiction on usury and usurious forms meant that they were, at best, extremely rare and their enforcement could prove to be difficult. Mortgage, however, was still necessary, particularly in a highly commercialized and monetarized economy like that of the Valpolicella, to provide investment capital and to cover owners against the problems and exigencies of rural and urban life. In common with many legal systems, the

Common Law of the Veronese used a legal fiction to reconcile the demands of the Church with those of everyday economic life: this compromise was the *Emptio cum Locatione*. The mortgagee borrowed a sum of money from the mortgagor: rather than executing a contract securing that loan and its interest upon the mortgagee's whole landholding, or upon a specific piece of land, the fiction was that the land had been sold to the mortgagor for the sum loaned. The new legal owner placed the former owner in possession as his tenant, in return for a rent which was, in effect, fixed at the equivalent of the interest due at the ruling rate; the contract gave the original owner the right to re-purchase the land at the end of (or during) a specified period – in effect to redeem the mortgage. Should the mortgagee fail to repay by the final date, the land, theoretically at least, passed into the ownership of the mortgagor; in many cases the mortgagor allowed a renewal of the right of redemption, obviously and surely significantly, happier to take a continuing income than to have land pass into his ownership. These rent/interest payments, often called *fitti affrancabili*, were a common feature of many landholdings and of many estates, and they could be continued for very lengthy periods.

Even this brief survey brings to the surface a number of major points about the role of land and of the land market in the Valpolicella. Despite its social role, which is undoubted and unchallenged here, land was, in essence, an economic commodity whose purchase and sale was undertaken for essentially economic as distinct from social reasons. At the highest levels of society land changed hands for its economic value and within a broad pattern of the economic structure and economic requirements of the family or household. With the legally enforced exception of entailed land, and even there only partially, there seems to have been little permanent tie between owners and particular pieces of land. Furthermore there seems to have been little social stigma attached to land sales. In general, then, land sales and land purchases at the upper levels of society seem to have been determined by economic strategies and not simply by desperation or decline. At the lower levels of society the same holds true: land was sold because it was convenient or profitable to do so, rather than because of desperation or disaster. Equally it is clear that the purchase and accumulation of land was not simply or even chiefly a question of the accumulation of land for land's sake, but the result of a clear idea of the economic value of particular pieces of land and their contribution to their own economy. As a corollary, it follows that there was no concerted drive by the rich to accumulate all land into their hands, except in so far as this was or might be to their own economic advantage. Land transfers and changing patterns of ownership were not necessarily a consequence of social or economic breakdown, or of a profound shift in the nature of the economy.

IV

The student of patterns of landownership in the Veronese is, in a sense, fortunate in the sources available. Inventories and other notarial enumerations provide some evidence, but above all it is on the records of land taxation that such a study must be based, albeit with a certain amount of scepticism resulting from the nature and origin of these records.

The fiscal structure of the Venetian Empire was, as always, a devolved one. The Councils in Venice set a total fiscal 'take' for the Empire, apportioned, usually on a historical basis, between the cities and other communities of the Empire. It fell to the cities and to their councils to raise the required quota from their resources. The major form of direct taxation involved in this, although most revenue seems to have been raised by indirect taxation, was a tax on the value of land and other real property, the *estimo*. The collection of the *estimo* was further delegated to the communes of the Territorio, including Verona itself. In allocating the proportion of the total to be raised between communities and between individual taxpayers within communities, the administrations resorted to what was in effect an enumeration of all landholding and all land values. Until the 1620s these enumerations were undertaken by the communities themselves, as they were later, and not reported to the centre. From the reassessment of the late 1620s onwards the detailed enumerations were submitted to and retained by a central office, a branch of the *Estimaria*, the agency charged with maintaining and enforcing such central control as there was in the system.

These central records – the *Antichi Estimi Provvisori* – form, then, the basis of this study. They are an invaluable collection of information, not merely on landholding but on a whole range of related topics. At their best and most complete they list each field, with its boundaries, an area calculated in some cases to the nearest square foot, and a book value for the land; they also list charges against the value of the land: *livelli*, *fitti* and *regalie*, for instance. Furthermore, they are a series; the *estimo* was reassessed and the lists prepared anew periodically throughout the seventeenth and eighteenth centuries.

In theory the *Estimi* should provide a clear and concise picture of the pattern of ownership through these two centuries. However, as so often is the case, the reality is rather less complete than the theory. The nature of the *estimo* and the way in which the enumerations were compiled makes it very difficult to be certain as to the accuracy – or rather the level of inaccuracy – of the returns. Any figures and any conclusions drawn from the *estimo* figures can only be treated as approximate. Equally, given the importance of rented land and of other sources of income, it must be restated that measurements of landownership as such are only a part, albeit an important part, of any individual or household's economic position.

The *estimo* was a tax on land values; the question, as always, was how were such values to be assessed. Two factors were perceived as crucial to this valuation: the area of land involved and its return (*rendita*). Area was, of course, relatively easily assessed. From the Middle Ages onwards, the Italian rural economy had been character- ized by very clear definitions in absolute terms of boundaries of fields, marked by boundary stones, hedges, ditches or *marogne*. Such defini- tions of boundaries form an important element in notarial documents and disputes over them are a major part of rural litigation. The *Estimi* in fact define boundaries in terms not of fixed physical features, but in terms of the boundaries of other landholders; rivers, cliffs and so on only appear where they mark an end of owned land. The same relativity of boundaries also marks notarial instruments of sale and transfer: it is *who* rather than *what* bounds a field or holding which is important. The boundaries of fields and holdings were, then, well- known and widely accepted; all that was necessary for the calculation of area was measurement. The science of geometry, properly so-called, was well developed in pre-modern Italy: from the Middle Ages, and earlier, the *Agrimensore* had been an important and respected figure in rural as well as in urban life. Indeed, so general was the knowledge of the bases of land measurement that they seem to have formed a part of the general education of a very wide range of sectors of society. Certainly, by the seventeenth and eighteenth centuries, if not earlier, leading men in villages were clearly capable of carrying out relatively complex calculations of field areas, in many cases of areas of irregular shape, and of providing a result which suggests considerable precision, in some cases accurate to less than twelve square yards in an acre.

Measurement was, then, no real problem, but what did inevitably cause real problems was the setting of a value on particular pieces of land. In theory this should have been simple. The *estimo* was based on the principle that rural land had a value which was based on its productivity and, therefore, on the return of the land. No allowance was made, in effect, for differences in land values caused by, for instance, geographical position. Except in so far as closeness to Verona led to differences in its use, suburban land outside the commune of Verona was valued at the same level as land of similar productivity thirty or forty miles from the city, despite the greater market demand for suburban land. It is worth emphasizing that the value set by the *estimo* upon land was not a market value but a 'theoretical' rateable value and, in that sense at least, it would be wrong to use the *estimo* as a measure of the asset-worth of any landowner. Certainly no attempt seems to have been made to relate *estimo* values to fluctuating prices in the land market.

The principle upon which the calculation of *estimo* value was made was basically simple. A calculation of the income which the owner or cultivator drew from the land was multiplied to give a 'capital' value. The basis of the multiplication remained essentially the same throughout the period of this study: the calculated *rendita* was regarded as the return at six per cent per annum on a capital sum which was the capital value of the land. Put in another form, the capital value represented sixteen and two-thirds years' return on the land. This six per cent figure was also used in calculating the capital value of *livelli*, *fitta* and *regalie* to be set against the income.

The outlines of the system were then, admirably clear cut and definite. The real problems, as always, arose when it came to transforming these principles into reality. At base lay the problem of determining the return of any piece of land. Obviously, given both the uncertainties of harvests and complex systems of rotation, single years were not enough: it was neccesary to calculate (or more strictly estimate) returns over a longer period ('un anno con l'altro'). Secondly, it is never clear in reality whether the figure which is taken for 'return' is a 'profit' figure, after the costs of cultivation are subtracted, or a 'gross yield' figure. Obviously, too, the returns of trees and vines growing in the field or along its boundaries have to be taken into account. Arable land was relatively easy to value as was, for instance, coppiced woodland in which there was a clear and quantifiable return for valuation. Meadow and pasture land presented a whole series of complex problems, however. Other than the return from the animals grazed on it – and they were assessed separately – and from olive or fruit trees which frequently grew in meadow or pasture land, the return of such land was indirect: some hay might be sold, and some income gained from renting grazing to others, but in general it was in terms of an internalized value to the landholder that pasture land and grazing should be seen, allowing him to feed and maintain the basic non-human power source in the economy and the major source of added soil fertility. Pasture and grazing land was, as already indicated, vital to the operation and survival of the *lavorente* system and was some of the most sought-after land in the rental and sale market; consequently it could hardly be excluded from the *estimo*. Its valuation was always difficult and contentious, and strikingly produced *estimo* values, particularly for pasture land, which were as high as or higher than values for all but the very best arable land.

The income from land was, however, only part of the story. The rules permitted the owner to set against the final value of the land any charges against the land. In particular *regalie*, *livelli* and *fitti*, secured on land, could be and were used to reduce the total value of the landholding, and hence the total liability to tax. One inevitable consequence of this was to favour the use of the *fitto* in particular as a way of borrowing in the short term at the time of the reassessment of the *estimo* as well as in the medium and long term. Early in the period, particularly in the seventeenth century, very large numbers of charges against land are recorded, so many in some cases that individuals, often apparently well-to-do, declared charges in excess of the total valuation of their land and effectively escaped taxation over the period to the next reassessment. This abuse, if such it can be called, was restricted by government action in the eighteenth century which effectively removed all but permanent *livelli*, usually to churches and other ecclesiastical corporations, from consideration. This form of tax evasion does create very real problems of interpretation, in particular if the *Estimi* are used in any attempt to gauge directly the wealth or poverty of individuals.

Descriptions of the problems of assessment could be multiplied, as indeed could descriptions of litigation over valuations, but it is already clear that the valuation of land for *estimo* purposes was both a delicate and highly specialized task. It must be emphasized again that the relationship between *estimo* values on the one hand and 'economic' and market values on the other is, at best, an indirect one; as a measure of the asset value of land or the wealth or otherwise of the owner, they should be used only with great caution and qualification.

In the Valpolicella, as in most of the Veronese, the task of dealing with the very real problems of assessment and valuation fell not upon salaried government officials, nor upon the growing professional body of *agrimensori* (although they were involved in the process in some of the larger communities) but upon elected amateur communal officials. In most communes the two *stimadori*, elected in rotation by the *vicinia* of their commune, were at once the most important and the most visible of the communal officials. Their functions were only partially concerned with the *estimo*, but were, in broader terms, to carry out land measurements and valuations; they were, for instance, frequently called into play as arbitrators between sellers and purchasers, or between the state and defaulters to value land and goods. The great strengths of the *stimadori* were their reputation as fair and unbiased figures and their wide-ranging local knowledge, vitally important in a situation in which land values and patterns of land use were extremely complex and extremely localized.

The great weakness of the *stimadori* was the inverse of their strength; they were inhabitants of the commune, elected by their fellow members of the *vicinia* and hence, and inevitably, involved in local faction and local tension. In a society in which patronage and connection was the key to social organization and articulation, the *stimador* was a potential patron figure and equally, the post of *stimador*, with both the prestige and the (admittedly small) remuneration it carried, was a useful element in any clientage system – the major patron exerting his influence to gain the post for his client. The *stimador* was expected to be as unbiased and as fair as the system allowed; it would be unreasonable and unrealistic to expect more of him. Hence, within the *estimo* for any commune there will be distortions, in valuation in particular, both in favour of the *stimador*'s networks and against opposing networks. In particular, sins of omission – the 'accidental' exclusion of pieces of land or elements in the *rendita* of the land are likely to be common. The *Estimi* are tax returns and tax returns in any age are notoriously suspect; in addition they are taxation returns compiled through the filter of an active patronage system in which favouring friends and penalizing enemies was a normal element in any situation.

The complexities of the situation are further compounded by the nature of the currency unit which was used to measure values. In common with all Veronese official accounts, the values of the *estimi* were not expressed in circulating currency, but in a money of account – the *Ducato*. The *Ducat* was originally a gold coin valued at six Venetian *lire* and four *soldi*, a rate of exchange which was maintained for accounting purposes despite fluctuations in the true metallic ratio between the currencies. The problem was further confused since most private accounts in the Veronese were kept not in Venetian *lire* but in Veronese *lire*, a metallic currency which also changed in value in relation to both the *Ducat* and the Venetian *lira*. The *estimo*, however, retained the conventional rates of exchange. While this is undoubtedly of value in comparing *estimo* values over a period of time, it does, once more, remove the *estimo* one further step from the reality of rural incomes and rural wealth. It is extremely difficult, and potentially dangerously misleading, to attempt to compare the wealth or income individuals and families over time by comparing the *estimo* values of their holdings.

A further feature of the *estimo* which makes its use both difficult and limited is its chronological nature. First, the *Estimo* presents us with a snapshot of the patterns of landholding at a single definite point in time; in effect it freezes the action at one point. In a land system which was as fluid and as lively as that of the Valpolicella, any moment may or may not be representative. In particular, it is clearly necessary to issue a warning against regarding the earliest *Estimo* which has survived in full form, that of the late 1620s, as being in some way normative, as representing landownership 'as it was' or even 'as it should be'. Given the high level of land transfers in the 1620s, it is clear that the late 1620s must be regarded as no more than a stage through which landownership passed rather than anything more significant. The problem of the snapshot nature of the *Estimo* is also compounded by the fact that the point of time at which the snapshot was taken varied from commune to commune, by as much as two years. The second chronological problem is that of the frequency of, and intervals between, revisions of the *estimo*. The frequency of land transfers inevitably made the *estimo* out of date; despite attempts by both communes and central administration to maintain some record of land transfers, the old books rapidly became inefficient bases for administration. Hence from time to time the central administration in Verona required the communes to revise their *Estimi* completely. The first general revision under the new system, in the late 1620s, came at the very end of the population growth of the sixteenth century; the pattern of landholding it described was to be devastated by the Plague of 1630. The crisis of the 1630s produced two, and in some communes three, revisions before the end of the decade. The greater stability of the seventeenth century produced revisions roughly every twenty years, starting in the early 1650s and ending with the revision of 1709–10. Despite the greater prosperity and the growing sophistication of government, the eighteenth century only produced two revisions – in the early 1750s and the later 1760s. This last was the final *Estimo* of the old type: no further revision was undertaken before the fall of the Republic, and the *Catasti* of both the French and Austrian dominations operated on a different basis which makes comparison impossible.

The *estimo* was based on the commune, that is to say the volumes of the *Estimi* for any commune record, more or less faithfully, the distribution of landownership within that commune. Land which lay outside the commune was the concern of some other commune and formed a part of the *Estimo* of that commune. Therefore, any land which any individual held by inheritance, purchase or dowry, in any commune beyond the one in question, was ignored and formed no part of that *Estimo*, but was listed and taxed in another commune. Had the commune been, as it may have been earlier, in any way a coherent and enclosed unit, this would have been an insignificant problem. However, the growth in population and extension of cultivation meant that the cultivated areas of most communes, particularly in the central block of the Valpolicella, marched directly with each other. Furthermore, the normal pattern of marriages, which saw men taking their wives from villages other than their own, meant that dowry holdings, and also holdings by inheritance, were not confined to single communes but spread much more widely. A smallholder in one commune might well be a major one in another or it was equally possible that the holder of small units in a number of communes might combine those holdings into a larger one while appearing, perfectly legitimately, as a smallholder in each commune. The *Estimi* do, to some extent, allow these multiple cross-communal holdings to be identified, but a number of features make this cross-correlation difficult and finally, almost certainly, incomplete. Names, for instance, can confuse the process horribly: many surnames are common to a number of villages, and the range of Christian names used is, in general, limited; it is often impossible to be sure whether the appearance of the same name in the *Estimi* of two communes indicates one man or two men with the same name. A problem which is exactly the reverse of this one also occurs. Names, in particular surnames, were not absolutely fixed, particularly in the seventeenth century, and it is possible and reasonably common for one man to have, perfectly legitimately, different surnames in different communes: hence different names may conceal the same person. The *Estimo* thus tends to exaggerate the number of smallholdings and to underestimate the average holding of individuals through this process of dispersal between a number of communes. Again it is clear that the *Estimo* can and should only be used as an indication of broad patterns of landholding and not, except in the most general of terms, as an indication of wealth or poverty.

The *estimo* was a communal tax and one commune – Verona itself – had a particular set of privileges and a peculiar way of drawing up its *estimo*. Like every commune, Verona had a quota of the total taxation allotted to it, and like every other commune, it allocated the quota amongst its citizens. It possessed, however, two advantages which the other communes did not. First, it was the Councils of the commune of Verona which allocated the quotas between the communes, including itself; hardly surprisingly the *estimo* of Verona was less demanding, *ducat* for *ducat* of value, than were those of the other communes. To have an assessment under the commune of Verona was financially advantageous, as well as conferring some of the other advantages of citizenship. These financial advantages, coupled with the drift of land into city hands, were so considerable that, by the late 1620s and early 1630s, the communes of the Territorio, and the Venetian Rectors were sufficiently worried about the shift of the burden of taxation on to fewer rural landholders that they instituted litigation against the city. A compromise was reached in 1633, and lasted to the end of the Republic, by which land which passed into the hands of citizens of Verona after that date would continue to be taxed and hence to appear in the *Estimi* of the rural communes.[2]

The *estimo* of Verona was different in another way. Unlike all the other communes, the citizens of Verona had the right to have all their land, wherever in the Veronese it lay, taxed under Verona rather than under the rural commune. Hence much land, and much of the land of the greatest landholders, never appeared in the *Estimi* of the rural communes but only in that of Verona. This extra-communal nature of the Verona *estimo*, coupled with the massively larger scale of the Verona assessment, meant that the relatively simple and straightforward system of the rural communes did not operate. In particular, although the commune of Verona had its own *stimadori* and although attempts were made to check the returns made from the city itself of land and houses within the city, the citizens of Verona were in effect allowed a form of self-assessment. Rather than a formal and properly controlled return by officials, the citizens of Verona were required to submit on their own account lists of their property, both in the city and the Territorio, and of their chargeable debts and other expenses, which then formed the basis of their assessment. Although these returns, the *polizze*, were made under oath it is quite clear that considerable concealment and creative accounting went on. As Professor Borelli has demonstrated, even allowing for the artificial nature of the calculations involved, most noble families made returns which seriously underestimated the income they drew from their estates outside the city.

Further, the way in which the *polizze* were drawn up precluded any standardization of their form, unlike the *Estimi* of the rural communes, which were formulaic and standardized, effectively from the beginning of the new system in the 1620s. As has been indicated earlier, the *polizze* have no standard form and no standard content; some are tremendously detailed, some are sketchy in the extreme. Furthermore, most do not include the results of the '*estimo*' calculation of value, but merely state a figure for annual or average *rendita*. In addition, the *polizze*, or rather their compilers, are concerned with estates – *possessioni* – rather than the often apparently arbitrary boundaries between communes. In many cases it is impossible – even where an area or a value is given for a whole estate – to allocate those areas or values between two or more communes, all involved in the same estate.

Even more than the rural *Estimi*, the *Estimi* of Verona suffer from chronological difficulties. Unlike the rural *Estimi* they are not a snapshot of landholdings at one point in time, but rather a kind of blurred picture covering a period of years, in which *polizze* were submitted; the worst offender in this case is the last Venetian *Estimo* of Verona, finalized in the mid-1740s. Administrative and political difficulties drew out the period over which the information was collected: the collection had originally begun in the 1720s and, by the time the *Estimo* was finalized – not completed since *polizze* were still being submitted in the 1750s – some taxpayers were submitting their second or third amendments to their first submissions. The Verona *Estimi* were also much less frequent and much less regular than those of the rural communes. The first *Estimo* of which details survive was made in the early 1650s. Two more were made in the early 1680s and the 1690s, while the only eighteenth century reassessment was that of the 1740s. It is true that the *Cancellaria* of the *Estimaria* maintained some records of transfers between the *Estimi*; they are incomplete and, at times, incomprehensible. The dates of the Verona reassessments do not, of course, coincide with the reassessments of the rural *Estimi*.

It is then impossible to combine the rural *Estimi* and the Verona *polizze* into a single range of data and, therefore, it is not possible to give an effective total picture of landownership in the Veronese from these or indeed any other source. All that they can produce by being combined is an impression of patterns of landownership and the changes within it. In particular they allow some indication of the shifting patterns of ownership and of unit size amongst the rural population, as distinct from that of the city. It cannot be emphasized too much that the picture which will develop from these sources is impressionistic. As has been indicated, the sources themselves do not allow the spurious certainty which statistics sometimes produce. It is impressions and hopefully broad trends which should emerge from these sources and from the use of them made here.

It is perhaps as well that it should be so. Landholding and landownership is the most easily recorded, the most easily quantified and the most stable element in the complex mix which was the Valpolicella economy. The temptation to place it centrally as virtually the exclusive measure of prosperity and wealth is, for that reason, great. However, it is misleading to accept its centrality, certainly without question or qualification. Landowning was not the only way of getting land for cultivation, nor was it necessarily the best way economically or socially for many individuals or families; other forms of landholding and other forms of income could offer better opportunities and better returns. For some families at least, landowning was only a minor part of their economic pattern and it would be wrong to elevate it into anything more. The *Estimi* and the *Polizze* give access to an important part of the economic mix, but it is vitally important to remember that it is only a part and that the picture the *Estimi* present is not an absolute or 'correct' one, but a version of the true picture compiled for specific purposes which are not necessarily those of the historian.

V

The most striking feature of the tenurial geography of the Valpolicella was its wide variety and diversity. In no way could the area be characterized as one of great estates nor yet as one of small-scale holdings exclusively. Although some communes were more dominated than others by large estates, even there no single estate seems to have been in a position to control absolutely or even in a limited way the supply of land in a commune or region. Equally striking is the widespread nature of land ownership: the number of landholders listed in the *Estimi* suggests that a high proportion of households owned at least some land. This, then, was not a simple 'landlord' or seigneurial society, nor yet was it a society of 'peasant' landowners.[3]

There are striking variations in patterns of landholding from commune to commune. At one extreme lie Breonio, Prun and Fane which, throughout the period of this study and beyond, were characterized by the almost complete exclusion of citizen landlords and by a very widespread pattern of landholding amongst the inhabitants of the communes. Ponton may be taken as the prime example of a commune with a very large proportion of property in the hands of a few outsider landlords, above all the Venetian Mocenigo family, which bought land in Ponton before 1628 and continued to hold it throughout the period. Even in Ponton, however, the Mocenighi were not the only great landlords nor was absolutely all the land in the hands of the great owners. Even the Mocenighi were not, even in the single commune of Ponton, in the position of a monopolistic rural magnate controlling the supply of land and the supply of employment within the community, with all that implies about rural control.

Most of the Valpolicella lay, however, somewhere between these two extremes: rather than being 'landlord' communes or 'peasant' communes, all the communities demonstrated a balance between the two, albeit a balance which shifted constantly. In very crude terms it is possible to say that, even at the beginning of the period, the higher communes – Breonio, Monte, Cavalo, Prun, Torbe and Fane – had a lower proportion of large outsider landholders, while the valley bottom and 'plains' communes – Negrar, S. Vito, Castelrotto, S. Pietro, S. Floriano, Gargagnago, for instance – tended to have, and to have increasingly, a relatively high proportion of their land in the hands of outsiders and outsiders who held large estates. It is not, however, a case of Braudel's 'mountain freedom': many of the lower level communes – Pescantina, Maran, Fumane, S. Ambrogio for instance – display a high level of local ownership in either larger or smaller units. Even where, as in Negrar, large units and outsider-held units were the rule, still large numbers of small landholders existed and survived to the very end of the period.

It is very striking that in virtually all communes, a high proportion of households seem to have held at least some land. Furthermore, although the size of units may have varied, the number of landholding households remained roughly stable between 1630 and 1766, although the later seventeenth and early eighteenth centuries saw a dip which was recovered in the mid-eighteenth century. It is clear that landownership of some kind was a feature of the economic structure of many families and households.

This varied and diffused pattern was not static. A high level of land transfer and mobility in landholding and land right was natural in this commercialized system. Of much greater significance historically, or at least historiographically, than the underlying and continual motion is any trend towards concentration of holdings, be it just the concentration of more and more land in fewer hands or a true process of consolidation of holdings into more economic units. This process of differentiation, if it can be called that, and of a transfer of ownership from 'rural' to 'urban' owners has been seen along with the rise of

new 'farmer' owners, identified by Berengo, as providing the key to
the social and economic decline which have been seen as typical of
this period. In broad terms, the declining economic position of the
'peasantry' saw control of the land passing from its hands into those
of the urban élite which was diversifying, or converting, its economic
base by investing in land, a commodity for which it had an almost
insatiable greed. In the wake of this process of transfer came the creation of a landless or almost landless peasantry, dependent upon an
increasingly rapacious landlord class for both employment and for
land which was rented to them on more and more unequal and unfair
terms, until a process of alienation and subordination reduced the
peasantry to a state of total penury and depression. The causes of this
process were many, but centred around rapid population growth, *(1)*
which it lay beyond the means of peasant agriculture to deal with; the
conscious desire of economic and social élites in Venice and Verona *(2)*
to invest in land as a more secure and profitable source of income and
store of wealth than commerce and finance had previously provided;
and the general decline and degradation of the economic and social *(3)*
system in the seventeenth and above all the eighteenth centuries.

   The use of the *Estimi* and the *Polizze* to estimate the course and
causes of any such process of transfer is an extremely difficult one.
The 'snapshot' nature of the *Estimi* means that it is never very easy
to be sure at what point, in a pattern of transfer, landholdings are
being recorded and fixed. The identification of owners and their location and origins by the *Estimi* is never either complete or consistent;
in particular the identification of individuals or families as living or
being based in Verona is always open to doubt, in particular given the
growing tendency for important families of rural origin to establish
Verona bases for themselves. One feature of the *Estimi* does, it is true,
make one part of the analysis easier, albeit possibly dangerously and
misleadingly so. The Compromise of 1633 meant that any land passing
from local to Verona hands remained listed in the *Estimo* for the rural
commune, and was not transferred to the Verona *Estimo* and hence
to the *Polizze*; land passing into noble hands in particular can thus be
very easily identified in the Communal *Estimi*. Unfortunately, this
gives a picture of a monolithic passage of land from the hands of the
peasants into City hands, without any countervailing process of
transfer. There is considerable evidence that land passing into the
hands of the nobility, and other city holders, was not in some way
extracted from the active local land market and, therefore, passed
back into local hands as frequently as it was transferred amongst the
noble and Veronese owners. Land which passed from citizen to local
hands remained, under the Compromise of 1633, taxed under the city:
the returns of these pieces of land – the *Polizze Distrettuali* – form
a separate series in the Archive of the *Estimaria*. They reveal not
merely a transfer of 'city' land between rural owners, but also a

Table 14 Proportion of taxable value of land taxed under communes held by residents of Verona (percentages)

	1653	1670	1690	1709	1752	1766
Negrar	—	17.33	50.37	66.22	64.74	58.04
S. Sofia	15.36	28.24	46.01	38.16	—	47.99
Castelrotto	2.13	3.64	10.40	11.92	5.39	8.16
Bure	—	—	22.63	29.77	55.47	47.39
Monte	—	28.94	26.65	18.16	13.44	12.75
Valgatara	8.26	15.94	29.64	32.31	32.85	34.48
Negarine	2.65	0.99	9.44	20.07	16.96	16.27

Source: ASVR, AEP, Reg: 600–1 (Negrar), 584 (S. Sofia), 599 (Castelrotto), 583 (Bure), 611 (Monte), 597 (Valgatara), 598 (Negarine)

transfer of land from city to rural owners. The 'monolithic and unstoppable flow of land to city owners' must be seen in this context of evidence of a much more complex, multi-directional flow.

The evidence for some communes is presented in Table 14. It has not been possible to calculate meaningful figures for all communes, given the difficulties of calculating total values and in many cases calculating the total value of the holdings of individuals. It must be emphasized that the percentages refer to the proportion of the total taxation value of the land in each commune's internal *Estimo* which was held by individuals or families identified or identifiable as citizens or residents of Verona; it does not include and cannot include any calculation or estimate of land held and taxed under the city of Verona. No attempt has been made to distinguish between 'new' and 'old' citizens, between that is to say long-established and new families in the city, some of whom were directly of rural origin and, indeed, from the communes in which their land lay.

A number of features can be distinguished. The first is, of course, the almost general increase in the proportion of land held by citizen and Verona resident landowners and the corresponding decline of local owners. One difficulty arises very clearly and very immediately: these figures are based on the assessed value of land, rather than on area or real value. There is some evidence that the transfer of land into city hands led to a raising of assessed value, for political rather than economic reasons. To some extent the increase in the proportion of land in city hands may be a result of an attempt by the tax assessors of the communes to shift the tax burden onto the shoulders of outsiders. It must also be emphasized that this transfer of value and of land into the hands of city men was not something which began in 1633: after all, if no other evidence were available, the crisis which led to the Compromise of 1633 was a consequence of the active transfer of land even before 1630. Certainly the sixty years before

1630 had seen a quite considerable increase in the share of land in the hands of urban owners.

Secondly, it is clear that the penetration of ownership by outsiders was of varying levels and at varying speeds over the communes of the Valpolicella. There was not a clear single or simple pattern by which land was transferred. Again there must be caution; the snapshot nature of the record and the not quite synchronized dating of the *Estimi* may distort the pattern of transfer. Nonetheless it is clear that no single event or collection of factors of general effect caused a sudden transfer nor a sudden and significant acceleration in transfer across the whole of the Valpolicella. Rather, the figures support other evidence which suggests that the timing and scale of transfers in any commune or, indeed, of purchases by individuals were determined by specific factors either within the local economies or within the development of the economies of individual families. There seems to be no clear single event or series of events of general application which led to an acceleration of transfers.

It is also clear that the movement of land into citizen hands was not necessarily a one-way process. Some communes, particularly in the eighteenth century, demonstrate a decline in citizen holdings, a decline which in some cases is concealed by the attainment of citizenship by previously locally-based families. As in so many other ways, the distinction between the city and country which was apparently so sharp and so clear cut, and which in the theory of the system was so absolute, turns out to have been much more confused and much more blurred. To talk in simple terms of a transfer of land from rural to urban hands is to misunderstand the fluid nature of society at its highest as well as at its lowest levels.

The extent of outsider penetration varied sharply from commune to commune. In some, more than half of the land which had not been in citizen hands had passed into city ownership by the later eighteenth century; in others, particularly the communes of the hill country, the proportion transferred was very much lower. Even within the lower areas, in which land was in more demand, the proportions varied very sharply. To some extent these figures may be misleading: in those communes where before 1630 a large proportion of land was already externally owned, relatively small shifts of landownership could produce large percentage changes. Nonetheless they do not indicate a land greed amongst purchasers which led them to buy any land which was available, but a very much more conscious and careful selection of land. Far from an indiscriminate and general land grab, what seems to have been going on, over time, was a clear and logical purchase of land by outsiders seeking to create or to develop effective holdings; this was no scramble by a city aristocracy seeking any home for its capital in an economy in which land had become the only safe investment, nor was it a rush for land as a social asset, separated from any economic meaning. The purchasers of land bought the land they did for, in their eyes, clear and logical reasons.

The literature which has discussed this transfer of land from rural to urban ownership in the seventeenth and eighteenth centuries has tended to do so in terms of a transfer into the hands of the 'nobility'. Such a statement is misleading in two ways. While, perhaps inevitably, a great deal of the land which passed into urban hands was bought by noble families, properly so called, this was not exclusively so. A fair proportion of the land passed into the hands of what can only be called urban bourgeois families, in particular, into the hands of successful traders, doctors or lawyers. The Bernardi family, for instance, who bought large amounts of land throughout the Valpolicella in the later seventeenth and eighteenth centuries had based their economic success upon their notarial business. This then was not simply a question of the city nobility seizing the opportunity to build (or rebuild) their traditional landholdings, but in one way at least, a more general urban search for land. Nor must it be thought that noble landholdings were, once they had been established, stable and permanent. Families like the Sigismondi Paletta or the Sbaddachia built up considerable holdings in the seventeenth century only to see them decline sharply in the eighteenth.

If it was not simply the nobility which bought land in the Valpolicella, it was by no means all the nobility which bought land. By no means all the nobility owned any land in the Valpolicella at the beginning of the seventeenth century and many families who did owned only small amounts of land, frequently dower land. These total outsiders very rarely, if at all, bought their way into Valpolicella land in the seventeenth and eighteenth centuries; where new families do appear it is usually by inheritance or by marriage. Even amongst the established Valpolicella noble dynasties land purchases were not consistent. Most, although by no means all, noble families gained some land, but the really spectacular increases were limited to relatively few families. The Rizzardi of Negrar, for instance, who had been important landowners in the commune before 1630, added some 100 pieces of land of varying size, value and quality in the next 120 years. In addition they bought land in neighbouring communes. Elsewhere the Ottolini family accounts for a high proportion of the land passing out of rural hands in the communes of the western Valpolicella. Land purchasing, again was highly selective and not something which was engaged in in a haphazard manner by every noble dynasty.

The other major factor in changes in landownership which figures frequently in the literature, the purchase of *Terra Firma* land either directly or through the *Beni Inculti* by Venetian noble families, seems to have been insignificant in the Valpolicella. Indeed, compared with areas nearer Venice, in particular areas to the north and east of the city, the Veronese seems to have attracted few Venetian noble purchasers. In the Valpolicella the only major Venetian landholder was the Mocenigo family who purchased an estate on the river bank at Ponton, which with its villa made them the dominant landholder in the commune. Elsewhere a few plots were held by inhabitants of Venice, usually of the citizen class, and there is no evidence of any major drive by Venetians to buy into the Valpolicella.

It is not clear what the social or economic effects of the transfers of ownership to outsiders were in the seventeenth and eighteenth centuries. Obviously the transfer of ownership implied a transfer of income from owner-producers in the Valpolicella to landlords in the city. In cases where the transfer of ownership involved a change in the method of exploitation there was, again, a change of obvious significance. It is not clear, however to what extent the sale of land involved a significant change for its former owner: in most cases, the transfer of land seems to have been piecemeal rather than total, with individuals selling off first one plot or field and then another. In many cases there is at least circumstantial evidence that they retained occupation of the land they had sold, subject now to the payment of rent or to sharecropping. The 'dismal revolution' which saw the transfer of ownership from countryside to town, really needs to be further clarified before it can safely be characterized, as it so often has been, as a social and economic disaster.

VI

The evidence of the *Estimi* and the other sources here considered point to another and possibly more significant development in the landownership and rural society of the Valpolicella. They permit, albeit imperfectly and only impressionistically, the construction of a picture of the distribution of landholdings between the individuals within a commune and, therefore, give some kind of picture of developing patterns of social and economic differentiation within rural society.

Two very major caveats must be entered at the beginning of this discussion. The first, and perhaps the most vital, is that differentiation was not something new in Valpolicella society: for as far into the past as it is possible to see clearly, there have been wealthy and poor families in every Valpolicella village. The early modern period did not see, and what is being discussed here is not, the development of differentiation, the breakdown of some previously equal and equalitarian society into a 'pre-capitalist' system. The leading families of the Valpolicella in the seventeenth and eighteenth centuries were the lineal successors of similar leading families from an earlier age. The second caveat arises from the nature of the evidence. In talking of differentiation in this context what in fact is being considered is different levels of land ownership. In many senses, land ownership is probably the best measure available of wealth and differentiation: land after all was still the most secure form of investment into which to sink liquid wealth. Taken over a period of time wealth was likely to show itself in landownership and growing wealth in growing owner- ship. However, this was a widely diversified economy in which many other sources of income and of wealth could be, and usually were, added to landowning. Equally, as the growing wealth of many *lavorente* families demonstrates, rented or sharecropped land could be as valuable and as important as owned land.

The distribution of landholdings by proportion of the total for every Valpolicella commune between 1628 and 1752 demonstrates a grow- ing polarization of landholding, with a growing number and a growing proportion of small or micro-holders on the one hand and a growing concentration of land in the hands of a few individuals and families on the other. To some extent, this is a consequence of the transfer of land into noble hands, but even when this is stripped out, the picture remains constructively the same. It is quite clear from this evidence that the local society of the Valpolicella was dominated by a network of leading village families, frequently intermarried, and dominating political and (increasingly) ecclesiastical office. The wealth of these families was not limited, any more than that of other families lower in the social structure, to land. Many put younger sons (and in some cases eldest sons) into non-agricultural employment: the Orlandi of S. Ambrogio, for instance, combined landownership with a long-running notarial business. It was these leading village families, too, which established, if not a monopoly at least a dominance, amongst the parochial clergy in the seventeenth and eighteenth centuries.

The wealth of the leading families can be seen not merely in their landholding but also in the quality of the houses they built, or rebuilt, for themselves in the seventeenth century and in the leading roles they seem to have played in, for instance, the rebuilding and re-equipping of the parish churches of the Valpolicella, and even more in the growth of the *Compagnie* – the religious confraternities which were such a major feature of the communal life of the pre-modern Valpoli- cella. Their wealth, however, also gave them temptations, the most significant of these being the attractions of Verona, both as a place of residence and as a place for economic activity. Certainly from the 1630s and before leading Valpolicella families had already established bases for themselves in Verona, at first in rented houses, usually in the quarters of the city in which Valpolicella migrants congregated, but increasingly spreading throughout the city. Many also developed economic as well as social bases in the city, becoming lawyers or traders in their own right and, ultimately, establishing a claim to citizenship of the city. As had happened to many leading Valpolicella families previously, the slow process of assimilation gradually transformed Valpolicella families with houses in Verona into Verona families with houses and interests in Valpolicella villages. The process was not new, nor unusual, and by the last third of the eighteenth century many, if not all of the leading village families, had transferred their interests effectively to the city, leaving behind in the villages the junior members (junior in status) of their clans to form a mass of moderately well-to-do to poor agriculturalists. What, however, was new and what constitutes in many ways the prime change in the fate of Valpolicella society in the late eighteenth century and subsequently, is that the leaders who had left had no, or very few, successors. Valpolicella society seemed to have lost the ability to create new leaders: far from seeing the appearance of differentiation, the eighteenth century seems to mark the atrophy of the mechanisms which made differentiation possible.

VII

The patterns of landownership, and the transfer of landownership which have been seen as central to the economic and social development not merely of the Valpolicella but of the whole of northern Italy, need to be considered not as free-standing facts on their own, but rather within the whole context of the economy and society. This was not a society or an economy which was land-centred in the way that, say, Russian peasant society was. Land was a commodity and a useful and a valuable one; it constituted the essential basis of one of the major forms of production, it was the most secure form of investment available. However, it was a commodity like other commodities, bought and sold as convenience or exigencies demanded. Its ownership conveyed no special legal or political status, nor did the status of tenant imply any form of feudal or other subjection. Individuals moved freely and apparently unscathed from landholding to non-landholding categories and, significantly, back again. This seems to have been as true for the rich as it was for the poor; there seems to have been little concern at any level of society to hang desperately on to land at all costs.

In that sense, then, despite the undoubted economic and social significance of land, it would be wrong to see statistics of landholding, even if they could ever be regarded as fully correct, as presenting anything other than a partial key to the operation and structure of Valpolicella society. Undoubtedly it constitutes an important part of the total picture, but it must be seen as part of a much wider complex of economic and social relations. It is, of course, significant that so much land passed into the hands of city men in the course of these two centuries, although that significance may well appear greater with hindsight than it did at the time. Certainly the transfer of the land into the hands of absentee landlords was, in the nineteenth century, to play a major part in the economic decline of the Valpolicella and indeed of the whole Veronese – to reduce its ability to respond to crisis and to remove its resilience at a time when resilience was profoundly needed. In the context of the eighteenth century economy on the other hand, the ownership of land was only one of a number of potential sources of wealth, and hence its transfer, even on a large scale, was only one factor of change in a diverse and ever-changing system.

7
The non-agricultural dimension

I

Specialization has become such an economic virtue since the Industrial Revolution and in the post-industrial world that our very categories of economies and societies are predicated upon specialization of functions not merely between regions but also between individuals and families. The world is divided into 'agriculturalists', 'industrial workers', 'merchants' and so forth. The consequences of economic and social change fall on groups or individuals as a consequence of their involvement in single activities.

This pattern, of course, holds for the industrial and post-industrial world: indeed one of the major features distinguishing an industrial society and economy may well be said to be this specialization and its consequent dependence on a specific and single economic activity. The realization that this is not necessarily the case with pre-industrial societies is one of the great advances in our approach to both economic and social history in recent years. That an agricultural economy and society in the pre-modern period does not mean that every individual and every family in that society is entirely and solely dependent upon the production of their fields or upon labour in the fields of others is a revolution in our understanding as great as, and in part related to, the realization that, in Western Europe at least, pre-industrial rural societies were not purely subsistence-based and that their populations were not immobile, tied to particular pieces of land and particular villages or communities by ties of economic, social or emotional servitude. In parallel with the mobility and adaptability of pre-modern societies also went, inevitably, their great variety and complexity.

Earlier chapters have demonstrated that, even in terms of land-ownership, the traditional categories do not fit the situation of the seventeenth and eighteenth century Valpolicella. The great legal categories, landlord and tenant, do not in reality say much about the actual distribution of land, of wealth or of income in the society. Furthermore, the evidence of patterns of cultivation and the system of agricultural production in general point to a very clear lack of specialization, and indeed, to a great element of diversity and risk-spreading. The Valpolicella was well-known as a wine producer, but that did not by any means imply that it was, as it was later to become, a wine monoculture, but only that in a mixed and fluctuating agricultural economy, wine production played an important but not dominant role.

The principle of diversity and risk-spreading, of ensuring as far as possible that economic success – and more immediately economic (and physical) survival – did not depend upon the vagaries of a single source of production was not, and could not be, limited to a purely agricultural economy. The diversity of pre-modern economies must also be insisted upon in another form: the absolute distinction between industrial and agricultural sectors in the economy, which has become enshrined at the very centre of modern perceptions of economies and of the process of economic development, is not one which holds for 'pre-industrial' societies. It may be possible to distinguish periods and areas in the pre-modern world in which that distinction is greater than at others: it could, for instance be argued that the later Middle Ages saw a much greater distinction between agricultural and industrial sectors, whereas the early modern period – here as in so many other ways less 'modern' than what went before – saw a much greater blurring and confusion of the two. The fundamental principle, however, remains good whatever the fluctuations of the balance: industrial and agricultural sectors in pre-modern economies may be analytically separable; certainly in southern Europe and, it seems clear over most of the rest of Western Europe in the early modern period, such a distinction is not one which can be made in terms of either the perceptions or the strategies of most of the economically-active population. It is not, of course, only a distinction between agricultural and industrial which has to be treated with caution; the same holds good for 'commercial' and 'service' sectors. Equally, the lack of this type of distinction applies to most levels of society: it was not just a function of 'peasant' or 'poor' society, but affected individuals at all levels – 'professional' and 'gentry' as well as cultivators.

It must again be emphasized that this lack of specialization was not the consequence of some kind of backwardness or economic primitiveness – a lack of a realization of the inevitable benefits which would come from specialization and concentration. The early modern economy was, as is its post-industrial counterpart, essentially functional; it did not behave in 'peculiar' ways through some perversity but because, within the terms and conditions of survival and profit which existed, those 'peculiar ways' provided the most efficient return and the most effective ways of achieving the common economic and social good.

That goal was, for much of the population of Europe and for much of the period, to be conceived in terms of survival and, if possible moderate plenty, rather than in terms of growth. Survival could be better guaranteed by a spreading of risk than by chancing all on a single element, however potentially profitable. The main threats to survival were, it is easy to see, agricultural failure – drought, storm, low production – or industrial depression, and it is quite clear 'by-employment' in industry, commerce or service offered some assurance of at least partial safety from the most disastrous effects of these. The world of weekly wages and monthly salaries forgets, however, the problems not merely of the trade cycle but also of the cycle of the seasons and the crises that they present in any agricultural or agriculturally-based society.

One area of pre-modern social history about which little is known and little is likely to be known is the whole question of housekeeping and household management, above all in less prosperous households. Even a relatively widely literate society like that of pre-modern northern Italy has left very little by way of record as to the details of the way or ways in which individuals and families managed their 'finances' – in kind as well as in cash – on a day-to-day basis, through the year. What can be deduced is very limited and arises more from an analysis of potential sources of income than from any direct information on the details of the management of actual households. Day-to-day management of the household, as distinct from the larger-scale 'investment' decisions, seems to have been largely in the hands of women, above all of the senior woman in the household (senior in terms of status rather than necessarily age). The problems which such management present in a basically agricultural system were clear and considerable. In a household whose source of income was solely agriculture, that is to say which was in essence a subsistence household, the income and the food supply were effectively the same; income management meant food management – and failure meant starvation. It is in the nature of agriculture, pastoral as well as arable, that the income it produces – harvests – come at a limited number of points in time throughout the seasons; in a single crop, specialized economy that income comes only once a year. The first concern then of the housekeeper is to apportion that income over the inter-harvest gap so that in the final days before the next income – harvest – a year away, there will be sufficient food to keep the family alive. This problem, daunting enough in itself, is made more difficult by two further elements in the context: the first is the problem of storage and the difficulties of keeping food – particularly meat and dairy products but also grain – edible through the inter-harvest period. The second, even more tremendous, is the uncertainty and fickleness of harvests: not merely do harvests vary considerably in their production, so that the housekeeper cannot know what next year's harvest will bring and hence whether food has to be saved to bolster future under-production, but in addition, the dates of harvest fluctuate with the weather – the housekeeper can never know in advance just how long any single inter-harvest period will be. Similar patterns, albeit in slightly different forms, are encountered when the direct consumption of food produced is replaced by the expenditure of cash gained from the sale of a single crop.

One way of reducing these problems is, as has been indicated earlier, to replace a single crop with a series of crops with staggered harvests. Not merely does this reduce the danger of total crop failure and hence of total disaster, but in addition it also spreads the inflows of crops (or cash) across the year: by reducing the length of each inter-harvest period it also reduces the potential for disastrous shortfall. As has already been pointed out, the cultivators of the early modern Valpolicella did not rely on a single August harvest home but could rely on a series of harvests: wheat in early summer and in autumn; maize and millets and the vintage in Autumn; the olive crop in November–December, and so forth. This spread may well have been one of the major factors in the relative stability of their economy.

The principle of diversity of income and of employment, and its functional advantages were not, of course, limited to purely agricultural activities. If it made sense to spread risks between crops within one economic sector, it also made sense to spread risks between economic sectors, to find industrial, commercial or service sources of income to complement agricultural employment. Not merely did this diversification reduce dependence on the vagaries of the agricultural economy (and of course on the fluctuations of the industrial and commercial economies), but, and this was surely as important, upon the iron discipline of the cycle of the seasons. Indeed, by their very nature, these 'by-employments' were counter-cyclical to the seasonal cycle: the times of greatest income in the agricultural year were also the times of the greatest demand for labour and, therefore, it was likely that by-employment would be most active, and other forms of income greatest, at times when the agricultural cycle was at its quietest.

Lying as it did close to a major urban centre and a major urban centre which had been, and still to some extent was, a major industrial and commercial centre, the Valpolicella was peculiarly able to take up employment, both locally and in the city. Later sections of this chapter will also demonstrate that both resource endowment and physical position gave its inhabitants a range of potential by-employments which was greater than that available in other less-favoured regions. Although the Valpolicella does, perhaps, illustrate a particularly clearly developed form of this mixed and non-specialized early modern economy, it is clear that the principles upon which it seems to have rested were of much more universal applicability; all that the wide range of opportunities available in and around the Valpolicella did was to make its economy more secure and its society more resistant to crisis and disaster.

II

Probably the most important of the complementary employments was a subordinate of agriculture itself – paid agricultural labour. The corollary of the peak and slump demand for agricultural labour inherent in its seasonal patterns was, of course, that from time to time during the agricultural year there were major shortages of labour. Furthermore, the importance of estates owned by distant owners involved the employment of paid labour. The paid labourer – the *braccente* – was a common figure in every Valpolicella commune and in the economy of every Valpolicella estate.

The existence of the *braccenti* raises the whole question of the existence of a class of 'landless labourers' or of a rural proletariat, and the related issues of its size and fluctuations. In fact, the implications of the diversified economy and society make this issue, in a very real sense, relatively unimportant. 'Landlessness' was not necessarily a permanent state but could be, and frequently was, no more than a temporary stage in the domestic economy. Furthermore, since this was an economy in which land and the income from it were only one of a number of potential or actual elements in a total economic complex, its lack or otherwise was not necessarily a matter of serious concern. Certainly 'landlessness' and the status of landless labourers did not necessarily imply actual or relative poverty but merely one pattern or group of patterns in a range of potential survival strategies. The sharp social and economic distinction historians and others love to draw between the landed peasantry and the landless labourer does not seem to have operated in either economic or social terms in Valpolicella society during the early modern period. Individuals and families moved back and forth between the two categories with a regularity and a smoothness which belies any idea that this was a division which marks any really deep fissure in society. It may be – indeed it probably was – the case that particularly in the later eighteenth century the number of the landless rose as the dual pressures of growing population and the concentration of landownership increasingly pushed marginal landowners out of landownership, or into the halfway state of ownership of houses, or parts of houses; but it is only with hindsight that that fluctuation can be seen as being the beginning of a long-term revolution in society and economy rather than just another swing of a pendulum which would sooner or later be reversed. To the historian it may be a clear-cut social revolution, a clear-cut social and economic crisis, but, within the traditional fluidity of pre-modern Valpolicella society, it must have appeared as something much less catastrophic, certainly not as a cause, actual or potential, of social breakdown.

It is not merely the fluidity of society that makes the distinctions between landed and landless, of 'peasant' and 'labourer' an unnecessarily sharp one, indeed an anachronism. The distinction can only be seen as crucial where land is the sole source of income, either of the landed or of the landless. In fact this is, for the Valpolicella and for many southern pre-modern economies, a gross distortion and over-simplification of a much more sophisticated system. Paid agricultural labour was not a monopoly of the landless or their families; such information as it is possible to extract on the identities of the *braccenti* and other wage labourers on – it is true – the larger estates of the Valpolicella indicates that the *braccente* may be landless, but he (or she) may also be a small or even a middling landowner: on the Dal Bene estate in Volargne in the 1770s, for instance, two of the five most frequently employed labourers had themselves small to medium holdings and at least two of the others were closely related to small landowners.[1] Nor was it the case that wage labour was associated with declining landowners: some *braccenti*-landowners do seem to drop out of landowning later in their lives but equally a number of *braccenti* do markedly increase their landowning. Even if the *braccente* was landless this does not, of course, exclude the possibility, indeed the likelihood, that he and his family would have further sources of income.

In general, agricultural wage-labour demand in the Valpolicella fluctuated with the seasons as, inevitably, it did throughout Europe – the highest demands for labour coming at sowing, harvest and vintage time. Here again the basic pattern was, or could be, modified by the great diversity of the economy. In the same way that the domestic economies of the lower levels of rural society were modified in the direction of diversity of activity, so too were those of the larger estates and for the same reasons. This had the effect of spreading demand for labour over a wide period of the year: the great traditional peaks of demand for labour, such as harvest, which in many parts of Europe produced labour shortages which could only be solved by large-scale seasonal migration of labour, were reduced, but to some extent at least the troughs of employment were also reduced by such activities as the cropping of woods or the collection of stones for lime-burning.

Despite this smoothing effect of diversification, agricultural labour was a fluctuating and uncertain form of employment. Even for those *braccenti* who were housed by estates, employment and payment was on a day-to-day basis rather than on any fixed form of payment.

Furthermore, by a tradition which continued until the end of the eighteenth century, the daily payments in the winter months (from
Martinmas to Easter) were lower (sixteen *soldi*) than in the summer
months (one *lira* a day), reflecting both the shorter day length and the
lower demand for labour in the winter. The dal Bene account books
allow, for a short period in the late 1770s at least, an indication of the
total employment an individual could expect and its distribution
through the year. This also allows a calculation of total income from
agricultural labour for a number of employees. It must be emphasized
that none of these employees was solely dependent upon their
payments from the dal Bene estate: some of them certainly also
worked for other estates and smaller landholders.[2] Some of them also
had land of their own. In addition, some forms of labour on the estate
were paid on a form of piece rate: wood collection was rewarded by
payment per hundred bundles; stone collection by payment per
basket, and so forth. At least two of the *braccenti* occupied estate
houses, albeit for a rent, and all received some payments and gifts in
kind.

Inevitably most information is available about the *braccenti* of the
larger estates: it must, however, be emphasized that it was not merely
the larger estates who employed *braccenti*, nor was it inevitable that
a *braccente* would work for a single employer, either throughout the
year or even during a single agricultural season. In the same way that
the Valpolicella had an active, fluid and socially undifferentiated land
market, so too it had an active and fluid labour market: the labourers
of the Valpolicella were not serfs nor indeed were they the wage-
slaves of single employers. Equally, the status of *braccente* was no
more exclusive than that of landowner or tenant, and hence *braccenti*
were able, possibly more able, to engage in by-employments. The
pattern of labour demand throughout the year made it possible to
combine wage labour at peak periods of the year with urban or other
outside employment.

If the idea of a specialized and separated group of landless labourers
must be abandoned so also must – at least without major emendation
– the idea of specialists within this group, dependent upon special
craft or agricultural skills. Undoubtedly there did exist a number of
specialist activities which, by their nature, did largely exclude their
practitioners from a full participation in the diverse economy. The
most obvious of these, in the Valpolicella as in other pre-modern
societies, were those involved with transhumant pastoralism. Drovers
and shepherds were, as their few surviving descendants are in the late
twentieth century, in a very real sense separated from the rest of
society. In particular, the need to take the flocks and herds onto high
pasturage for the summer and then down to the plains in the winter,
and the need to move constantly, gave to these pastoral domestic
economies a higher form of specialization than was necessary or

desirable in more settled households. The wandering drover or shepherd is a romantic as well as a mildly threatening figure in the traditions of the Valpolicella as elsewhere, but the picturesqueness and strangeness of these outsiders can very easily lead the historian astray. Even in the most pastoral regions of the Valpolicella, the high hills of Breonio or the valley scrubland of the *Campagna* in the commune of Pescantina, the great mass of families and households were not involved in large-scale or long-distance migration; the true transhumant shepherd was, then as now, a rarity and more likely to be based, if such a word can be used, in either the Alfaedo region or in the lowland regions where the sheep and cattle wintered.

Most agricultural specialisms did not involve any migration away from the home base and represented not a different exclusive employment, but rather a further addition to the range of opportunities which any individual who had them possessed. In fact, in the Valpolicella the potential for agricultural specialization was relatively limited. In contrast with the plains, for instance, the lighter soils and smaller fields of the Valpolicella meant that the demand for skilled ploughmen, able to operate the heavy ploughs and large ox teams which were needed in the plains, was much reduced. Indeed it seems to have been the case that ploughmen from the Valpolicella were in demand, as migrant workers, in the plains.

Some specialist agricultural occupations and skills did, however, exist. One example is the skills and knowledge which were necessary for the proper management and harvesting of wood. The combination of population growth, particularly in the major urban centres, and disafforestation had led to a major shortage of wood in the Veneto and indeed in the whole of northern Italy from the later Middle Ages. For the Venetian state the problem was in essence one of a shortage of timber for naval construction, a problem made worse by the gradual loss of the maritime empire in the eastern Mediterranean. The real problem was, however, a much more immediate one for most of the population: the shortage of wood meant not merely a shortage of building materials, although that could be serious, but more seriously still a shortage of fuel, since most house and commercial activities were fuelled either by wood or, less usually, by charcoal. From the fourteenth century at least, the supply of firewood to Verona had been of major concern and a source of major profit: the *Radiroli* – the shippers of wood (and other bulk goods) into the city – had become one of the wealthiest *Arte* of the city and from their numbers had sprung one of the major noble dynasties of the Veronese, the Bevilacqua.[3]

By the seventeenth and eighteenth centuries much of Verona's supply of wood came from beyond her territories, imported by river from the Trentino and beyond.[4] The Valpolicella did, however, retain some woods and hence some commercial interest in the trade, even though the major Veronese supply areas lay elsewhere, in particular on the slopes of the Val d'Adige. The Valpolicella supplies, lying chiefly in Monte, Cavalo, Mazzurega and to some extent Breonio, were relatively small and relatively difficult to exploit because of their distance from the major transport arteries and also because they were in rapid decline: the growing soil erosion which occurred in the later seventeenth century and even more drastically and dramatically in the eighteenth, was almost certainly a consequence in part of growing disafforestation.

The management of woodland and in particular of coppiced woodland – which most of the Valpolicella woodlands were – is a complex and specialized craft. Equally, the problems of extracting the cut wood from the forests, often over narrow and steep tracks, involved special skills. Hence the skilled *boscher* was a man in demand, and a man whose special skills could and did command special payment. Even here, however, it is clear that the *boscheri* did not constitute some kind of special and separate aristocracy of labour. Significantly, it is often difficult to identify *boscheri* with any amount of certainty; where they can be identified it is quite clear that they were not simply specialists relying on a single skill and activity to bring in their livelihood, but rather were full and active participants in the economy of diversification – owning land, working as unskilled *braccenti*, and also engaging in commercial and industrial activities.

Little is known about the ways in which *braccenti* were recruited. It is clear that some, particularly on the larger estates, occupied estate houses and, it must therefore be presumed, were regarded by the estate owner as being permanently available for labour. Most, however, lived in non-estate houses, either their own or rented from other villagers. How they were recruited, either by the large estates or by the lesser owners and tenants in the village, is largely unknown. It can safely be hazarded that in some cases kinship links, of blood or marriage, played a role, and certainly they seem to have been important in attracting individuals and families from neighbouring or more distant villages to migrate into Valpolicella communes, presumably in search of work.

III

Paid agricultural labour was, then, for many households – landed as well as landless – an important element in the household economy, not merely providing extra income but also reducing the riskiness of the situation by introducing a counterweight to the cycle of the seasons as well as to the longer-term agricultural cycle. Central to the whole system, however, is the premise that this was not merely an agricultural system, that the distinction between agricultural and non-agricultural employment, significant though it might be in theory, was in practice untenable.

The industrial decline of the cities of the Veneto, as in Lombardy, was not merely a decline in industrial production and its transfer to the countryside; it also marked important changes in the nature of industry and industrial employment.[5] The textile industries, which in Verona as elsewhere in the Veneto were the main industrial activity for much of the later Middle Ages, had developed on essentially modern lines, with specialist urban workers concentrating on industrial production, and organized into craft guilds which to some considerable extent owed their power and influence to their members' heavy dependence upon craft employment for their income. In many ways the cities of Renaissance Italy began to develop the sort of specialized labour force which is closely associated with industrialization. During the sixteenth and more particularly the seventeenth century, this modernizing pattern broke down; as industry moved out of the cities – and out of the control of the guilds – into the countryside, so the nature of the labour force changed, not merely in its location but also in its commitment to industry as a specialized employment. The process of the creation of a 'modern' working pattern and of an industrial labour force went sharply and clearly into reverse. The industrial worker became an agriculturalist with industrial interests, or, more truly, a multi-purpose, multi-functional worker with agricultural, industrial and other concerns.

Industrial and industry-related activities played a role in the economy of the seventeenth and eighteenth century Valpolicella just as they did in every region of the Veronese. Indeed it can fairly be said that one of the major elements in the prosperity of the region during this period, and one of the few factors which helped to carry it through the economic and agricultural catastrophes of the nineteenth century, was the existence of an industry-related sector. Again it must be made clear that it was not a single industrial activity but rather a series; if individuals and households did not specialize neither did regions, at least not to the extent that the operation of the law of comparative advantage would imply. The inhabitants of the Valpolicella had a range of varied opportunities and they made the most of the range; a single-industry economy is just as vulnerable as a single crop one.

Unusually, the prime industrial activity of the Valpolicella during the seventeenth and eighteenth centuries was not the spinning and weaving of textiles, transferred from the city. The industrial crisis of Verona in the sixteenth century had been a double one. As elsewhere, guild and state regulation and rising costs had driven the traditional woollen industry out of the city: in fact, those regulations and the pattern of taxation drove textile production not merely out of the city but also out of the Territorio, to Mantua and above all to the towns of the Trentino, in particular Ala and Rovereto. Related to this was a shift from wool to silk as the major textile industry of the region.[6]

By the 1630s silk had replaced wool as the region's major export. Here again the major centres of finishing lay, to the fury of the Venetian state, beyond her borders, in the Trentino towns in particular, to which large numbers of craftsmen migrated and to which large supplies of raw silk were illegally exported.

It was the production of raw silk, the rearing of silkworms and, to some extent, the reeling of the threads from the cocoons that constituted the most general industrial activity of the Valpolicella. The history of raw silk production is closely linked with the decline of wool production and the replacement of spinning, in particular. Unlike wool-spinning, however, raw silk production was a widespread activity, both geographically and, more significantly, socially. Despite its nineteenth century association in the Valpolicella with poverty, silk production in the seventeenth and eighteenth centuries was an occupation of a very wide range of households from the very poorest to those noble households and estates where the servants produced silk on behalf of their employers. The nobility and the greater estate-holders were also involved in silk production in that the estates frequently acted as bulkers and wholesalers for the produce of their tenants, and indeed of the small independent holders, and also as providers through the *soceda* system of the eggs (*semenza*) which were the necessary raw material of the trade.

Silk production had a large number of advantages for the agriculturalist. The initial cost of production was small: the eggs and the racks (usually home-made) on which the worms were placed to feed and grow. The food for the worms – mulberry leaves – could either be grown (and the surplus sold) or purchased: the feeding pattern meant that relatively small amounts of leaves were purchased over a period of time, rather than one major investment at one point. The larger producers, however, frequently and increasingly bought up or rented the entire leaf production of a number of trees for a lump sum at the beginning of the season. The equipment necessary to remove the silk from the cocoons was simple and inexpensive, until the development in the middle and later eighteenth century of mechanized systems using water power. The silk production period – late March to early to mid-May – covered a relatively dead period in the agricultural calendar, and produced a form of income at a period when other sources were few and when the income from earlier harvests was approaching its end.

It must again be emphasized that the production of silk cloth was not carried on in the rural Valpolicella, but only the production of the raw material. Furthermore, the weaving took place, very largely, outside not merely the Valpolicella but also the Veronese. Ala, and above all Rovereto in the territory of the Prince-Bishop of Trento were, for much of the early modern period, the major consumers of Valpolicella silk. In passing it is worth pointing out that the smuggling of silk to the Trentino, either up the Adige Valley or over the high passes of the northern Lessini, in particular the Rocca Pia, provided another valuable source of supplementary income, particularly for the people of the higher communes and of Alfaedo.

Silk production could be carried on everywhere, both geographically and socially; that was its strength and indeed its importance. That the income from silk production was important is clear, if from no other evidence than from the difficulties which its decline in the nineteenth century produced for an increasingly impoverished rural economy. The narrowing of opportunities in the nineteenth century affected industrial as well as agricultural employment.

If silk production was general, the Valpolicella had other industries and other industrial employments, albeit ones not as widespread nor as generally significant. After its wines, the fame of the Valpolicella came, in the early modern period as today, from its stone and above all from its marbles. The pink *rosso ammonitico* of S. Ambrogio was used for building and for paving in Verona and in Venice: its fame spread beyond the Veneto, to Germany and to France, and the transport of stone by raft and barge was one of the major trades of the Adige to and below Verona. The S. Ambrogio quarries were the most famous of the Valpolicella sources but there were also quarries in S. Giorgio, Fane, Torbe, Prun and a number of other communes.[7]

Surprisingly little is known of the stone trade and its workers in the early modern period or indeed in the Medieval period. Little indeed seems to be knowable about it: as with so much of the non-agricultural economy of the Valpolicella, stone cutting and the stone trade operated on a purely verbal basis or, more likely on the basis of written but unregistered contracts. Such information as is available is partial and indirect. To some extent this may be explained by the organization and structure of the quarries and their operation. Unlike the large-scale, semi-state organization of, for instance, the marble quarries at Carrara,[8] the Valpolicella quarries seem to have been small in scale, reflecting the nature of the marble beds, and largely locally owned, as adjuncts to normal landownership. Even where, as in Volargne, quarries were in the hands of large estates, the quarries themselves were small and played a relatively small part in the estate economy.

Even in those communes, such as S. Ambrogio, where stone-working was important, there is a further difficulty. Veronese dialect makes no clear distinction between the stone cutter – the quarry worker – responsible for the extraction of the raw stone – and the carver and dresser of stone – the producer of the finished product, whether sculpture, tombstone or paving stone. For both of these very different occupations the word *tagliapietra* (more usually, particularly in the earlier part of the period *taliapreda*) is used, making clear distinctions impossible.

The occupational census of S. Ambrogio in the 1620s suggests that a fair proportion of the male population was employed in some kind of stone-cutting.[9] Stone-cutting was a skilled and at times dangerous occupation, involving the splitting of regular sized and shaped blocks of stone from the vein and its safe removal and transportation by horse, sledge or cart first to the road and then to the river. A skilled occupation but not, in general, a specialized or exclusive one. Both the S. Ambrogio evidence and such later evidence as is available, suggests that stone-cutters were normally agriculturalists, often landowners themselves, who worked in the quarries as a complement to their agricultural income. Stone-cutting was a seasonal activity, dependent upon the right weather conditions to split the rock and upon the right conditions to allow the stone to be transported. For those with the skills to be involved in it, the stone trade again provided a useful and profitable adjunct to their other sources of income.

More is known about another stone-based industry – the burning of stone for lime. There was a continuous and growing demand throughout the early modern period for lime: for mortar, for plaster, for rendering and many other uses. The limestone of the Valpolicella was a perfect source for lime. The kilns (*fornasse*) were normally sited on or near the river bank, since it was by river that the great mass of the burnt and slaked lime was transferred to Verona and beyond. *Fornasse* were usually the property of the relatively well-to-do; many of the noble estates bordering on the Adige had their own *fornasse*, and lime kilns and their exploitation, coupled with building and owning the boats in which the lime was shipped, played an important part in the growing wealth and significance of, for instance, the Bonvicini family of Pescantina.

The operation of the *fornasse* was a skilled and specialist task. The *fornassa*, however, required two forms of raw material: wood to provide the heat and the stones themselves – the raw material of the lime. Both required collection and transportation, and both therefore provided a further complementary element in the economy. Stone collection could be done at almost any time in the year, particularly since the transportation was largely done in baskets by hand rather than by wheeled transport. On the large estates estate workers were often set on this task, but both the dal Bene[10] and Bonvicini[11] accounts indicate that numbers of casual workers were taken on, particularly in the weeks and days before the burning of the kiln. The smaller kilns seem to have depended very largely upon more casual labour. Here again, although it is as always, very difficult to be precise, it does not seem to have been the case that 'stone-picking' and poverty went together. As far as it is possible to determine the identity of the casual workers involved, there does not seem to be any suggestion that it was only the landless or the poor who sought or accepted this form of employment: small and even medium landowners and their families appear, along with the landless and craftsmen.

Two areas of industrial employment, one general, one relatively localized, have been discussed here. They do not, by any means exhaust the possibilities and the range of industrial employment available in the early modern Valpolicella. They do, however, illustrate the importance of industrial employment within this 'agricultural system' and the reasons why the movement of industry into the countryside was so significant. Not merely did industry provide additional income, but it also provided an income which could help to fill in the income-less periods of the year and which might also, on occasions at least, provide a counterweight to the fluctuations of the agricultural cycle. This was a complementary form of income too: not merely did industrial employment help out a fluctuating agricultural income, but the reverse was also true – that agricultural income helped protect the 'industrial worker' from the problems generated by the fluctuations in trade and demand which certainly did not begin with the Industrial Revolution and the Trade Cycle. In such a system and in such a context 'industrialization' and 'specialization', far from being a strengthening of the economy, an improvement in the position of the individual or household, constituted a severe weakening.

IV

Industry and industrial employment were not the only forms of diversification and of complementary income possible in this system. This was not in any way a simple subsistence economy largely dependent upon primary production, with a small exchange sector. As always it is easy to fall into the error of believing that a tertiary sector in the economy is a late development. The economy of the early modern Valpolicella was one in which commerce and tertiary employment played a major role, and in which individuals and households could and did complement their income by engaging in trade or the provision of services.

The commercial and market structure of rural northern Italy, that is to say outside the larger cities, is relatively unknown. Until recently the very existence of a marketing structure outside the regulated city and town markets was virtually denied; the medieval communes were, in effect, believed to have concentrated commercial power and control so firmly in their own hands that markets and, indeed, commercial structures elsewhere were destroyed. It is clear that, although the city markets and city services did distort the commercial structure and commercial development of the areas around them, and in particular of areas like the Valpolicella which lay close to the city, nonetheless a local marketing structure did develop and survive even in a region like the Valpolicella.

Two elements of that structure can be identified. The history of the periodic markets of the Valpolicella is little known and even less studied. A number of centres – Pescantina, Negrar, Fumane, for instance – held weekly or bi-weekly markets; some of the smaller centres may well have held unofficial markets on a weekly or monthly basis. The trade of these periodic markets seems to have been limited to the exchange of local production and to a 'mountebank' trade, provided either by city traders or by itinerants from elsewhere in the Veronese or from beyond its borders. Most market trade, particularly from the closer regions of the Valpolicella seems, however, to have passed through the markets of Verona, either the controlled markets within the city or the uncontrolled and nominally illegal ones in the suburbs, such as the one at the Porta S. Giorgio on the road to the Valpolicella.

In terms of complementary income, markets as such were relatively insignificant. Much more important was the growing permanent commercial sector, the development that is of shops open on a more or less regular basis in the small towns and villages of the Valpolicella. Here again evidence is patchy, scarce and biased towards certain types of enterprise. The *Estimi* list, albeit in a rather haphazard sort of way, shops and shopkeepers; *Patrimonio* provides, for the families of potential ordinands, some indication of the commercial and craft sources of income. The vicars and their deputies were charged, as one of their duties, with controlling weights, measures and qualities in certain types of shop: in fact they seem to have concentrated on inns, wine shops and bakeries. All these sources point clearly, however, to the existence of a wide range of commercial operations working on a permanent basis in most villages: they also point to an increase in the number of these outlets, particularly in the eighteenth century.

Many of the shops, it is true, were relatively specialized and involved a certain element of capital investment: bakeries, mills and inns for instance. What, however, is striking is the growing number of what can only be described as village general stores, selling fats, wine, salt, flour and a range of other goods. In most cases the shop premises seem to have been converted parts of village houses; the shopkeepers were villagers seeking a complementary income. There is, perhaps, a tendency for shopkeepers to be widows, but that should not conceal the fact that in most cases they were members of relatively prosperous village families, obviously seeking yet another complementary source of income.

As with industrial employment, commercial and service employment could be both specialized and general. The small shopkeepers of the villages represent one end of this spectrum, while at the other are to be found specialist service practitioners such as the *Parons* of

Pescantina.[12] The *Parons* (the dialect word, which is the same as the French *patron*, can best be translated as 'skipper') were the most specialized and the most exclusive of all the service-sector workers of the Valpolicella, specializing in river navigation and transport. The Adige was the main internal artery of the Veronese as well as its major export route; in the seventeenth and eighteenth centuries it was navigable by both boat and raft for the whole of its course in the Veronese except at the time of the autumn and spring low waters. Boat, as distinct from raft, navigation was a very skilled and specialized craft and one upon which the economic prosperity of the city of Verona depended. The control of river navigation had, by the seventeenth century, come in theory to be the monopoly of two local guilds of sailors: the *Arte* of the *Burchieri* of Pescantina which had established and defended a monopoly of navigation on the river above Verona[13] and its sister *Arte* of *Burchieri* at Zevio which effectively controlled the navigation of the lower river. Strikingly, and despite an almost continuous series of law suits, river navigation was only indirectly controlled by Verona and its council.

The group of the *Parons* of Pescantina who, particularly in the seventeenth and early eighteenth centuries, constituted perhaps the major element in the society and economy of their home town was, like most of the guild-crafts, essentially closed by the statutory requirements of the *Arte*. Furthermore, river navigation was an expensive business. The boats used were small and light, but their initial cost was high and their construction a skilled affair. Few *Parons*, if any, built their own boats but bought them from specialized builders, in particular in the seventeenth century from the Bonvicini family who controlled the major boatyard in Pescantina, and who were willing and able to sell boats to *Parons* on credit in return for a share of their profits. Boats seem to have been used and repaired over long periods. The current of the Adige, particularly in times of spate, is strong and hence some form of traction was necessary to allow the boats to move upstream; this traction was normally provided by horses, two to each boat, which pulled the boat upstream and then either sailed or walked downstream. Draught horses were expensive and hence the capital cost of river trade was high, which of course was one reason why involvement in it tended to be hereditary.

If any sector of the Valpolicella economy, and any group within it, was to be exclusive and specialized, surely the *Parons* should have been it. Both skill and the cost of entry to and survival in their craft argue for specialization. It is an indication of the all-pervading nature of the diversified economy that there is little to suggest that the *Parons* were navigators pure and simple. It goes without saying that the *Parons* had to be landowners to some extent, if only to provide their horses with grazing, but in fact it is clear that they were also agriculturalists and landowners on some scale; indeed one possible explanation of their decline in the eighteenth century may well be the gradual transfer of more and more *Paron* wealth into landholding.[14]

Even the most skilled and specialized of all the service crafts then were involved in landowning, in a diversification of their economy. The same holds true of the whole range of service crafts: millers, smiths, bakers, for instance. Virtually all of them diversified their service income with agriculture in its many forms or, to put it the other way around, were agriculturalists who complemented their agricultural income with service and industrial employment.

V

The greatest diversification was offered by Verona and its employment opportunities. It would be totally impossible to write a social or economic history of the Valpolicella without considering the city and its relationship to the rural system. Despite Italy's high level of urbanization in the seventeenth and eighteenth centuries, there was no clearer distinction between rural and urban than there was in any part of Europe. Trade, finance, culture and above all people flowed constantly to and fro between city and countryside; in the same way that the distinction between agricultural and industrial was not an absolute one, but rather a question of degree, so too the distinction between rural and urban was a relative one.

The influence of the city could be felt in a wide range of ways. For much of the Valpolicella, for instance, Verona constituted the major market, both as a consumer of local production and also as the central place in which goods were exchanged and imports obtained. The survival of local markets in the Valpolicella and the growing importance of permanently established village shops did little to reduce Verona's importance. It was still to Verona that most people from the Valpolicella came for their larger purchases of goods somewhat out of the ordinary. Verona was also the major administrative centre, the seat of the major law courts and the centre of most services: it was to Verona that people from the Valpolicella came to seek an advocate or a doctor and, although by the eighteenth century many of the communes had their resident notaries, it was still to Verona that most people went for notarial services.

The role of the city was, however, greater than purely that of an administrative, commercial and service centre as far as the Valpolicella was concerned. Even after its great decline in the early seventeenth century Verona still offered a wide range of employment possibilities and a wide range of ways in which a family's economy could be diversified. As with all pre-modern cities, Verona relied on immigration to maintain its population levels. All attempts to calculate a rate of migration between the Valpolicella and Verona have failed: the records are simply not sufficient or sufficiently clear to allow any really clear answer. It is undoubtedly the case, on the basis of purely impressionistic evidence, that large numbers of men and women from the Valpolicella migrated into Verona. It is equally clear that their periods of migration varied very sharply: indeed it is possible to point to what were effectively commuter workers from the Valpolicella communes nearest to the city who migrated into the city on a daily or almost daily basis in search of employment, largely unskilled. Most migrants seem to have stayed on a longer-term basis, however, although many of them returned to their home communes (and to their agricultural activities) both regularly and frequently. Some stayed much longer and established themselves on a more permanent basis.

It is certainly possible, on the basis of the *Anagrafie*, the periodic censuses of the city population, to identify clusters of Valpolicella settlers in the city.[15] As in many other towns, migrants tended to congregate in areas of the city where there were already people from their home villages or home areas, in whose houses they could find lodging and, on occasion, work. In Verona there appear to have been concentrations of Valpolicella settlers in the *contrade* of S. Steffano, Ponte Pietra and, to a lesser extent, S. Lorenzo – areas geographically close to the likely first point of entry of the settlers into the city, although this may be no more than coincidence. There were also smaller concentrations of Valpolicella settlers around the city palaces of the noble families who had land in the Valpolicella and who, it may be guessed, brought workers from their estates into the city to work in the *palazzi*.

Urban employment, either short or medium term, was obviously a further element in the diversification of rural household economies: one or more members of the household could seek city employment to complement the agricultural or industrial income of themselves or of other members of the household. The Valpolicella's geographical position, close to the city and with great ease of access, obviously gave it major advantages in this respect. It would be wrong, again, to see this seeking of urban employment as being either a breakdown of the rural system, of the destructive effects of urban development and growth upon a rural system, or as a sign of the poverty or desperation of a rural labour force compelled to pillage an urban economy which was by its nature inimical and alien. Equally it seems wrong to characterize the urban economy and the rural economy as being in some sense parasitic on each other; rather they were, and clearly were in the seventeenth and eighteenth centuries, integrated and complementary.

The integration of urban employment into rural economies was not simply a matter for the poorer sectors of rural society. Many of the village-leader families discussed earlier established what can best be called city branches – sons (and daughters) established in the city in urban functions, as merchants, notaries or other professions, and providing both an urban base and also potential urban income for the wider family. Unfortunately there is at present very little evidence which permits any form of penetration of the internal organization of these middle-ranking families, but there is some evidence which points to what can best be called a loose joint family structure in which several branches of a family, a group of brothers for instance, effectively divided a diversified family economy amongst themselves – one becoming the 'farm manager', one heading the family's urban activities, one possibly engaging in a learned employment like notarial work, one going into the church and so forth – producing as it were, a family conglomerate, like all conglomerates offering a range of possibilities for income and profit, and, more significantly, a range of protection against crisis in any one area.

VI

The aim of this chapter has not been to provide a complete and comprehensive picture of the commercial and industrial economy of the Valpolicella, which would take far more space than is here available, but merely to illustrate the ways in which that economy fitted into and complemented the agricultural economy which has traditionally been seen as the basic economy to which all the others were subservient. In fact the idea of a subservient economy, although it fits well with the modern concern with specialization, distorts the structure and the organization of the pre-modern economy. This was an economy in which all the parts have to be seen fitting together on an equal basis rather than as a central activity and subservient ones.

Above all, the basis of the economy lay in the avoidance of risk and the avoidance of over-commitment; it was not in any sense a specialized economy nor one which was, in modern terms, capable of immense development through concentration on a single activity. The great difference between modern and pre-modern economic perception lies, surely, in this differing view of specialization: specialization in the early modern period, as the experience of the specialized grain economy of northern France, for instance, demonstrated, was not a good thing but very much a bad one. Specialized economies, economies which in modern terms were 'progressive' or 'developing' were lunatic and, at an individual as well as at a regional level, to be avoided as far as possible. The most successful of the economies of the early modern period, such as the Valpolicella economy, were those which most minimized risk and, therefore, increased security, stability and ultimately, survival; they were, therefore, in modern terms, the less successful, the most conservative, the most resistant to change. Perhaps, then, the great changes which came over the economy of north-western Europe in the period from the mid-seventeenth to the later nineteenth centuries were not a measure of their success but of their failure to match up to the brilliant flexibility and adaptability of economies such as that of northern Italy.

8
Conclusion: the decline of the system

The system which has been described in this study was, in many ways, beautifully adapted and tuned to deal with the specific problems it faced. Having said that, it must be made clear that this created no economic or social Utopia. The system reduced the chances of major crisis, for the whole economy and for individuals, but it did not, and could not, totally remove it. Equally, although it could guarantee stability and reasonable prosperity, it was, by its very nature, incapable of creating the great quantum leaps in prosperity which were created by industrialization. Furthermore, the survival of the system depended upon a series of conditions which were not necessarily permanent and which, in particular, could not survive the development of and competition from more specialized economies elsewhere.

In the seventeenth and eighteenth centuries this system produced a high level of prosperity for the Valpolicella but, in the early to mid-nineteenth century that prosperity had collapsed and by the late nineteenth century the Valpolicella, along with most of the rest of the Veneto, presented a horrifying picture of profound rural poverty, only less bad than the poverty of the Italian south. What had gone wrong?

In part that decline can be explained in terms of the traditional sorts of economic movement. The rapid growth of population in the eighteenth century inevitably had its penalties; greater population pressure undoubtedly meant that a resource pool which was growing more slowly than population was spread more thinly and that, therefore, the margin between survival and catastrophe became narrower, as the subsistence crises of the late eighteenth century so sharply demonstrated. The growing problems of soil erosion and soil exhaustion, related in part to deforestation, which had been obvious from the early eighteenth century if not before, added to the precarious state of agriculture as did the decline in the number of animals consequent upon more concentrated land use.

Political change and warfare also took their toll. Along with the rest of the Veronese, the Valpolicella shuttled backwards and forwards between Austrian and French control following the extinction of the Republic in 1797, only to settle finally into Austrian control in 1814. Political and institutional change meant not merely that the external structures of the society and the economy were shaken, but also that production and marketing were disrupted. Furthermore, new political structures meant new, and higher taxes, and less freedom of activity. The brief, false dawn of agricultural revival under the Napoleonic Kingdom of Italy was brought catastrophically to an end by the famine and inflation of 1815–16 from which the Valpolicella – and indeed the rest of the Veronese – never fully recovered. Instead of the stability and resilience in the face of crisis which had characterized the eighteenth century economy, that of the nineteenth century showed little if any ability to recover. When from the mid-century onwards, agricultural depression coupled with the economic disasters related to the Unification of Italy, hit the north Italian economy, its only reaction was deeper ammiseration and emigration.

The real problem of explanation is not, in fact, the explanation of decline or the explanation of the sort of crises which the economy faced, but rather the explanation of the loss of resilience, the loss of the ability to respond to crisis in any other way than to collapse. Why did an economy and a society which previously had been able to deal relatively effectively with social and economic crises every bit as deep as those of the nineteenth century, of a scale and a nature sufficiently great to have overwhelmed more modern and progressive societies, suddenly, become apparently unable to cope?

The answer, as this study has attempted to demonstrate, lies in the nature of the pre-modern Valpolicella and the mechanisms it was able to adopt to deal with problems. Those solutions, the reverse of the modern economist's theoretical prescriptions for success, lay above all in a widely diversified and non-specialized economy. But this solution was dependent upon the availability and profitability of a wide range of possible sources of income and profit in the countryside. In crude terms, the decline of economies like that of the Valpolicella came as a result of the decline and final disappearance of all but a few of such possible sources.

It is only at this point that the conflict between the specialized and the diversified, which in a sense is the fundamental conflict between the industrial world and its predecessors, comes fully into play. In dramatic terms, this was the conflict between a thrusting 'enterprise economy' based upon risk-taking and change and a much more staid, risk-avoiding economy, seeking in diversification a stability and security which, certainly to begin with, the new economy could not provide. Conflict it certainly was and, in the end, one which – for good or evil – the old economy lost. In particular, the law of comparative advantage finally drove out of profitability most of the complementary sources of income which had been available, and placed a growing premium on specialization in both production and employment. For the overall world economy, or indeed for the European economy as a whole, this was progress, but for individual families in areas like the Valpolicella it marked the greatest economic catastrophe of their history. No longer did they have a balanced and a mixed economy in which, in past time, many had been able to prosper: significantly it was in the urban 'modernized' sector rather than in the increasingly depressed and socially despised rural sector that new families, new clans of wealth and influence, developed in nineteenth and twentieth century Italy.

The early modern Valpolicella was no Utopia, nor was it a model to be held up as a solution to the problems of the post-industrial world. Its people were moderately prosperous, more so perhaps than many other people in pre-modern Europe, and certainly far more prosperous than their descendants in the nineteenth and early twentieth centuries. Their lives were, nonetheless, despite the stabilizing effects of the system which has been described here, lived always at the psychological, if not the physical, edge of catastrophe. They were not creating some neat academic system within a given framework but rather were fighting a constant and desperate battle for survival – a struggle in which, in the last resort, the penalty for failure was destitution and annihilation. It is from that very present fear that industrialization has saved the developed world and that, rather than technological change or even improvement in living standards, is its chief contribution to the human good.

Notes

Abbreviations

The following abbreviations are used throughout.

ASVE   Archivio di Stato, Venezia
ASVR   Archivio di Stato, Verona
ASCVVR   Archivio Storico della Curia Vescovile di Verona
AEP   Antichi Estimi Provvisori
SFM   S. Fermo Maggiore
VVP   Atti dei Vicari della Valpolicella
SMC   S. Michele in Campagna
PE   Patrimonium Ecclesiasticorum

1. Introduction

1. F. Braudel, *The Mediterranean and the Mediterranean World in the Age of Philip II* (tr.) S. Reynolds, 2 vols (London: 1972), pp. 91-4, 98-101.
2. W. W. Rostow, *The Stages of Economic Growth: a Non-Communist Manifesto*, 2nd edition (Cambridge: 1971).
3. Frederic C. Lane, *Venice, A Maritime Republic* (Baltimore and London: 1973), pp. 285-94.
4. The 'decline' is well summed up in Stuart Woolf, *A History of Italy 1700-1860: The Social Constraints of Political Change* (London: 1979), pp. 13-26.
5. For seventeenth and eighteenth century Venice see Lane *op.cit.* pp. 423-36.
6. The complex and difficult literature on this period is discussed in: James S. Grubb, 'When Myths lose power: four decades of Venetian Historiography', *Journal of Modern History*, 58 (1986), pp. 43-94.

2. Verona, the Veronese and the Valpolicella

1. M. Braubach, *Prinz Eugen von Savoyen*, Band I (Munchen: 1963), pp. 318-20.
2. D. G. Chandler, *The Campaigns of Napoleon* (London: 1967), pp. 53-131.
3. See G. M. Varanini, *Il Distretto Veronese nel Quattrocento: Vicariati del Comune di Verona e Vicariati Privati* (Verona: 1980).
4. E. Turri, *Dietro il Paessagio: Caprino e il Monte Baldo; ricerche su un territorio comunale* (Verona: 1982).
5. For instance Erbe: ASVR, AEP, Reg 446-7.

6. G. F. Viviani, *Ville della Valpolicella* (Verona: 1974).
7. G. M. Varanini (ed.), *La Valpolicella dal Duecento al Quattrocento* (Verona: 1985).
8. The Veronese legal system has been little studied; see F. Vecchiato, 'Problemi del'ordinamento guidiziario a Verona in Epoca Veneta', in *Studi Storici Veronesi Luigi Simeoni*, xxx-xxxi (1980-1), pp. 1-37.
9. On the Vicarate of the Mountains see *Capitoli per il buon governo delli tredici communi della Montagna* (Verona: 1724), reprinted in *Taucias Gareida*, 32 (1977), pp. 5-15 and Varanini, *Il Distretto Veronese . . .*, pp. 86-7.
10. See F. Carcereri, 'L'amministrazione della Valpolicella attraverso documenti a stampa di epoca veneta', in *Annuario Storico della Valpolicella* (1982-3), pp. 127-48.
11. Some indication of these activities can be found in ASVR, VVP, *passim*.
12. See, for instance, ASVR, AEP, Reg 591.
13. Benedetto dal Bene, *Giornale di Memorie* (1770-1796) (ed.) Giuseppe Biadego (Verona: 1883) and ASVR, dal Bene, Reg 109.
14. On the Casa della Valpolicella see: Varanini, *La Valpolicella dal Duecento al Quattrocento*, p. 105 and E. S. Righi, 'Iscrizioni relative alli antichi vicari della Valpolicella esistente nella residenza municipale di S. Pietro in Cariano', in *Archivio Storico Veronese*, I (1879), pp. 302-9.
15. On this see: ASVR, SFM, Processo 640.
16. See below pp. 59-60.
17. See for instance ASVR, AEP, Reg 339.
18. See N. W. Simmonds (ed.), *Evolution of Crop Plants* (London: 1976), pp. 108-11.
19. See James Casey, 'Spain: a failed transition', in P. Clark (ed.), *The European Crisis of the 1590s: Essays in Comparative History* (London: 1985), pp. 209-28.
20. See Lamberto Paronetto, *Valpolicella Splendida Contea del Vino* (Verona: 1981).
21. G. F. Viviani, *op.cit.*
22. ASVR, VVP, Reg 279: 31/8/1694.
23. ASVR, VVP, Reg 317: 5/11/1778.
24. M. Lecce, 'Le condizioni zoo-tecnico-agricola del territorio Veronese nella prima meta del '500'', *Economia e Storia*, I (1958).
25. ASVR, VVP, Reg 276, 14/1/1690.
26. ASVR, dal Bene, Reg 110.
27. ASVR, VVP, 277, 27/4/1691.
28. Recipes for salting pork and for making salami can be found in a number of monastic account books, for instance ASVR, S. Spirito, 29.
29. ASVR, AEP, Reg 609.
30. ASVR, AEP, Reg 596-7.
31. See Chapter 7.
32. M. Elvin, *The Pattern of the Chinese Past* (London: 1973), pp. 298-316.
33. G. Sancassani, *L'Archivio di Stato di Verona: gli Archivi Veronesi dal Medioevo ai giorni nostri* (Verona: 1961).
34. ASVR now holds catalogues of some, but not all, Valpolicella communal archives; in most little more than a single page is devoted to pre-nineteenth century records.
35. The dal Bene Archive is now in ASVR, the Sagramoso and Rizzardi archives are still in private hands.

3. The performance of the economy

1. The *Relazioni* are preserved in ASVE, Collegio V (Secreta); the relevant Veronese buste are 32 and 50. The Relazioni have been edited and published under the general editorship of Amelio Tagliaferri : A. Tagliaferri (ed.), *Relazioni dei Rettore Veneti in Terraferma: IX Podesteria e Capitanato di Verona* (Milano: 1977).
2. On the early history of the Ufficio di Sanita see: G. Sancassani, 'Le lettere dell'Archivio della Sanita di Verona', in *Notizie degli Archivi di Stato*, VIII, 2-3, 1948.
3. ASVE, Collegio V (Secreta), B.50, Michiel Priuli, 1626.
4. ASVR, AEP, Reg 545.
5. ASVR, AEP, Reg 609.
6. ASVR, Sanita, Reg 191.
7. ASVE, Collegio V (Secreta), Bragadino, 1627.
8. Ibid., Valier, 1639.
9. ASVR, SFM, Processo 441.
10. ASVR, SFM, Reg 118.
11. ASVR, SFM, Reg 124.
12. ASVR, SFM, Processo 593.
13. E. Le Roy Ladurie and J. Goy, *Tithe and Agrarian History from the Fourteenth to the Nineteenth Centuries: An Essay in Comparative History* (tr.) S. Burke (Cambridge: 1982).
14. ASCVVR, Pievi, S. Giorgio, Scritture Varie.
15. Ibid., Stampe: RR. Chierichi contra Avanzi ad laudem.
16. On the Fonte see F. Vecchiato, *Pane e Politica Annonaria in Terraferma Veneta tra secolo XV e secolo XVIII: Il caso di Verona* (Verona: 1966).
17. On Legnago see: C. Boscagin, *Storia di Legnago* (Verona: 1966).
18. E. Le Roy Ladurie, *Les Paysans de Languedoc*, 2 vols (Paris: 1966); Henry Kamen, *Spain in the Late Seventeenth Century* (London and New York: 1980); and Domenico Sella, *Crisis and Continuity: The Economy of Spanish Lombardy in the Seventeenth Century* (Cambridge and London: 1979).

4. The system of agricultural production

1. On the early history of the *Accademia* see: G. Sandri, 'L'Accademia di Agricoltura, Scienze e Lettere di Verona', in *Atti dell'Accademia di Agricoltura, Scienze e Lettere*, sV, XIII (1935).
2. Lorenzi's book has been recently republished in facsimile with an introduction by Gian-Paolo Marchi: abate Bartolomeo Lorenzi, *Della Coltivatione de'Monti*, Verona 1778 (reprinted Verona: 1971).
3. A leading role in the collection not merely of folk traditions and folk sayings but also of details of agricultural practices and methods has been played by Dino Coltro: for example his *Paese Perduto: la cultura dei Contadini Veneti*, 4 vols (Verona: 1975). Eugenio Turri, in his *Villa Veneta: conte, sior, paron, castaldo, lavorente, bacan: agonia del mondo mezzadrile e messagio neo-tecnico* (Verona: 1977) and elsewhere has also provided a series of interesting insights into the Valpolicella of the 1930s and 1940s.
4. See above p. 30.
5. ASVR, dal Bene, Reg 207, 221.
6. See Chapter 6.

7. 1628, 1633, 1639, 1652, 1671, 1691.
8. 1710, 1752, 1766 (partial).
9. On the reassessment of 1745 see: *Libro Preparatoria per l'Estimo Reale principiato ano 1728 e terminato 1745, Estratto delle Relazioni fatte de Proclami e Mandatti sopra la renovatione del Estimo Reale, 1732*, and *Preparatoria pro Aestimo praesenti et incipiendo 1732*, all in ASVR, AEP, Reg 1.
10. These 'forgotten' returns form the major part of the *Polizze Obliti*.
11. See below p. 150.
12. G. Borelli, *Un Patriziato della Terraferma Veneta: la Nobilta Veronese nel Sei- e Settecento* (Verona: 1972).
13. Sancassani, *op.cit.*
14. The category *Uffizi Veneti* in the index to the *Atti dei Rettori Veneti* in ASVR provides many examples of this.
15. On the history of the notarial archive in Verona see: G. Sancassani, *Documenti sul Notariato Veronese durante il Dominio Veneto* (Verona: n.d).
16. The cleric's annual income from his 1000 ducats would, of course, be larger than the *bracente*'s, because, as will be pointed out later (pp. 167–8) the *bracente* could only expect to be employed on half the days in the year.
17. A nominal catalogue of the *Patrimonio*, by year, indicating name of ordinand and place of origin (ed. Fr. M. Trivulzi, A. Brusco and P. J. Musgrave) is in the process of completion. The completed sections cover the periods 1569 (when the records begin) to 1720 and 1815–60 (when the Curia's own index begins). For the eighteenth century, as yet uncovered, a series of contemporary nominal indexes, which, however, do not indicate place of origin, allow some access.
18. For a more detailed discussion of the issues raised in this paragraph, see P. J. Musgrave, *The Social Origins of the Italian Clergy* (forthcoming).
19. See above, Chapter 2.
20. ASVE, Collegio V (Secreta), busta 50, Andrea Vendramin.
21. Lecce, see Note 24 to Chapter 2.
22. See: P. Laslett, *The World We Have Lost*, 2nd edition (Cambridge: 1971).
23. Marshall Sahlins, *Stone Age Economics* (Chicago: 1972).
24. W. W. Rostow, see Note 2 to Chapter 1.
25. See: E. Labrousse, P. Leon, P. Goubert, J. Bouvier, C. Carriere, P. Harsin, *Histoire Economique et Sociale de la France: Tome II: Des dernieres temps de l'age seigneurial aux preludes de l'age industriel (1660–1789)* (Paris: 1970), pp. 105–8.
26. For the sources of these figures see Table 6, Chapter 3, above.
27. For the S. Giorgio tithe returns see pp. 54–64 above.
28. Gianni Fae, *S. Giorgio di Valpolicella Ingannapoltron* (S. Giorgio Valpolicella: 1982), pp. 49–53: G. M. Cambie, 'La Festa de le Fae', in P. P. Brugnoli, *S. Giorgio di Valpolicella* (Verona: 1975).
29. ASVR, AEP (Polizze Citta, 1653), Reg 31, 402.
30. ASVR, AEP, Reg 123, p. 458 (Montenari).
31. ASVR, AEP (Polizze Citta, 1745), Reg 121, 28.
32. On Monte Baldo see: E. Turri, *Caprino e Monte Baldo . . .*; on the Vicarate of the Mountains see above p. 15.
33. ASVR, AEP, Reg 120 (Polizze Citta, 1745), 251.
34. On the Bevilacqua see: G. Sandri, *I Bevilacqua e il Commercio del Legname tra il Val di Fiemme e Verona nel secolo XIV* (Venezia: 1940).
35. On rice cultivation and technology see: M. Lecce, *La Coltura del Riso in Territorio Veronese (Sec XVI–XVIII)* (Verona: 1958).

36. See for instance ASVR, AEP, Reg 89, 429, polizza of Sinibaldo q Alessandro Sinibaldi.
37. ASVR, AEP (Polizze Citta), Reg 28, p. 380 (Maffei), p. 727 (Sbadacchia), Reg 46, p. 435 (Trivesol), Reg 49, p. 800 (Badili), Reg 52, p. 147 (dal Bene), ibid., p. 226 (Morando), Reg 53, p. 702 (Turcho), Reg 55, p. 557 (Sinibaldi), ibid., p. 645 (Capetti), ibid., p. 727 (Tomasini), Reg 82, p. 80 (Suttori), Reg 83, p. 602 (Manfredi), ibid., p. 929 (Badili), Reg 86, p. 211 (Morani), Reg 87, p. 547 (Rocco), ibid., p. 599 (Sartorari), ibid., p. 909 (Minali), Reg 89, p. 749 (Soardi), Reg 90, p. 266 (Sagramoso).
38. ASVR, AEP, Reg 120, p. 251.
39. ASVR, AEP, Reg 29, p. 427. For further information on the mills see: G. Borelli (ed.), *Una Citta e il suo Fiume: Verona e l'Adige*, 2 vols (Verona: 1977), and Dino Coltro, *L'Adige* (Verona: 1989). Specifically on the mills of the Valpolicella see: Pierpaolo Brugnoli and Giovanni Viviani (eds), *Invito a Molina* (Verona: 1982), pp. 34-7.
40. See p. 40 above.
41. See, for instance, ASVR, AEP, Reg 137, p. 202 (Ferrari).
42. ASCVVR, PE, 1603, Hierolamus Bennassuti.
43. Ibid.
44. ASCVVR, PE, 1605, Bernardinus Maragis.
45. ASCVVR, PE, 1603, Antonius de Vicis.
46. ASCVVR, PE, 1615, Augustinus de Zoccis.

5. Units of exploitation

1. ASVR, AEP, Reg 586 (Breonio).
2. ASVR, AEP, Reg 129, p. 644.
3. ASVR, dal Bene, Reg 100.
4. ASVR, dal Bene, Reg 207, 217, 221 for instance.
5. The volume of late seventeenth and eighteenth century Valpolicella contracts ('Scritti et Affitanze del Nob: Sig Co Ruffino Campagna et Scritti Lavorentie et Affittanze diverse di Val Policella') preserved as ASVR, Campagna, 1176, seems to have been intended as a pattern book for the instruction of the landlord.
6. See F. McArdle, *Altopascio: A Study in Tuscan Rural Society* (Cambridge: 1974).
7. See Stuart Woolf, 'The Economic Problems of the Nobility in the Early Modern Period: the example of Piedmont' in *Economic History Review*, 2nd series, XVII, 2 (1964) pp. 267-83.
8. For a detailed breakdown of the location of the lands of some of the major noble families see G. Borelli, *op.cit.*
9. See below pp. 145-7.
10. See for instance: ASVR, AEP, Reg 53, p. 664 (Barzisa), ASVR, AEP, Reg 121, p. 541 (Mosconi), ASVR, AEP, Reg 122, p. 179 (Ottolini), ASVR, AEP, Reg 86, p. 64 (Perez).
11. ASVR, AEP, Reg 53, p. 664 (Barzisa).
12. ASCVVR, PE, 1677, Francescus Carrara, ibid., 1685, Iohannes Quintarelli, ibid., 1689, Antonius de Muraris.
13. ASCVVR, PE, 1643, Antonius de Melchioris, ibid., 1691, Iohannes Baptista Scamperle (Fumane), ibid., 1692, Petrus Spadae (Maran), ibid., 1683, Franciscus Barbieri, ibid., 1695, Petrus de Bacillieris (Breonio).
14. See ASVR, AEP, Reg 117, p. 600. (Fontana).
15. ASVR, AEP, Reg 121, p. 541.

16. For example the estates of Ottolino Ottolini in Bure: ASVR, AEP, Reg 122, p. 190.
17. See, for example, the Polizza of Giovanni Battista Salvi: ASVR, AEP, Reg 117, p. 624.
18. ASVR, SFM, Reg 252.
19. See for instance the possessions of Francesco Sacchetti in Negarine, where two plough teams seem to have been usual: ASVR, AEP, Reg 130, p. 204.
20. ASVR, AEP, Reg 134, p. 209.
21. ASVR, AEP, Reg 138 (Polizze Obliti 1745), p. 881.
22. ASVR, AEP, Reg 121, p. 572.
23. G. F. Viviani, *op.cit.*
24. See Chapter 6.
25. ASVR, AEP, Reg 123, p. 271.
26. ASVR, AEP, Reg 124, p. 198.
27. ASVR, AEP, Reg 28, p. 53 (Betteloni), p. 364 (Spolverini), p. 380 (Maffei), p. 458 (Cavalli), p. 487 (da Monte), ibid., Reg 29, p. 148 (Fioravanti), ibid., Reg 31, p. 451 (Campeti), ibid., Reg 32, p. 39 (Parma), p. 222 (Rambaldi).
28. ASVR, AEP, Reg 82, p. 166.
29. ASVR, AEP, Reg 84, p. 58.
30. ASVR, AEP, Reg 83, p. 572.
31. ASVR, AEP, Reg 87, p. 666.
32. ASVR, AEP, Reg 83, p. 598.
33. ASVR, AEP, Reg 47, p. 552.
34. ASVR, AEP, Reg 46, p. 334.
35. See pp. 47–8.
36. ASCVVR, PE, 1659, Jacobus Dusi, 1677, Francescus Conati, 1679, Antonius Peroni, 1683, Iohannes Bustaglio, 1685, Iohannes Quintarelli, 1686, Thaddeus Pigari.
37. ASCVVR, PE, 1675, Bartolomeus Moraia.
38. ASCVVR, PE, 1690, Francescus Faciotti.
39. See Varanini *La Valpolicella tra '200 e '400*, pp. 180–204.
40. P. J. Jones, 'La Storia Economica', in *Storia d'Italia: dalla Caduta del Impero Romano al Secolo XVIII* (Torino: 1974).
41. ASVR, AEP, Reg 91, p. 889 (Facolta Olivieri).
42. ASVR, AEP, Reg 28, p. 380 (Maffei).
43. ASVR, AEP, Reg 87, p. 599.
44. ASVR, AEP, Reg 121, p. 467.
45. ASVR, AEP, Reg 466–7 (Erbe), 502 (Villa Bartolomea).
46. See G. M. Varanini, *Il Distretto Veronese*, p. 171.
47. The only 'bourgeois' records which deal with the Valpolicella which seem to have survived are the Alessandri and Bonvicini papers, both now in ASVR. Unfortunately, they are only indirectly concerned with the management of land, and both of the families drew rather more of their wealth from commercial and business activities in the city than from their estates: the Bonvicini from commerce, in particular on the Adige, and the Alessandri from their role as notaries.
48. McArdle, *op.cit.*
49. Even the aristocratic nuns of S. Michele in Campagna raised pigs and silk worms: ASVR, SMC, Reg 124.
50. See for instance: ASVR, VVP, Busta 350, Scritture Varie, Gironimo Suttori contro Domenico Fainel, lavorente.
51. Ibid.
52. ASVR, SFM, Reg 124.
53. Contracts, such as that which forms the basis of the lengthy, complicated

and only partly legible document which is part of ASVR, Bonvicini, 113, and which deals with the Bonvicini estates at Ca d'Aprile in the Basso.

54. See for instance Suttori's allegations against Fainel: ASVR, VVP, 350.
55. See for instance: ASVR, AEP, Reg 28, p. 455 (Noris), ibid., Reg 126, 186 (Roveretti).
56. For example: ASVR, S. Leonardo in Monte, Reg 28, S. Fermo Maggiore, Reg 441, S. Catterina Martire, Processo 435, Campagna, Reg 442.
57. ASVR, AEP, Reg 53, p. 727.
58. ASVR, AEP, Reg 120, p. 237.
59. ASVR, AEP, Reg 131, p. 536.
60. See, for instance, ASVR, AEP, Reg 82, p. 166 (Sigismondi Paletta).
61. The literature on this debate has been well summed up by J. S. Cohen and Francesco L. Galassi in 'Share-cropping and Productivity: "feudal residues", in Italian Agriculture, 1911', in *Economic History Review*, 2nd series, XLIII, 4 (1990), pp. 646–56. Specifically on the Veronese see: G. Borelli, 'Dei contratti agrari nel Veronese tra '500 e '600: aspetti e problemi', in *Il Mondo Rurale Veneto attraverso i contratti agrari: Il Territorrio Veronese nei secoli IX–XX* (Verona: 1982), pp. 118–37.
62. *Affittanza* must be clearly distinguished from the type of payment called *livello* and usually translated 'lease'. A *livello*, usually a *livello perpetuo*, is a charge on land, usually of a charitable or pious nature, although on occasions a recognition of previous services or an installment payment on debt. The *livello* did not imply any idea of ownership or superior tenure on the part of the recipient, but was merely a charge on the land which was transferred along with the land. The recipient of a *livello* gained no rights over the land in question, nor did he have to be consulted before the land could be transferred. Where the *livello* represented in effect a payment on a mortgage, designed to escape the restrictions on usury, the arrangements for the transfer of the *livello* might be more complex but they still did not represent any form of legal ownership. There was a growing tendency in the mid-eighteenth century for owners of land to buy out the rights of *livello* holders for capital sums.
63. For instance the estates of S. Fermo Maggiore, see pp. 51–2.
64. ASVR, AEP, Reg 82, p. 166.
65. Ibid.
66. See Chapter 6.
67. It was not only the bourgeois who were buying land at this period; some of the more successful noble landholders were also extending their holdings at the expense of their fellow nobles as well as of the smaller scale local landowners: perhaps the best examples of this in the Valpolicella were the Ottolini and, even more, the Rizzardi: ASVR, AEP, Reg 600–1 (Negrar), 602 (S. Vito).
68. See Brian Pullan (ed.), *Crisis and Change in the Venetian Economy* (London: 1968).
69. ASVR, SFM, Reg 180.
70. Ibid., Reg 189.
71. Ibid., Reg 198.
72. Ibid., Reg 204.
73. Ibid., Reg 212.
74. Ibid., Reg 223.
75. Ibid., Reg 230.
76. Ibid., Reg 236.
77. Ibid., Reg 244.
78. ASVR, AEP, Reg 82, p. 166.
79. See, for instance, ASVR, AEP, Reg 28, p. 456 (Noris).

80. ASVR, AEP, Reg 82, p. 166.
81. ASVR, AEP, Reg 83, p. 572.
82. ASVR, dal Bene, Reg 217.
83. See, for instance, ASVR, dal Bene Reg 109 and ASVR, Bonvicini, Reg 439.
84. On 23 November 1638, for instance, the nuns of the Abbey of S. Martino at Avesa paid 6 *lire* 15 *soldi* for a pair of shoes for the wife of their *gastaldo*: ASVR, S. Martino d'Avesa, Reg 19.
85. The dal Bene estate had a long tradition of importing workers from Soave to its Volargne lands and also of moving Volargne workers to Soave: ASVR, dal Bene, Reg 111.
86. See, for instance the dal Bene *Giornali* for 1776–7 and 1777–8 and below, Chapter 6: ASVR, dal Bene, Reg 207 and 221.

6. The ownership of the land and its vicissitudes

1. See: G. Borelli, 'Nozze e doti in una famiglia nobilare durante la prima meta del XVIII secolo', in *Economia e Storia*, 3 (1971), pp. 321–42.
2. On the Compromise of 1633 see: *Transatione sguita tra la magnifica Citta di Verona and il spettabile Territorio MDCXXXIII 27 Novembre in materia de beni stabili passati da Distrittuali in Cittadini e da Cittadini in Distrittuali dal 1575 per tutto l'anno 1633*, in ASVR, Comune, Reg 798.
3. The succeeding discussion is based upon the Estimi for the Valpolicella communes and the Polizze for the City Estimi:

ASVR, AEP, Registri
Estimo Territoriale

388	Arbizzano
582	S. Pietro in Cariano
583	Bure
584	S. Sofia
585	Semonte
586	Breonio
591	Volargne
592	Fumane
593	Cavalo
594	Mazzurega
595–6	Marano
597	Valgatara
598	Negarine
599	Castelrotto
600–1	Negrar
602	S. Vito
603–4	Pescantina
605	Prun
606	Fane
607	Mazzan
608	Torbe
609	S. Ambrogio
610	Gargagnago
611	Monte
612	Ponton
613	S. Giorgio

Estimo Citta

28–32	Polizze 1653
36	Polizze Distrettuali 1653
42–57	Polizze 1682
59–64	Polizze Distrettuali 1682
71	Polizze Distrettuali Obliti 1682
76–91	Polizze Citta 1696
92–7	Polizze Distrettuali 1696
98	Polizze Obliti 1696
116–35	Polizze Citta 1745
136–45	Polizze Obliti 1745
146–55	Polizze Distrettuali 1745 .
175–7	Polizze Obliti Distrettuali 1745

Veneti

289	Polizze 1696
290–1	Polizze 1740
292	Polizze 1745
293	Polizze 1680

Estimo Clero

328	Polizze Abbazie ed altro 1680
329–30	Polizze delle Chiese di Citta 1680
331-2	Polizze de Chierigati 1680
333	Polizze delle Capelle di Citta 1680
334–5	Polizze Monasteri 1680
336	Vescovado 1724
337	Chiese di Citta 1724
338	Capelle 1724
339	Pievi 1724
340	Chierichi 1724
341	Chiese e Capelle 1724
342	Chiese di Villa 1724
343	Monasteri 1724
344	Polizze del Vescovado 1763
345	Polizze delle Chiese di Villa 1763
345[bis]	Polizze delle Chiese di Citta 1763
346	Polizze delli Chierichi 1763
347	Polizze delle Pievi di Citta e Villa 1763
348	Polizze delle Capelle di Citta e Villa 1763
349	Polizze delli Monasteri 1763

7. The non-agricultural dimension

1. ASVR, dal Bene, Reg 207, 221.
2. Ibid.
3. See p. 103.
4. See Sandri, *op.cit.*
5. See P. Kriedte, H. Medick, J. Schlumbohm, *Industrialisation before Industrialisation* (tr.) S. Burke (Cambridge: 1982).
6. See: M. Lecce, *Vicende dell'Industria della lana e della seta a Verona delle origine al XVI secolo* (Verona: 1955) and A. M. Girelli, *Il setificio Veronese nel Settecento* (Milano: 1969).

7. G. de Poli, *Marmi Veronesi* (Verona: n.d).
8. C. Klapisch-Zuber, *Les Maitres du Marbre: Carrara, 1300–1600* (Paris: 1969).
9. ASVR, AEP, Reg 609.
10. ASVR, dal Bene, 207, 221.
11. ASVR, Bonvicini, Reg 439.
12. On the river trade and the Parons see: C. F. Zamboni, *La Navigazione sull'Adige in rapporto al commercio veronese* (Verona: 1925), G. Faccioli, *Verona e la navigazione atesina: Compendio Storico delle attivita produttive dal XII al XIX secolo* (Verona: 1925); G. Canali, *I trasporti sull'Adige da Bronzolo a Verona e gli Spedizioneri di Sacco* (Gleno: 1939); T. Fanfani, 'L'Adige come arteria principale del traffico tra Nord Europa ed emporio realtino', in G. Borelli (ed.), *Una Citta e il suo Fiume: Verona e l'Adige*, 2 vols (Verona: 1977), II, pp. 569–620 and G. M. Varanini (ed.), *La Valpolicella nella prima eta moderna (1500–c1630)* (Verona: 1987), pp. 187–9.
13. ASVR, Arte dei Burchieri, processo 177.
14. ASVR, AEP, Reg 603-4.
15. ASVR, Anagrafie.

Select bibliography

1. PRIMARY SOURCES

(a) Archivio di Stato, Venezia
The best guide to the Archive in Venezia remains A. da Mosto, *L' Archivio di Stato di Venezia*, 2 Vols (Venezia: 1939).
Collegio V (Secreta)

(b) Archivio di Stato, Verona
The best guide to this, the major archive used in the present study, is G. Sancassani, *L'Archivio di Stato di Verona: gli Archivi Veronesi dal Medioevo ai giorni nostri* (Verona: 1961), although it does not include a number of major private sources deposited in the Archivio since the late 1950s.

State Records
Anagrafie
Antico Archivio del Comune:
    (a) Registri
    (b) Processi
Antichi Estimi Provvisori
Arte e fraglie
Atti dei Rettori Veneti
Atti dei Vicari della Valpolicella
Camera Fiscale
Registri di Battesati e Morti
Ufficio del Registro
Ufficio di Sanita

Ecclesiastical Records
S. Bartolomea della Levata
S. Cattarina Martire
S. Croce
S. Daniele
S. Fermo Maggiore
S. Fermo in Braida
S. Giorgio Maggiore
S. Giorgio Sopra Garda
SS. Giuseppe e Fidenzio
S. Leonardo in Monte
S. Lucia
S. Maria degli Angeli
S. Maria in Organo
S. Maria della Scala

S. Martino d'Avesa
S. Michele in Campagna
Redentore
S. Spirito
S. Zeno Maggiore

Private Archives
Alessandri
Bonvicini
Campagna
dal Bene

(c) Archivio Storico della Curia Vescovile di Verona
The Archive of the Curia is fortunate in having a first rate modern guide: F. Segala, *Guida Storico-Archivistico dell'Archivio della Curia Vescovile* (Verona: 1987).

Presentationes et Collationes
Amministrazione Economica della Diocesi:
   Pievi: S. Giorgio
            S. Floriano
            Negrar
Patrimonium Ecclesiasticorum

2. SECONDARY SOURCES

No complete bibliography of the Valpolicella exists, although one is planned under the auspices of the Centro per la Documentazzione Storica della Valpolicella. Local history is now one of the major areas of growth in Italian historiography, boosted by the growing awareness of locality and of local allegiances which has characterized the last two decades. New material, frequently produced by local committees or by local school-teachers or their students now appears regularly; although this material is of very variable quality, at its very best it provides information of major importance. No bibliography of the Valpolicella can, thankfully, be regarded as complete; the best sources for the most recent material are the following journals:
Civilta Veronese (successor of Vita Veronese)
Annuario Storico della Valpolicella
Studi Storici Veronesi Luigi Simeoni
   In the same way, the literature on the local history of the rest of the Veronese is constantly expanding and the following bibliography makes no pretence at completeness.

(a) Valpolicella.
Benedetto del Bene: *Giornale di Memorie (1770-1796)* ed. Giuseppe Biadego (Verona: 1883).
P. P. Brugnoli, *S. Giorgio di Valpolicella* (Verona: 1975).
Pierpaolo Brugnoli and Giovanni Viviani (eds), *Invito a Molina* (Verona: 1982).
F. Carcereri, 'L'amministrazione della Valpolicella attraverso documenti a stampa di epoca veneta', in *Annuario Storico della Valpolicella* (1982-3).
Gianni Fae, *S. Giorgio di Valpolicella Ingannapoltron* (S. Giorgio Valpolicella: 1982).

Lamberto Paronetto, *Valpolicella Splendida Contea del Vino* (Verona: 1981).

E. S. Righi, 'Iscrizioni relative alli antichi vicari della Valpolicella esistente nella residenza municipale di S. Pietro in Cariano', in *Archivio Storico Veronese*, I (1879), pp. 302–9.

Eugenio Turri, *Villa Veneta: conte, sior, paron, castaldo, lavorente, bacan: agonia del mondo mezzadrile e messagio neo-tecnico* (Verona: 1977).

G. M. Varanini (ed.), *La Valpolicella dal Duecento al Quattrocento* (Verona: 1985).

—, *La Valpolicella nella prima eta moderna (1500–c1630)* (Verona: 1987).

G. F. Viviani, *Ville della Valpolicella* (Verona: 1974).

(b) Verona and the Veronese

G. Borelli, 'Nozze e doti in una famiglia nobilare durante la prima meta del XVIII secolo', in *Economia e Storia*, 3 (1971), pp. 321–42.

—, *Un Patriziato della Terraferma Veneta: la Nobilta Veronese nel Sei- e Settecento* (Verona: 1972).

—, *Una Citta e il suo Fiume: Verona e l'Adige*, 2 vols (Verona: 1977).

—, 'Dei contratti agrari nel Veronese tra '500 e '600: aspetti e problemi', in *Il Mondo Rurale Veneto attraverso i contratti agrari: Il Territorrio Veronese nei secoli IX–XX* (Verona: 1982), pp. 118–37.

C. Boscagin, *Storia di Legnago* (Verona: 1966).

A. Canali, *I trasporti sull'Adige da Bronzolo a Verona e gli Spedizioneri di Sacco* (Gleno: 1939).

Dino Coltro, *Paese Perduto: la cultura dei Contadini Veneti*, 4 vols (Verona: 1975).

—, *L'Adige* (Verona: 1989).

G. Faccioli, *Verona e la navigazione atesina: Compendio Storico delle attivita produttive dal XII al XIX secolo* (Verona: 1925).

A. M. Girelli, *Il setificio Veronese nel Settecento* (Milano: 1969).

M. Lecce, *Vicende dell'Industria della lana e della seta a Verona delle origine al XVI secolo* (Verona: 1955).

—, 'Le condizioni zoo-tecnico-agricola del territorio Veronese nella prima meta del '500', *Economia e Storia*, I (1958).

—, *La Coltura del Riso in Territorio Veronese (Sec XVI–XVIII)* (Verona: 1958).

Abate Bartolomeo Lorenzi, *Della Coltivatione de'Monti* (Verona: 1778), (reprinted Verona: 1971).

G. de Poli, *Marmi Veronesi* (Verona: n.d).

G. Sancassani, *Documenti sul Notariato Veronese durante il Dominio Veneto* (Verona: n.d).

G. Sandri, *I Bevilacqua e il Commercio del Legname tra il Val di Fiemme e Verona nel secolo XIV* (Venezia: 1940).

A. Tagliaferri (ed.), *Relazioni dei Rettore Veneti in Terraferma: IX Podesteria e Capitanato di Verona* (Milano: 1977).

E. Turri, *Dietro il Paessagio: Caprino e il Monte Baldo; ricerche su un territorio comunale* (Verona: 1982).

G. M. Varanini, *Il Distretto Veronese nel Quattrocento: Vicariati del Comune di Verona e Vicariati Privati* (Verona: 1980).

F. Vecchiato, *Pane e Politica Annonaria in Terraferma Veneta tra secolo XV e secolo XVIII: Il caso di Verona* (Verona: 1966).

—, 'Problemi del'ordinamento guidiziario a Verona in Epoca Veneta', in *Studi Storici Veronesi Luigi Simeoni*, xxx–xxxi (1980–1), pp. 1–37.

C. F. Zamboni, *La Navigazione sull'Adige in rapporto al commercio Veronese* (Verona: 1925).

(c) Other Works

M. Braubach, *Prinz Eugen von Savoyen, Band I* (Munchen: 1963).

F. Braudel, *The Mediterranean and the Mediterranean World in the Age of Philip II*, (tr.) S. Reynolds, 2 vols (London: 1972).

D. G. Chandler, *The Campaigns of Napoleon* (London: 1967).

James Casey, 'Spain: a failed transition', in P. Clark (ed.), *The European Crisis of the 1590s: Essays in Comparative History* (London: 1985), pp. 209–28.

J. S. Cohen and Francesco L. Galassi in 'Share-cropping and Productivity: "feudal residues", in Italian Agriculture, 1911', in *Economic History Review*, 2nd series, XLIII, 4 (1990), pp. 646–56.

James S. Grubb, 'When Myths lose power: four decades of Venetian Historiography', *Journal of Modern History*, 58 (1986), pp. 43–94.

P. J. Jones, 'La Storia Economica', in *Storia d'Italia: dalla Caduta del Impero Romano al Secolo XVIII* (Torino: 1974).

Henry Kamen, *Spain in the Late Seventeenth Century* (London and New York: 1980).

C. Klapisch-Zuber, *Les Maitres du Marbre: Carrara, 1300–1600* (Paris: 1969).

E. Le Roy Ladurie, *Les Paysans de Languedoc*, 2 vols (Paris: 1966).

Frederic C. Lane, *Venice, A Maritime Republic* (Baltimore and London, 1973).

P. Laslett, *The World We Have Lost*, 2nd edition (Cambridge: 1971).

E. Le Roy Ladurie and J. Goy, *Tithe and Agrarian History from the Four-teenth to the Nineteenth Centuries: An Essay in Comparative History* (tr.) S. Burke (Cambridge: 1982).

F. McArdle, *Altopascio: A Study in Tuscan Rural Society* (Cambridge: 1974).

Brian Pullan (ed.), *Crisis and Change in the Venetian Economy* (London: 1968).

W. W. Rostow, *The Stages of Economic Growth: a Non-Communist Manifesto*, 2nd edition (Cambridge: 1971).

Domenico Sella, *Crisis and Continuity: The Economy of Spanish Lombardy in the Seventeenth Century* (Cambridge and London: 1979).

Marshall Sahlins, *Stone Age Economics* (Chicago: 1972).

N. W. Simmonds (ed.), *Evolution of Crop Plants* (London: 1976).

Stuart Woolf, 'The Economic Problems of the Nobility in the Early Modern Period: the example of Piedmont', in *Economic History Review*, 2nd series, XVII, 2 (1964), pp. 267–83.

—, *A History of Italy 1700–1860: The Social Constraints of Political Change* (London: 1979).

Index